Preliminary Edition
MATHEMATICS
FOR ELEMENTARY TEACHERS
via problem solving

JOANNA O. MASINGILA
Syracuse University

FRANK K. LESTER
Indiana University

PRENTICE HALL Upper Saddle River, NJ 07458

Acquisitions Editor: *Sally Denlow*
Production Editor: *Robert Walters*
Production Coordinator: *Alan Fischer*
Managing Editor: *Linda M. Behrens*
Cover Manager: *Paul Gourhan*
Cover Designer: *Liz Nemeth*

© 1998 by **PRENTICE-HALL, INC.**
Simon & Schuster/A Viacom Company
Upper Saddle River, NJ 07458

Printed in the United States of America

10 9 8 7 6 5 4 3 2

ISBN 0-13-888488-9

Prentice-Hall International (UK) Limited, *London*
Prentice-Hall of Australia Pty. Limited, *Sydney*
Prentice-Hall Canada, Inc., *Toronto*
Prentice-Hall Hispanoamericana, S.A., *Mexico*
Prentice-Hall of India Private Limited, *New Delhi*
Prentice-Hall of Japan, Inc., *Tokyo*
Simon & Schuster Asia Pte. Ltd., *Singapore*
Editora Prentice-Hall do Brasil, Ltda., *Rio de Janeiro*

BRIEF CONTENTS

iv

CONTENTS

PREFACE

Give a child a fish and you feed her for a day. Teach a child to fish and you feed her for life.

The ancient Chinese saying above tells us how important it is to have good teachers for our children. Indeed, there are few professions or occupations that are as important to the welfare of our society and culture as teaching. The purpose of the activities in this book is to help you develop a deep and lasting understanding of the mathematical concepts, procedures, and skills that are essential to being able to teach young children, in particular children in the elementary grades. We believe that if you develop such deep and lasting understanding, you will be well prepared to teach mathematics to many children and thereby helping to prepare them to lead productive, informed lives once their school days are over.

The Way Mathematics Is Taught Is Changing

Those who would teach mathematics need to learn contemporary mathematics appropriate to the grades they will teach, in a style consistent with the way in which they will be expected to teach.

All students, and especially prospective teachers, should learn mathematics as a process of constructing and interpreting patterns, of discovering strategies for solving problems, and of exploring the beauty and applications of mathematics.

(Everybody Counts: A Report to the Nation on the Future of Mathematics Education, 1989, pp. 64 & 66)

The two quotes shown above are taken from a report written nearly 10 years ago for the United States' National Research Council by a group of concerned mathematics teachers. The authors of the report insisted that it was time to change the way that mathematics is taught at all levels, kindergarten through university. Since this report was written, the nature of mathematics instruction has begun to change. In the past, mathematics instruction was viewed by many as an activity in which an "expert"—usually the teacher—attempted to transmit her or his knowledge of mathematics to a group of students who usually sat quietly trying to make sense of what the expert was telling them. This passive transmission view has been replaced by a new view where mathematics is seen as a cooperative venture among students in which they are encouraged to explore, make and debate conjectures, build connections among concepts, solve problems growing out of their explorations, and construct personal meaning from all of these experiences.

The activities contained in our books have been created with the new view of mathematics teaching and learning promoted by the American Mathematical Association of Two-Year Colleges (AMATYC) and the National Council of Teachers of Mathematics (NCTM). In particular, we developed the activities with the following documents in mind: AMATYC's publication, *Crossroads in Mathematics: Standards for Introductory College Mathematics Before Calculus*, and the NCTM's publications, *Curriculum and Evaluation Standards for School Mathematics, Professional Standards for Teaching Mathematics, and Assessment Standards for School Mathematics.*

From these four documents we developed a set of principals to guide the development of all activities.

- *All Activities Are Based on the NCTM Standards.*

Special emphasis is placed on the four primary standards of the NCTM: *problem solving, communication, reasoning,* and *connections.* First and foremost, students should be engaged in the solution of thought provoking, real world problems. Not only should students learn to solve problems, but they should also learn mathematics *via* problem solving. The second major standard is *communication.* Knowing mathematics is of little value if one cannot communicate mathematical ideas to other people. NCTM's third major standard is *reasoning.* Among other things, reasoning deals with the ability to think through a problem and to carefully evaluate any solution that has been proposed. The fourth of the major standards involves making *connections.* To really understand mathematics, one must be able to see connections between various mathematical ideas, and between "school" and "real world" mathematics.

- *Solving Problems Regularly and Often Is an Essential Part of Developing a Good Understanding of Mathematics.*

In order for you to improve your ability to solve mathematics problems, you must attempt to solve a variety of types of problems on a regular basis and over a prolonged period of time. We also believe that ability to solve problems goes hand-in-hand with the development of an understanding of mathematical concepts, procedures, and skills. Put another way, as you solve problems you will develop better understanding of the mathematics involved in the problems. And, as you develop better understanding of mathematical ideas, you will become a better problem solver.

- *Problem Solving Involves a Very Complex Set of Processes.*

There is a dynamic interaction between mathematical concepts and the processes used to solve problems involving those concepts. That is, heuristics, procedural skills, control processes, awareness of one's cognitive processes, etc. develop concurrently with the development of an understanding of mathematical concepts.

- *The Teacher's Role in Fostering Healthy Problem-solving Performance Is Vitally Important.*

Problem-solving instruction is likely to be most effective when it is provided in a systematically organized manner under the direction of the teacher. Our philosophy is that the role of the teacher changes from that of a "dispenser of knowledge" to a "facilitator of learning." With respect to problem solving and reasoning, this implies that the teacher does very little lecturing on how to solve specific types of problems and much more posing and discussing of a wide variety of non-routine and applied problems. The teacher also focuses on helping you make connections between the mathematics you are learning and its application to the workplace or home.

- *Cooperative, Small-group Work Is Encouraged.*

The standard arrangement for working on the activities in the *Activity Book* is for you to work in small groups. Small group work is especially appropriate for activities involving new content (e.g., new mathematics topics, new problem-solving strategies) or when the focus of the activity is on the process of solving problems (e.g., planning, decision making, assessing progress) or exploring mathematical ideas.

• *Assessment Practices Are Closely Connected to Instructional Emphases.*

We believe that the teacher's instructional plan should include attention to how your performance will be assessed. In order for you to become convinced of the importance of the sort of behaviors that a good problem-solving program promotes, it is necessary to use assessment techniques that reward such behaviors. As a result, we encourage teachers to use various alternative assessment methods such as providing opportunities during tests for you to work with a group of your classmates to solve certain problems on the tests. We also encourage teachers to assess your ability to discuss your understanding of mathematical concepts and procedures in writing and orally.

A Very Important Feature of the Activities in This Book

As indicated above, the activities in the *Activity Book* have been designed to engage you in doing real mathematics through small-group exploration. We have two mottoes that should be followed:

- Mathematics is best learned by active, "hands-on" exploration of real problems.
- If "two heads are better than one," then three or four heads are even better!

These mottoes arise from our conviction that the best learning occurs when you are engaged actively in making sense out of problematic situations. Thus, it is your responsibility to make sense out of the activities, rather than wait for the teacher to tell you what is important or how to solve the problems.

Consequently, the activities in this book include almost no explanations with them. It will be your responsibility to work with the students in your group (some students like to refer to their groups as "teams") to solve problems and develop good understanding of the mathematics involved. The teacher's job will be to encourage you, to offer gentle assistance to you without too much specific guidance. This may be a new experience for you and it may even be a bit uncomfortable for you at first. But, be patient! As you gain experience working in a group with others rather than depending on the teacher to tell you everything you should know, you are likely to find that you are becoming more and more independent of that teacher and increasingly in control of your own learning.

Other Special Features of the This Book

The *Activity Book* contains several other features that further distinguish it from more traditional mathematics books. First, in the front of this book you will find a matrix that shows how the topics included in the *Activity Book* correlate with those found in several of the most popular traditional mathematics textbooks for prospective elementary teachers. In addition to containing very different sorts of activities (as described above), each chapter also contains a chapter overview and outline, a list of "Words, Concepts, and Procedures to Know," and sets of exercises and problems to supplement those found in the activities.

References

American Mathematical Association of Two-Year Colleges. (1995). *Crossroads in Mathematics: Standards for Introductory College Mathematics Before Calculus.* Memphis, TN: Author.

Mathematical Sciences Education Board (National Research Council). (1989). *Everybody Counts: A report to the Nation on the Future of Mathematics Education.* Washington, DC: National Academy Press.

National Council of Teachers of Mathematics. (1989). *Curriculum and Evaluation Standards for School Mathematics.* Reston, VA: Author.

National Council of Teachers of Mathematics. (1991). *Professional Standards for Teaching Mathematics*. Reston, VA: Author.

National Council of Teachers of Mathematics. (1995). *Assessment Standards for School Mathematics*. Reston, VA: Author.

Joanna O. Masingila

Frank K. Lester

Comparison of Topics in Traditional Books with Topics in our
Activity Book and *Resource Manual*

Traditional Chapters	Traditional Topics	Where Found in *Activity Book*	Where Found in *Resource Manual*
Introduction to Problem Solving	The Problem Solving Process	Chapter 0; Activities 1.1-1.10	Chapter 1 Explanations
	Strategies	Activities 1.1-1.10	Chapter 0; Chapter 1 Explanations
			Additional Items: Historical/Social/ Cultural Notes on Problem Solving
Sets, Functions, and Logic	Describing Sets		
	Set Operations		
	Functions	Activities 8.7	Chapter 8 Explanations
	Logic		
		Additional Items: Activities 8.1-8.6, 8.8-8.14 that explore patterns and functions	*Additional Items:* Historical/Social/ Cultural Notes on Patterns and Functions
Numeration Systems	Numeration Systems	Activities 2.1-2.5	Historical/Social/ Cultural Notes on Numeration
	Addition and Subtraction of Whole Numbers	Activity 3.3	Chapter 2 and 3 Explanations
	Multiplication and Division of Whole Numbers	Activity 3.3	Chapter 2 and 3 Explanations
	Algorithms for Whole-number Addition and Subtraction	Activities 3.6, 3.8, 3.9	Chapter 3 Explanations
	Algorithms for Whole-number Multiplication and Division	Activities 3.7, 3.10	Chapter 3 Explanations
		Additional Items: Activities 2.6-2.10 that explore place value ideas through different bases; Activities 3.1-3.2 that explore sets of numbers and their properties; Activities 3.11-3.12 that use algorithms to solve problems	*Additional Items:* Explanations on Numeration Ideas; Historical/Social/ Cultural Notes on Operations

Integers and Number Theory	Integers and Operations of Addition and Subtraction	Activities 3.4	Chapter 3 Explanations
	Multiplication and Division of Integers	Activities 3.5	Chapter 3 Explanations
	Divisibility	Activities 4.7-4.8	Chapter 4 Explanations
	Prime and Composite Numbers	Activities 4.1-4.4	Chapter 4 Explanations
	Greatest Common Divisor and Least Common Multiple	Activity 4.9	Chapter 4 Explanations
	Clock and Modular Arithmetic	Activities 4.10-4.12	Chapter 4 Explanations
		Additional Items: Activities 4.5-4.6 that explore special types of primes; Activities 4.13-4.16 that explore ways of representing number theory ideas and proofs	*Additional Items:* Historical/Social/ Cultural Notes on Number Theory
Rational Numbers as Fractions	The Set of Rational Numbers	Activity 7.14	Chapter 6 Explanations
	Addition and Subtraction of Rational Numbers	Activities 6.12-6.14	Chapter 6 Explanations
	Multiplication and Division of Rational Numbers	Activities 6.12-6.16	Chapter 6 Explanations
		Additional Items: Activities 6.1-6.8, 6.10-6.11 that explore three models to represent fractions; Activity 6.9 that explores the density of the set of real numbers	*Additional Items:* Historical/Social/ Cultural Notes on Fractions
Exponents and Decimals	Integer Exponents and Decimals	Activity 7.4	Chapter 7 Explanations
	Operations on Decimals	Activities 7.6-7.7	Chapter 7 Explanations
	Real Numbers	Activities 7.12-7.14	Chapter 7 Explanations
		Additional Items: Activity 7.5 that explores why the decimal point placement rules work	*Additional Items:* Historical/Social/ Cultural Notes on Rationals and Irrationals

Applications of Mathematics	Algebraic Thinking	Activities 8.5-8.8, 8.12-8.13	Chapter 8 Explanations
	Word Problems	Activities 8.1-8.10	Chapter 8 Explanations
	Lines in a Cartesian Coordinate System	Activity 10.13	Chapter 8 Explanations; Chapter 10 Explanations
	Ratio and Proportion	Activities 7.1-7.3	Chapter 7 Explanations
	Percents	Activities 7.8-7.11	Chapter 7 Explanations
	Computing Interest	Activity 8.10	Chapter 8 Explanations
		Additional Items: Activities 8.9, 8.11 that explore iterated functions; Activity 8.14 that explores distance versus time motion	
Probability	How Probabilities are Determined	Activity 5.5	Chapter 5 Explanations
	Multistage Experiments with Tree Diagrams and Geometric Probabilities	Activities 5.1-3	Chapter 5 Explanations
	Using Simulations in Probability		
	Odds and Expected Value	Activity 5.5	Chapter 5 Explanations
	Methods of Counting	Activity 5.6	Chapter 5 Explanations
		Additional Items: Activity 5.4 that explores fairness	*Additional Items:* Historical/Social/ Cultural Notes on Probability
Statistics	Statistical Graphs	Activities 5.7-5.10	Chapter 5 Explanations
	Measures of Central Tendency and Variation	Activity 5.8	Chapter 5 Explanations
	Normal Distributions	Activity 5.7	
	Abuses of Statistics	Activity 5.11	Chapter 5 Explanations
			Additional Items: Historical/Social/ Cultural Notes on Statistics

Introductory Geometry	Basic Notions	Activity 9.3	Chapter 9 Explanations
	Polygonal Curves	Activities 9.7-9.10	Chapter 9 Explanations
	Linear Measure	Activities 9.5, 9.11, 10.1-10.4	Chapter 10 Explanations
	More about Angles	Activities 9.6	Chapter 9 Explanations
	Geometry in Three Dimensions	Activity 10.10	Chapter 10 Explanations
	Networks		
		Additional Items: Activities 9.1-9.2 that explore the importance of precision of language	*Additional Items:* Historical/Social/ Cultural Notes on Geometry
Constructions and Similarity	Congruence through Constructions	Activity 9.4	Chapter 9 Explanations
	Other Congruence Properties	Activities 9.12	Chapter 9 Explanations
	Other Constructions	Activity 9.4	
	Similar Triangles and Similar Figures	Activity 9. 13-9.14	Chapter 9 Explanations
	Trigonometry Ratios via Similarity		
		Additional Items: Activities 9.15-9.16 that explores proving geometry ideas; Activity 9.17 that explores spherical geometry	*Additional Items:* Historical/Social/ Cultural Notes on Geometry
More Concepts of Measurement	Areas of Polygons and Circles	Activities 10.2-10.3, 10.6, 10.8	Chapter 10 Explanations
	The Pythagorean Theorem	Activity 10.5	
	Surface Areas	Activities 10.9, 10.11	Chapter 10 Explanations
	Volumes	Activities 10.9, 10.12	Chapter 10 Explanations
	Mass and Temperature		
		Additional Items: Activity 10.7 that explores the circumference to diameter ratio	*Additional Items:* Historical/Social/ Cultural Notes on Measurement

Motion Geometry and Tessellations	Translations and Rotations	Activities 10.14-10.15	Chapter 10 Explanations
	Reflections and Glide Reflections	Activity 10.16	Chapter 10 Explanations
	Size Transformations		
	Symmetries		Chapter 10 Exercises & More Problems
	Tessellations of the Plane	Activities 10.17-10.18	Chapter 10 Explanations
			Additional Items: Historical/Social/ Cultural Notes on Measurement

Acknowledgments

Although it is impossible to completely acknowledge all the people who have helped us in writing this textbook, we want to thank some people specifically. Since these materials were developed out of two projects funded by the National Science Foundation (one at Indiana University and one at Syracuse University), there have been a number of people who developed activities and ideas for activities that have contributed to this textbook. We are grateful to these people and want their contributions recognized here: Jean-Marc Cenet, Rapti de Silva, K. Jamie King, Norman Krumpe, Diana V. Lambdin, Sue Tinsley Mau, Francisco Egger Moellwald, Preety Nigam, and Vânia Santos. Other persons helped us in the latter stages of writing this preliminary edition by generating exercises and solutions. We thank them for their help: Dasha Kinelovsky, Sandra Reynolds, and Robert Wenta.

We also thank the following persons who reviewed our manuscript. Their comments and suggestions have helped us make this a better textbook: Rita M. Basta (California State University-Northridge), George Csordas, (University of Hawaii), Dale Oliver, (Humboldt State University). Finally, we thank our editor, Sally Denlow, for her encouragement and desire to publish a reform textbook for prospective elementary teachers.

Chapter 0: Learning Mathematics via Problem Solving

Chapter Overview:

Mathematics instruction has changed rather dramatically in recent years. A passive transmission view of the teacher's role has been replaced by one involving students as active participants in the act of "doing" mathematics. This new vision is one where mathematics is seen as a cooperative venture in which students are encouraged to explore, make and debate conjectures, build connections among concepts, solve problems growing out of their explorations, and construct personal meaning from all of these experiences.

This chapter provides a discussion of the philosophy underlying teaching and learning "via problem solving." Also included are brief discussions of key ingredients of the materials contained in the *Activity Book*, namely: the importance of emphasizing big mathematical ideas, cooperative learning, reflective writing, alternative assessment, and different classroom roles for both instructors and students.

Chapter Outline:

The Changing Nature of Mathematics Instruction

The Role of Problem Solving in Instruction
 Teaching About Problem Solving
 Teaching For Problem Solving
 Teaching Via Problem Solving

Important Ingredients of the Activities in the Activity Book
 "Big Ideas" in Mathematics for Prospective Elementary Teachers
 Cooperative Learning
 Reflective Writing
 Assessment: Emphases and Practices
 Instructor's and Students' Roles in Learning Mathematics Via
  Problem Solving

Bibliography

THE CHANGING NATURE OF MATHEMATICS INSTRUCTION

Mathematics instruction has changed rather dramatically in recent years. In the past, mathematics instruction was viewed by many as an activity in which an "expert" attempted to transmit her or his knowledge of mathematics to a group of mostly passive students, typically by means of lectures. This passive transmission view has been replaced by one involving students as active participants in the act of "doing"—that is, creating, exploring, testing, verifying, etc.— mathematics. This new vision is one where mathematics is seen as a cooperative venture in which students are encouraged to explore, make and debate conjectures, build connections among concepts, solve problems growing out of their explorations, and construct personal meaning from all of these experiences.

The emphasis in the activities in this book is on learning mathematical concepts and processes by doing mathematics and, in particular, by solving problems. Also, this active doing of mathematics takes place in an environment of cooperation among small groups of students in which the teachers plays the roles of guide, coach, question asker, and co-problem solver.

THE ROLE OF PROBLEM SOLVING IN MATHEMATICS INSTRUCTION

Most mathematics educators agree that problem solving is a very important, if not the most important, goal of mathematics instruction at every level. Indeed, some have even gone so far as to insist that: "Problem solving should be the focus of school mathematics" (National Council of Teachers of Mathematics [NCTM], 1980, p. 1), and "Problem solving is a central focus of the mathematics curriculum" (Mathematical Sciences Education Board, 1990, p. 31). Since about 1980, problem solving has been the most written about topic in the mathematics curriculum in the United States. And, most teachers agree that the development of students' problem-solving abilities is a primary objective of instruction.

The question arises: "How can we make problem solving the focus of mathematics instruction?" We have found it useful to think about the answer to this question by distinguishing among three approaches to problem-solving instruction: (a) teaching *about* problem solving, (b) teaching *for* problem solving, and (c) teaching *via* problem solving. (See the article, "Developing Understanding in Mathematics via Problem Solving," in the 1989 yearbook of the National Council of Teachers of Mathematics for a more thorough discussion of these three approaches to problem-solving instruction; Schroeder & Lester, 1989).

Teaching *About* Problem Solving

The teacher who teaches *about* problem solving emphasizes the various phases or stages that are involved in the process of solving mathematics problems. The best known model of this sort was proposed by the eminent mathematician, George Polya, more than 50 years ago (Polya, 1945). Briefly, Polya's model describes a set of four interdependent phases that are involved in the process of solving mathematics problems: understanding the problem, devising a plan, carrying out the plan, and looking back. Teachers who teach *about* problem solving encourage their students to use the phases, which according to Polya, expert problem solvers use when solving mathematics problems. These teachers also encourage their students to become aware of their own progression through these phases when they themselves solve problems. Additionally, they are taught a number of "heuristics" or "strategies" from which they can choose and which they should use in devising and carrying out their problem-solving plans. Some of the several strategies typically taught include: looking for patterns, solving a simpler problem, and working backwards. Teaching *about* problem solving usually includes experiences actually solving problems, but it always almost involves a great deal of discussion of the problem-solving process and teaching about how problems are solved.

Teaching *For* Problem Solving

Teachers who choose to teach *for* problem solving are interested in teaching so that the mathematics being taught can be applied in the solution of both routine and non-routine problems. The teacher interested in teaching *for* problem solving thinks the primary purpose for learning mathematics is to be able to use it. Consequently, students are exposed to many examples of mathematical concepts and structures and given many opportunities to apply mathematics in solving problems. Further, teachers who teach *for* problem solving are very concerned about their students' ability to transfer what they have learned from one problem context to others. A strong believer in this approach would suggest that the primary reason for learning mathematics is to be able to use the knowledge gained to solve problems.

Teaching *via* Problem Solving

In teaching *via* problem solving, problems are used not only for their value in helping students learn mathematics, but also as the primary means for doing so. Adherents of this approach begin instruction on a mathematical topic with a problem situation that embodies key aspects of the topic, and mathematical techniques are developed as sensible methods to use to solve problems. The learning of mathematics in this way may be viewed as a development from the concrete (a "real world" problem which serves as an instance of the mathematical concept or technique) to the abstract (a symbolic representation of a class of problems, and techniques for operating with that representation).

Unlike the other two approaches, until recently teaching *via* problem solving was a conception that had not been adopted by many teachers. But, teaching *via* problem solving is the approach that is most consistent with the recommendation of the NCTM *Standards* that: (a) mathematics concepts and skills be learned in the context of solving problems; (b) the development of higher level thinking processes be fostered through problem-solving experiences; and (c) mathematics instruction take place in an inquiry-oriented, problem-solving atmosphere (NCTM, 1989).

The materials included in the *Activity Book* and the *Resource Manual* have been designed with four main goals in mind:

1. To help students develop adult-level perspective and insights into the nature of mathematics taught in the elementary school;
2. To improve students' ability to engage in mathematical thinking and reasoning;
3. To increase students' ability to use their mathematical knowledge to solve problems; and
4. To expose students to learning mathematics via problem solving.

[Additional references: Lester & Mau (1993), Lester et al. (1994)]

IMPORTANT INGREDIENTS OF THE ACTIVITIES IN THE *ACTIVITY BOOK*

Five features characterize the activities: (1) *"big mathematical ideas"* serve as important organizers for the course; (2) *cooperative learning* is an essential part of regular instruction; (3) *reflective writing* is considered a useful tool to help students make strong connections among the mathematical ideas they encounter and consolidate their mathematical understanding; (4) *assessment* is a continuous activity engaged in by both the teacher and students to the extent that it becomes a natural part of instruction; and (5) the new view of instruction requires that both the *teacher and students assume different roles* in daily classroom activities.

"Big Ideas" in Mathematics for Prospective Elementary Teachers

The term "big idea" refers to those themes that pervade several areas of mathematics and which serve to make connections among mathematics topics. These big ideas, then, are recurring, unifying themes in mathematics. With respect to identifying KEY big ideas to emphasize in the activities, we decided that to be a big idea an idea should:

1. Help students make connections among what may for them seem like unrelated topics;
2. Help students make connections between the world of mathematics and the real, everyday world, and
3. Provide ample opportunities for students to develop a greater appreciation for and understanding of the beauty of mathematics and mathematical activity.

Notwithstanding our belief that it is not so important to be concerned about selecting a specific set of themes, it is useful to take a look at what others think the big ideas in mathematics are. In particular, we found three books to be especially helpful: *The Mathematical Experience* (Davis & Hersh, 1981), *On the Shoulders of Giants* (Steen, 1990), and *The Growth of Mathematical Ideas: Grades K - 12* (NCTM, 1959). A brief overview of each of these books illustrates how the authors think about big mathematical ideas.

The Mathematical Experience. The authors of this powerful treatise on the nature of mathematics and mathematical activity, Philip Davis and Reuben Hersh, identify both inner and outer issues related to doing and studying mathematics. Their outer issues have to do with the utility of mathematics. Their inner issues seem to be closest to our notion of big ideas. They are as follows: abstraction, aesthetics, algorithmic vs. dialectic mathematics, formalization, generalization, infinity, math objects & structures, pattern, order & chaos, proof, symbolism, and unification.

On the Shoulders of Giants. The authors of this widely-read book on the nature of contemporary mathematics discuss two types of ideas: *connective themes* and *deep ideas* (that nourish the branches of mathematics). Both types seem to be related to our view of big ideas. Their *connective themes* include: algorithms, classification, exploration, inference, measurement, symmetry, and visualization. Their deep ideas include the notions of: mathematical structures, attributes, actions, abstractions, attitudes, behaviors, and dichotomies.

The Growth of Mathematical Ideas: Grades K - 12. The authors of the 24th yearbook of the NCTM insisted that "teachers . . . plan so that pupils continually have recurring but varied contacts with the fundamental ideas and processes of mathematics" (p. 2). Their list of big ideas includes the following: language & symbolism, mathematical modes of thought, measurement & approximation, number & operation, probability, proof, relations & functions, and statistics.

Some Thoughts about Big Ideas

Of course, each of the authors considered above used somewhat different terminology, but there was considerable agreement that the number of truly big ideas is relatively small. Moreover, it is interesting to note that traditional branches of mathematics (e. g., algebra, geometry, calculus) were not viewed by any of the authors as being big ideas in themselves and mathematical "actions" seemed to be as important as mathematical "structures."

Our own thinking, guided by a consideration of the ideas expressed in the three volumes mentioned above, has led to a conceptualization of the big ideas in terms of three dimensions: *structures, actions*, and *tactics*. Each dimension contains big ideas that exemplify a fundamental theme, process, or aim of mathematical activity.

Structures include mathematical ideas and entities such as equivalence, function & relation, measurement, number & operation, shape & space, and pattern & order, among others. The structures identified here are almost arbitrary; many other (perhaps better) structures could have been chosen. This is consistent with the notion that the specific big ideas are not nearly as important for these courses as the idea that there are unifying themes that pervade many branches of mathematics.

The *actions* refer to the sorts of activities that individuals engage in when they are doing mathematics and, as often as not, they are the goals of mathematical activity (e.g., creating a generalization, developing a useful mathematical model). These actions help distinguish mathematical activity from other kinds of intellectual activity. Among the actions that seem to be particularly relevant for courses for prospective teachers are verifying, generalizing, modeling, representing, and composing/decomposing.

The *tactics* dimension includes tools that help the individual do mathematics. More specifically, tactics assist the person doing mathematics in implementing mathematical *actions*. The four tactics we have chosen are conjecturing, creating & using algorithms, using problem-solving strategies, and developing & using appropriate language and symbolism, but there may be other equally as important tactics.

Finally, we reiterate the tentative, incomplete nature of these dimensions and the big ideas contained within them. However, they provided a framework for us in our development of the activities and materials in the *Activity Book* and *Resource Manual*. Samples of big ideas within each of the three dimensions are shown in Table 1. [*Note*: Big ideas associated with each chapter of the *Activity Book* are identified at the beginning of each chapter in the chapter overview.]

Table 1
Sample Big Ideas in Mathematics

Structures	Actions	Tactics
Equivalence	Generalizing	Creating/using algorithms
Function/relation	Representing	Conjecturing
Measurement	(De)composing	Using heuristics
Number & operation	Verifying	Using language & symbolism
Shape & space	Modeling	

Cooperative Learning

The philosophy behind the appropriate use of the materials in the *Activity Book* requires that students—rather than the teacher— must bear the primary burden for making sense of mathematical ideas, for constructing mathematical arguments, and for providing mathematical explanations. Shifting the burden in this way is accomplished by organizing each class session in a very different way from the usual university mathematics class: During much of each class period students work cooperatively in small groups to wrestle with problems that challenge them, to develop new and deeper understandings of fundamental mathematical concepts, and to talk about their new ways of thinking.

On the first day of class the instructor should group students into cooperative groups of about four students each. Since most students will not yet know each other, typically initial groups are formed by merely suggesting that four students who are sitting near one another put their desks together for small-group work. Students are then expected to keep working each day with the same group of people until the teacher indicates that it is time for a change of groups (usually every 3 or 4 weeks).

When the time comes, some instructors find it best to form new groups totally at random. One way to do this is to put a pile of playing cards near the door and to instruct students to take a card as they arrive at class on the day when groups are to be changed. Then those four who have the same card number (for example, 7 or 2 or Queen), regardless of suit, form a group. Of course, the instructor will have to take extra cards out of the deck ahead of time so that the appropriate number of groups of four cards remain—for example, if there are 24 students in the class, an instructor might remove from the deck all cards except those from Ace through 6. This will leave 24 cards, six sets of four cards each.

There may be times when random assignment to groups does not seem appropriate. For example, if there are one or two students in a class who have trouble working together, the instructor may want to assign groups so that these students are separated. Or the instructor may want to arrange groups so that neither the best students (nor the weakest students) are concentrated in one group. Near the end of the semester, an instructor may choose to ask each student to turn in a list of individuals they would like to work with and may form groups deliberately to include students who have expressed an interest in working together.

The role of the instructor in class is quite different from in more traditional mathematics classes. Rather than preparing a lecture, the instructor is usually responsible for a three-part lesson: (a) providing a brief introduction to the day's activities, (b) circulating about the room while students work in small groups and making appropriate comments to the groups, (c) leading wrap-up whole-class discussions where various groups share their thinking about the problem and the instructor helps everyone consolidate their thinking about their work. [This type of wrap-up often occurs several times throughout the class period, as well as at the end of each class.]

Before students begin work in their groups, the instructor should talk briefly to the entire class, introducing the activity of the day, explaining any new terminology or special instructions, and indicating how this activity fits into the larger context of the course. Note that this introduction is not a time for telling how to solve the problem at hand: **Solving the problem is the task of the students working in their small groups.** Students will probably be frustrated at first with small group work because they are accustomed to being told by their teachers exactly what to do. By contrast, the problem-solving activities challenge students to do their own thinking and the instructor's role is merely to introduce the activity and to guide students to discover their own solutions.

As the instructor circulates around the room while students are working in small groups, he or she must assume the role of question asker, problem poser, and careful listener; the students are the problem solvers and explainers, not the instructor. No matter how many times the instructor tells the students that *they* must be the problem solvers, they will only believe it if the instructor demonstrates it by his or her actions in the classroom. Four tenets should guide the instructor's behaviors:

- *Don't be an answer giver.* Try not to provide right/wrong judgments or to tell students how to proceed on a problem. If you do, they will always be waiting for you to tell them the next time, instead of thinking for themselves. If students ask, "Is this right?" ask them how they might decide for themselves. Some appropriate replies are "What do your group members think?" or "Can you find another way to verify your answer?"

- *De-emphasize correct answers.* Try to help students understand that you are more interested in depth of understanding, in ability to communicate mathematical ideas clearly, and in reasonable thinking than simply in correct answers. As you move from group to group, avoid asking "What did you get?" Instead ask questions that require explanation such as "Can you tell me what you've been thinking?" or "What strategies have you been using to approach this problem?"

- *Be prepared with appropriate hints.* There is more than one way to solve nearly every problem. When students are stuck, the instructor may need to provide a hint, but the hint should build on whatever progress the group has already made. For example, if students have been experimenting with specific numbers, it might be appropriate to suggest organizing findings in a table so that a pattern may become more apparent. If students are stuck because a problem has very large numbers or seems too complicated, it might be good to suggest trying some simpler cases first. It is usually not appropriate to provide a hint that merely provides students with the first (or a subsequent) step in a problem solution because this is often tantamount to telling students how to solve the problem.

- *Be prepared with problem extensions.* Some groups in the classroom will work faster than others. The experienced instructor helps these students (and eventually all students) to think beyond the task at hand. For example, it is often useful to ask students how they would solve the problem if conditions were changed (numbers different, question different, more constraints, etc.) or to ask them if they can work from their specific solution to a solution for a generalization of the problem.

One of the most important parts of the class is the wrap-up discussion that takes place after small groups have worked on problems. Once again, the instructor must guard against playing too prominent a role. There is no point in telling the class how their groups should have solved the problem. An instructor who does this will find that groups soon have no motivation to work on their own: Why should students struggle to work a problem if they know the teacher will explain it later? The wrap-up discussion should be a session where all groups have a chance to tell what approaches they tried, how successful or unsuccessful they were, and what conclusions they drew from their efforts. The best discussions are those in which the students do most of the talking—comparing approaches, arguing, and trying to convince one another of the validity of their findings. The instructor's role is to orchestrate this discussion so that everyone has an opportunity to participate, so that everyone can hear and understand what others are saying, and so that some closure is reached by the end of the discussion. Although it is important to allow everyone to contribute (even those whose solutions are incorrect), it is also important not to leave students hanging at the end, uncertain as to what makes sense and what doesn't. At the end of an ideal problem discussion, students will have reached their own conclusions about the validity of various problem solutions and will have a good sense of how the day's work fits into the bigger picture of the mathematical concepts being studied in the course.

[Additional References: Davidson, 1990; EQUALS, 1989; Weissglass, 1990]

Reflective Writing
Reflective thinking occurs both inside and outside the classroom. Inside the classroom, students reflect as they work to understand a problem, evaluate their solution processes, decide if their solutions make sense, justify their generalizations, connect mathematical concepts, understand a problem solution different from their own, extend a problem, monitor their thinking processes, and communicate their ideas to other students and the teacher. When students are encouraged and expected to be reflective in their work, they become better at thinking reflectively, their understanding of the content improves, they are more creative and insightful in their problem solving, their motivation for learning increases, and they begin to look for, and make, connections between mathematical concepts (Borasi & Rose, 1989).

Outside of the classroom students can continue their reflective activity through reflective writing. Reflective writing benefits students in four ways: (a) therapeutic value, (b) increased learning of content, (c) improvements in learning and problem-solving skills, and (d) change in one's conception of mathematics. Reflective thinking and writing are meaning-making processes that involve the student in actively building connections between what they are learning and what they already know.

In general, there are two broad types of reflective writing assignments that are used to give students the opportunity to reflect on their feelings and thoughts and communicate these in written form. The first type is an assignment that encourages the students to come to terms with their feelings and beliefs about mathematics. Some examples of this type are as follows:

- Write a brief description of your thinking as you played the games "Poison" and "What's My Number?"
- Discuss how you think mathematics fits with the real world. How do you think new mathematics is created? Has this changed your definition of mathematics?

The second type of reflective writing assignment asks the students to explain a mathematical idea or procedure. It forces the students to ask themselves, "Do I really understand this?" Several examples of open-ended assignments of this type are listed below.

- Explain why the Sieve of Eratosthenes works, in general, in identifying prime numbers.
- What do you consider to be the three most important features of a numeration system? Why?
- Verification is a big mathematical idea. What is the essence of this idea and why is it so important?

Throughout the course the reflective writing provides a record of the student's development through time, which provides new awareness and stimulus for reflection. This record also allows the teacher to enter into a dialogue with the student by responding to, challenging, and encouraging reflectiveness.

Assessment: Emphases and Practices

Assessment is perhaps the most worrisome aspect of any mathematics course for both the instructor and students, due in part to the fact that assessment is commonly associated (often exclusively) with grading and in part to the all-too-often mysterious nature of the instructor's assessment practices. We encourage the instructor to explain carefully to the students the various sources of data to be used for grading. These sources of data might include class participation, tests and quizzes, homework, reflective writing, and group projects. From the confluence of these data sources, the instructor assigns each student a grade that indicates the extent to which he or she has reached the goal of the course, namely, to develop good understanding of key mathematical ideas and to be able to communicate these ideas clearly and efficiently to others.

Assessment Is Not Just a Matter of Grading

Yet instructors should not think of assessment only in terms of assigning grades. Another just as important reason for assessment is to help the instructor build an accurate mental picture of the understandings held by students and to enable him or her to adjust instruction accordingly. Thus, assessment is an ongoing process in the classroom. For example, whenever the instructor is circulating throughout the room during small group work, he or she should be assessing the progress of the various groups, trying to get a picture of student understandings, and making mental plans so that the wrap-up discussion or the next class session may be orchestrated to help students deepen their understandings. Another source of assessment data for the instructor is the students' reflective writing. By reading students' writing, an instructor gets additional insight into which topics have been understood and which need more attention or a more focused discussion.

Still another reason for assessment is to indicate to students what is considered important. Because being able to communicate about mathematics is an important goal of the course, instructors must allow sufficient time for students to talk about mathematics and to write about it. And they must offer thoughtful reactions to students' communicative efforts, so that the students can see that their efforts to explain their ideas are valued.

Recommended Assessment Practices

Because teaching via problem solving requires a different type of instructional approach and different expectations of students, it also demands new ways of assessing student growth. In particular, it requires using more than just tests and quizzes for assessment. For example, if one accepts the position that assessment should be embedded in classroom work and should be aligned with classroom methods, then it makes sense that group assessment would be used in a class where group problem solving is the norm. A second reason for using alternative assessment techniques is that use of a variety of methods can provide a much richer vision of what students think, believe, and know than that obtained from any single method alone. Finally, in a course for prospective teachers, it is especially important that use of alternative assessment be modeled. As a result of a dozen or more years of schooling, many college students have developed the notion that the most important forms of assessment provide grades and serve to differentiate students from their peers. However, we would like to develop prospective teachers who have a broader view of assessment—who understand that, in the long run, grades are less important than how an individual's understanding is being deepened. Let us consider some alternative assessment techniques that we have used successfully. See Lambdin Kroll, Masingila & Mau (1992), Lester & Lambdin Kroll (1991), Mathematical Sciences Education Board (1993), and Stenmark (1991) for considerably more information about alternative assessment in mathematics classes.

Classroom Observation and Interaction. Classroom observation and interaction can be used as an alternative form of assessment. If students solve problems and discuss mathematical ideas in small groups, an instructor can watch and listen carefully while circulating from group to group. From a compilation of such observations, a more complete picture of students' understandings can be constructed than from any batch of test papers—and, as a result, more appropriate decisions concerning future instruction can be made.

Instructors can also gain important insights about the climate in their classroom as they interact with small groups of students: Are students confident? Frustrated? Involved? What beliefs about mathematics are being fostered by the work that students are doing? It is important to take time to think about how students feel and what they believe about the mathematics they are learning. Furthermore, when an instructor poses thought-provoking questions to a group of students working together, and demands responses that provide clear explanations of students' reasoning, students soon learn the importance of considering *why* mathematics makes sense rather than focusing solely on answers. They begin to appreciate the necessity of being able to communicate using precise mathematical language. Thus, the use of observation and interaction as assessment tools not only benefits the instructor, but also helps students develop an appreciation for what is really important in the learning and teaching of mathematics—an appreciation that is particularly important if the students are prospective teachers who are, themselves, to become reflective practitioners.

Although the use of a variety of assessment techniques helps instructors make decisions and aids in communicating expectations to students, it is also true that a major reason for assessing student work is to judge progress and assign grades. Grades in our mathematics course for teachers are based in part on sources that sound like they would be quite traditional (e.g., quizzes, tests, and class participation), and in part on other, more obviously non-traditional aspects of the course such as group presentations, written reflections, and concept maps. Yet, even quizzes and tests may need to be assessed in new and different ways, when the methods of teaching are non-traditional.

Group Problem Solving during Tests. The NCTM *Standards* stress the importance of aligning assessment techniques with teaching methods. Since so much class time will involve students working in cooperative groups, tests should consist of both an individual component and a group problem solving component. The group portion of each test involves two phases. In phase one, students work in small (pre-assigned) groups to solve a problem and to write a single group solution. In phase two, individuals are expected—on their own—to be able to answer individual questions about the group's solution and to solve problem extensions. (See Lambdin Kroll, Masingila & Mau, 1992, for a detailed description of how cooperative work on tests can be graded.)

Having a group portion on each test emphasizes to students several underlying messages of the course: that mathematics is not a solitary endeavor, that there are a variety of alternative approaches to problems, and that clarity of communication is important. Moreover, group problem solving provides an opportunity for students of every ability level to work together and to contribute to a common goal. Assessment of problem solving in groups also makes the point that prospective teachers need to consider themselves responsible not only for their own learning, but also for that of the others in the group. They should already consider themselves teachers in training.

Group Presentations and Group Projects. Another source of assessment data can be provided by group projects and presentations. In working on group projects outside of class, we have found that many students—for the first time—find themselves doing mathematics without continuous monitoring by a teacher. After having worked cooperatively to complete a project, students are expected to communicate to their peers and their instructor (in a group report to the class and in individual written reflections) their own self assessments of the mathematics concepts they used and the difficulties they encountered in accomplishing the project. In their presentation to the class, students must, in a professional manner, explain concepts and field questions about their mathematical thinking in the task. Thus, group presentations provide instructors with new layers to add to their multidimensional assessment of students' understanding, as well as providing students with still another situation where they must engage in reflection and self assessment.

Notebooks: Reflective Writing, Class and Homework Activities. Prospective teachers in our mathematics classes keep a notebook that contains a variety of documents including activities from the *Activity Book*, homework assignments and quizzes, as well reflective writing assignments. The notebooks serve two assessment functions: they help students become more aware of their own strengths and weaknesses, and they provide an avenue for confidential one-to-one communication with the instructor.

Instructor's and Students' Roles in Learning Mathematics via Problem Solving

As we mentioned earlier in this chapter, the instructor's role in a course emphasizing learning mathematics via problem solving is drastically different from the role he or she assumes in a more traditional, lecture-based course.

Students' must accept different roles also! No longer are they allowed to sit passively and simply "absorb" information transmitted to them by the instructor. Students are expected to listen to, respond to, and question the teacher and one another. They should also be reflective thinkers to become aware of how they themselves learn mathematics. Validity of particular representations and solutions should be determined by mathematical evidence and argument, whether working in large or small groups, and not by seeking the "right" answer from the teacher. It is probably inevitable, then, that some student frustration will arise in this environment because of prior student beliefs about the nature of mathematics and expectations about the proper role of the teacher. It is ultimately the task of the student to try to make sense of her or his mathematical experiences.

We realize, however, that role changes of this sort are not easy to make. One reason for the difficulty is that many instructors feel comfortable being "in charge" (of both the content to be taught and the students) and may have painstakingly developed lecture notes over the years that they are loath to give up. There is also the matter of the teacher needing to learn how to adopt an appropriate balance, sensing when to intervene and re-direct student exploration and when to allow the student to stumble along. A teacher who gives detailed directions may be sending the message that students are to be dependent on her for all knowledge. But a teacher who gives almost no direction increases the possibility of student frustrations rising to a debilitating level. Thus, the teacher's role is that of a guide, not that of an authority. The teacher chooses which problems and activities to use as a means for introducing material and guides the discussion of these problems, but the teacher does not pronounce solutions. This is fundamentally different from what has been considered appropriate teacher behavior in the past.

At the same time, college students have experienced years of training in which the teacher was the authority and the teacher's word was as close to the "truth" as was possible. As a result, many college students expect the teacher to tell them what to learn and how to learn it. That is, they have not developed autonomous learning behaviors that they will one day hope to develop in the children they will teach.

A heavy reliance on cooperative learning removes the teacher as the authority figure and minimizes the possibility of students blindly emulating the teacher's modeled techniques and solutions. Students are forced into helping each other develop their own deeper understanding of mathematical principles and mathematical autonomous learning behaviors.

The overarching responsibility of the teacher is to establish a mathematical community in the classroom where everyone's thinking is respected and in which reasoning and discussing mathematical ideas and meanings is the norm. Within this community, the teacher's insightful questioning can play an important role in stimulating student thinking so that there are opportunities for students to examine and question their beliefs about mathematics, to have their misconceptions challenged, and to seek clarifications, strategies, and verifications without direct teacher intervention.

The traditional mathematics classroom is teacher-centered. In a typical teacher-centered class, the first activity is for the teacher to check answers for the previous day's assignment. Second, the more difficult problems are worked by the teacher or students at the chalkboard. Then, a brief explanation is given by the teacher of any new material and problems (exercises) are assigned for the next day. The remainder of class is devoted to working on homework while the teacher is available for answering questions. This type of instruction implies that there is a specific mathematical knowledge that the teacher has and through modeling what the teacher does and through passive absorption, students will acquire this knowledge.

In summary, a course following a learning via problem solving approach requires new and different roles for both instructors and students, roles that are negotiated throughout the semester. Table 2 contrasts a course emphasizing learning via problem solving with a traditional college mathematics course.

Table 2
Contrast Between a Traditional Approach and a Learning via Problem Solving Approach

Approach to College Mathematics Instruction	
Traditional Approach	**Learning via Problem Solving Approach**
Teacher's Role	
• Lectures • Assigns seat work • Dispenses knowledge	• Guides and facilitates • Poses challenging questions • Helps students share knowledge
Student's Role	
• Works individually • Learns passively • Forms mainly "weak" constructions	• Works in a group • Learns actively • Forms mainly "strong" constructions

BIBLIOGRAPHY

Davidson, N. (Ed.). (1990). *Cooperative learning in mathematics: A handbook for teachers.* Menlo Park, CA: Addison-Wesley.

Davis, P. J., & Hersh, R. (1981). *The mathematical experience.* Boston: Birkhäuser.

EQUALS. (1989). *Get it together: Math problems for groups—grades 4 - 12.* Berkeley, CA: Lawrence Hall of Science.

Johnson, D.W., & Johnson, R.T. (1990). Using cooperative learning in math. In N. Davidson (Ed.), *Cooperative learning in mathematics* (pp. 103-125). Menlo Park, Ca: Addison-Wesley Publishing Company.

Lambdin Kroll, D., Masingila, J. O., & Mau, S. M. (1992). Cooperative problem solving: But what about grading? *Arithmetic Teacher, 39*(6), 17-23.

Lester, F. K., & Lambdin Kroll, D. (1991). Implementing the Standards—Evaluation: A new vision. *Mathematics Teacher, 84*(4), 276-284.

Lester, F. K., Masingila, J. O., Mau, S. T., Lambdin Kroll, D., Santos, V. P., & Raymond, A. M. (1994). Learning how to teach via problem solving. In D. A. Aichele (Ed.), *The professional development of teachers of mathematics.* 1994 yearbook of the National Council of Teachers of Mathematics. Reston, VA: NCTM.

Lester, F. K., & Mau, S. T. (1993). Teaching mathematics via problem solving: A course for elementary teachers. *For the Learning of Mathematics, 13*(1).

Mathematical Sciences Education Board/National Research Council. (1990). *Reshaping school mathematics: A philosophy and framework for curriculum.* Washington, D. C.: National Academy Press.

Mathematical Sciences Education Board/National Research Council. (1993). *Measuring up: Prototypes for mathematics assessment.* Washington, DC: National Academy Press.

National Council of Teachers of Mathematics. (1959). *The growth of mathematical ideas K - 12.* (24th yearbook of the Council). Reston, VA: Author.

National Council of Teachers of Mathematics. (1980). *An agenda for action: Recommendations for school mathematics for the 1980s.* Reston, VA: Author.

National Council of Teachers of Mathematics. (1989). *Curriculum and evaluation standards for school mathematics.* Reston, VA: Author.

Polya, G. (1945). *How to solve it.* (2nd ed.). Princeton, NJ: Princeton University Press.

Schroeder, T. L., & Lester, F. K. (1989). Developing understanding in mathematics via problem solving. In P. R. Trafton (Ed.), *New directions for elementary school mathematics* (1989 Yearbook of the National Council of Teachers of Mathematics) (pp. 31-42). Reston, VA: NCTM.

Steen, L. A. (Ed.). (1990). *On the shoulders of giants: New approaches to numeracy.* Washington, DC: National Academy Press.

Stenmark, J. K. (Ed.) (1991). *Mathematics assessment: Myths, models, good questions, and practical suggestions.* Reston, VA: National Council of Teachers of Mathematics.

Weissglass, J. (1990). *Exploring elementary mathematics: A small-group approach for teaching.* Dubuque, IA: Kendall/Hunt.

Chapter 1: Getting Started in Learning Mathematics via Problem Solving

Chapter Overview:

In this chapter you will begin to see just how different this course is from any other mathematics course you have taken. The activities in this chapter focus on three things: (1) learning how to *work in a small, cooperative group* on real mathematical investigations, (2) becoming *less dependent on your instructor* for answers and direction, and (3) learning about certain key *problem-solving strategies*. All of this will be done in the context of playing various strategy games and exploring solutions to some interesting problems. Throughout the activities you will be gaining valuable experience in how to collaborate in a productive way with others without relying on your instructor. You will also be looking for patterns, guessing and checking, making conjectures, using logical reasoning, and making organized lists.

Big Mathematical Ideas:

> problem-solving strategies, generalizing, verifying, using language & symbolism

NCTM Standards Links:

> *K - 4:* Mathematics as problem solving; Mathematics as reasoning; Mathematical connections; Patterns & relationships

> *5 - 8:* Mathematics as problem solving; Mathematics as reasoning; Mathematical connections; Patterns & functions

Chapter Outline:

Activity 1.1—What's My Number?

In your group, form two teams. One team will play against the other team in the group.

1.   One team, say team A, writes a 3-digit number on a piece of paper (e.g., 982).

2.   All digits in the number must be different.

3.   The other team, say team B, tries to determine the number that has been written on the paper.

4.   They do so by naming any 3-digit number.

5.   In return, team A tells them the number of correct digits and the number of correct places in their guess.

6.   Team B continues to name numbers until they determine the correct number.

Play several games of What's My Number? Alternate which team forms the number and which team guesses the number. You will want to have an organized method of keeping track of your guesses and the information you receive from the other team. Try to determine strategies that minimize the number of guesses you need.

Activity 1.2—Poison

Form two teams in your group. One team will play against the other team in the group. Your instructor will give you 10 color tiles. Place the 10 tiles between the two teams and follow these rules:

1. Decide which team will go first.

2. When it is your team's turn, you must take 1 or 2 tiles from the table.

3. Alternate turns until there are no tiles remaining on the table.

4. The team who takes the last tile, the "poison" one, is the loser.

Play several games of Poison and try to determine a strategy for winning.

Activity 1.3—Cereal Boxes and Patio Tiles

PROBLEM 1:

Part A: Stacking Cereal Boxes

A store clerk was told she had 45 cereal boxes to be stacked in the display window and all of the boxes had to be used. The manager told the clerk that the boxes had to be in a triangle like the one shown below. The sales clerk wondered how many boxes needed to be placed on the bottom row to build the triangle using all the boxes.

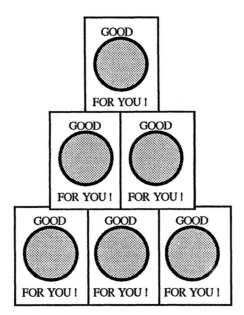

Part B: Stacking More Boxes

Suppose the clerk had to stack 200 boxes of cereal in a triangle like the one above. Now how many boxes would be on the bottom row? What if the clerk had B boxes to stack?

PROBLEM 2: Laying Blocks in a Patio

A patio was to be laid in a design like the one shown. A man had 50 blocks to
use. How many blocks should be placed in the middle row to use the most
number of blocks?

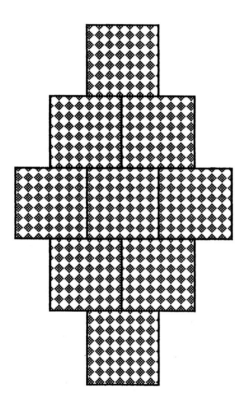

Generalize your answer to the patio block problem.

PROBLEM 3: Looking for Similarities

How are problems 1 and 2 alike? How are they different?

Talk over your solutions with your group. Decide what gave you trouble and why. Ask yourselves questions such as: "What did we do that helped us get started in the right direction? What did we do that gave us trouble? Why?"

Activity 1.4—The Mathematics in the Pages of a Newspaper

Newspapers usually consist of large sheets of paper that are printed and folded in half to form the pages of a newspaper.

1. Suppose you had a sheet of paper that you folded in half. How many pages would be formed with one such sheet of paper? How many pages would be formed with two such sheets?

2. If, starting with 1, you numbered the pages of the single sheet that was folded in half, what would be the numbers that appeared on either side of the sheet? Answer the same question if you had two sheets of paper arranged as in a newspaper.

3. What is the sum of the page numbers on the same side of the sheet for the single sheet? What is this sum for the double sheet ?

4. What is the sum of all page numbers for the single sheet? For the double sheet?

5. If you had 10 sheets of paper in the newspaper, how many pages would you get?

    What would be the page numbers that would appear on the innermost sheet? What would be their sum?

    What would be the sum of the page numbers that appeared on any one side of a sheet of paper?

    What would be the sum of all the pages in the newspaper?

6.   Answer questions #2-5 if you had 100 sheets of paper.

7.   If your newspaper had to have 28 pages, how many sheets of paper would you need?

What would be the sum of the page numbers that appeared on any one side of a sheet of paper?

What would be the page number that appeared on the same side of the sheet as page 8?

8.   Answer the above questions if your newspaper had 50 pages.

9.   Pat pulled out one full page from the Travel section of the New York Times. If the left half of the page was numbered 4 and the right half was numbered 19, how many pages were there in the Travel section? Had there been 18 pages in the section, then which page would have appeared opposite the page numbered 6?

Activity 1.5—Family Relations

The following is part of a family tree. Answer the questions that follow based on the tree given below. Make sure that you state the relationship as precisely as possible.

Key

**** ---- denotes a marital relationship
——— --- denotes a sibling relationship
| --- denotes a parent to child relationship
|

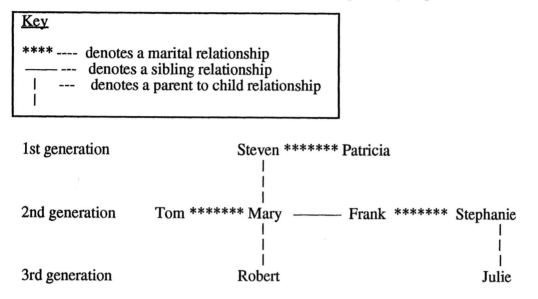

1st generation   Steven ******* Patricia

2nd generation   Tom ****** Mary ——— Frank ****** Stephanie

3rd generation   Robert   Julie

1.   How is Patricia related to Frank?

2.   How is Steven related to Stephanie?

3.   How is Julie related to Patricia?

4.   How is Mary related to Stephanie?

5.   How is Tom related to Steven?

6.   How is Frank related to Tom?

7.   How is Tom related to Stephanie?

8.   How is Robert related to Tom?

9.   How is Julie related to Mary?

10. How is Robert related to Frank?

11. If Stephanie met her husband's sister's father on Tuesday, whom did she meet?

12. If Tom called his wife's brother's daughter, whom did he call?

13. If Frank invited his mother's grandson for dinner, whom would he have invited?

14. If Robert visited his mother's brother's wife yesterday, whom did he visit?

Activity 1.6—Constructing Numbers

Using each of the ten digits no more than once, construct the numbers described below.

1. largest 7-digit odd number with a 9 in the ten's place

2. largest 10-digit even number containing more than 50% odd digits

3. smallest 6-digit even number with a 1 in the thousands place

4. largest 8-digit even number

5. smallest 9-digit even number

6. number closest to half a billion

7. smallest 6-digit multiple of 5 containing no digits less than 6

8. number closest to half a million that contains no digits less than 4

9. largest 10-digit number that is a multiple of 10

10. smallest 7-digit number containing no digit between 1 and 5

11. largest 6-digit even number that is a multiple of 5 and uses no digits between 4 and 9

12. smallest 10-digit odd number with more than 75% of the digits greater than 4

13. largest 6-digit multiple of 9 that is odd

14. largest odd number using only digits that alone are considered prime numbers

15. number closest to a quarter billion that contains only even digits

Activity 1.7—The Valentine's Day Party

Three married couples met at a local restaurant for a Valentine's Day dinner party. As each couple arrived, individuals meeting for the first time would shake hands. Each person met a different number of people (0 - 8) for the first time, except for Tom and Joyce Martin, who each met the same number of people. How many hands did Joyce Martin shake?

Activity 1.8—The Puzzle of the Hefty Hippos

Every year the members of the Hefty Hippos Weight Watchers' Club host a volleyball tournament against another group of serious dieters. The tournament has been held on July 4th for the past six years, this year being no exception. The tournament has been such a success that the HHWWWC was able to purchase uniforms for all players last year. When they tried on their uniforms four weeks before this year's tournament, they decided that they had better lose a little weight. They started to meet once a week at the local gym to work off the extra weight they had gained since last year. As an incentive to lose weight, the group decided that the hippo who lost the least amount of weight by the day of the tournament would have to pay for beer and pizza for everyone. On the morning of the tournament the hippos went down to the nearby warehouse to use the heavy duty scales. But the scales started at 300 kg, more than any of them weighed (these were no ordinary hippos). What were they to do? Heloise, a hippo of some considerable mathematical prowess, came up with a solution. She said that they merely needed to weigh all possible pairs of hippos and then determine each hippo's weight from these weights. The weights of all possible pairs were as follows (in kilograms, of course): 361, 364, 376, 377, 380, 389, 392, 393, 396, 398, 408, 411, 414, 426, 430. How much did each hippo weigh? (You may assume that all weights are whole numbers)

Activity 1.9—Making Dice

Each of the shapes given below can be folded to make a die. In each of them, three numbers are missing. Fill in the missing numbers so that the numbers on opposite faces always add up to 7.

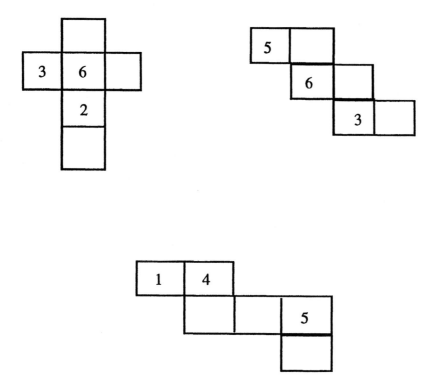

Create two similar shapes yourself and exchange them with your partner and have him or her complete them.

Activity 1.10—The Tower of Hanoi

You are given five disks of varying sizes. Stack these disks so that they increase in size with the largest at the bottom. Imagine that these disks are stacked on a peg and that there are two other empty pegs on the table, placed side by side. The goal is to transfer all the five disks to one of the other pegs using the fewest possible moves, while observing the rules below.

1. Move only one disk at a time.

2. No disk may be placed on top of one smaller than itself at any point of time.

Fill in the table below and make a conjecture about the fewest possible number of moves for N given disks. Test your conjecture for small values of N. How would you test it for large values of N? Explain your strategies for making and testing your conjectures.

Number of disks	Fewest possible number of moves

Things to Know from Chapter 1

Words to Know
- devise a plan
- implement a plan
- look back and review a solution
- look for a pattern
- problem solving
- guess and check
- solve a simpler problem
- strategy
- understand a problem
- use a visual aid
- use algebra
- work backwards

Concepts to Know
- what it means to understand a problem
- what it means to devise a plan
- what it means to implement a plan
- what it means to look back and review a solution
- what it means to be systematic in solving a problem
- what it means to persevere in solving a problem
- what it means to monitor your thinking when solving a problem

Procedures to Know
- guess and check strategy
- solve a simpler problem strategy
- use a visual aid strategy
- use algebra strategy
- work backwards strategy
- work systematically

Exercises & More Problems

Exercises

1. 1, 2, 4, ___, ___, ___   Find the next three terms.

2. A, B, B, A, B, B, A, ___, ___, ___   Find the next three terms.

3. 5, 6, 14, 29, 51, 80, ___, ___, ___   Find the next three terms.

4. 2, 3, 9, 23, 48, 87, ___, ___, ___   Find the next three terms.

5. ▢, ▢▢, ▢▢▢, ▢▢▢▢ , ___, ___, ___   Find the number of segments required for each of the next three terms.

6. Make up two patterns where the object is to find some missing terms.

7. Name four problem-solving strategies you have learned and implemented in this chapter.

8. List and explain the four steps of problem solving that were introduced in this chapter.

Critical Thinking

9. a. Rebekah needed exactly 6 cups of water for a recipe, but she had only two cups that could measure 5 cups and 8 cups of liquid respectively. How could she use these two to get the exact amount she needs?
   b. Could Rebekah get exactly 1 cup of water using the two cups she had?
   c. What other amounts are possible to get using the two cups?

10. June and her friend bought an 8-gallon barrel of cider that they wanted to share equally. However, the only other containers that they had were a 5-gallon container and a 3-gallon container. How could they use these to separate the cider?

11. Suppose you have an inexhaustible supply of 5 cents and 8 cents stamps.
    a. Which of the following amounts can you make up using the stamps you have? Show the combinations that you would use to make up the amounts that you can.

    7¢, 13¢, 14 ¢, 17¢, 18¢, 31¢, 41¢, 43¢, 52¢, 78¢, 164¢

    b. List all the amounts between 1¢ and 100¢ that cannot be made using these stamps.

12. Compare problems 9 and 11.
    a. What similarities do you see between the two problems?
    b. What differences do you see?

13. Moses had $23,560 in his bank account at the beginning of this year. Each month, starting with January, he withdraws half the amount of money that is left in the account.
    a. How much money will be left in his account at the end of October?
    b. When will the money in the account become less than $10? Less than $1?
    Show your methods of obtaining the solutions clearly. You may give all the answers correct to the nearest cent.

14. You have eight coins that look alike, but one is heavier than the others. Using a balance scale, what is the minimum number of weighings that you need in order to determine the heavier coin? Explain your answer.

15. Adam wants to make 3 waffles. He has a griddle iron that can hold at most two waffles at a time, and each side of a waffle takes three minutes to get cooked. What is the minimum amount of time that Peter will take to cook all the three waffles?

16. A spider is trying to climb a wall that is 15 feet high. In each hour, it climbs up 3 feet, but falls back 2 feet. In how many hours will it reach the top of the wall? Explain your answer.

17. Which of the following numbers is larger? Explain your answer.

$$(1 + 2 + ... + 1000) \times 999 \quad\text{or}\quad (1 + 2 + ... + 999) \times 1000$$

18. Sara inspected the horses and hens in her farm one morning. Afterwards, she could not remember how many animals of each kind she had, but knew that the total number of these animals was 27, her own age in 1997. She also knew that the total number of legs of the animals was 70, the year in which she was born. How many horses does Sara have? You may assume that each animal has the usual number of legs. Outline clearly the strategy you used to answer this question.

19. Three boxes with lids are placed on a shelf. Of the three boxes, one contains all white balls, one contains all red balls, and one contains a mix of red and white balls. The three boxes are labeled, "White Balls," "Red Balls,", and "Red and White Balls," but all three are placed incorrectly. By pulling out a single ball from any one of the three boxes, how can you determine the correct label for each box.

20. Diana has a sheet of paper that is 8 1/2 inches x 11 inches in size. How can she cut off a square that is 6 inches x 6 inches, using only the paper?

21. Six friends Eric, Harry, Kevin, John, Tom, and Max are comparing their weights. Kevin is 32 pounds lighter than Harry. Tom is 26 pounds heavier than Eric. Harry is 4 pounds lighter than Tom, but 17 pounds heavier than John. Max is halfway between the heaviest and the lightest person. Arrange the six friends in decreasing order of their heights. If Eric's weight is 130 pounds, find the weight of the other five people.

22. The bus system of the Longwinded Bus Company runs in a strange way. On most routes, the buses only run in one direction. Thus, to travel from one town to another, passengers may have to go through several other towns. The following statements show the bus routes between ten destinations.
   - From Stratford, buses travel to Temple and Hastings. (This means that passengers can go from Stratford to Temple or Hastings but they cannot travel back on the same route).
   - From Temple, buses go to Mapletown.
   - From Blissville, buses go to Oakwood, and buses also go from Oakwood to Blissville.
   - Buses go from Pinesville to Brackport and Williamsburg.
   - Mapletown gets buses only from Temple.
   - From Morgantown, buses travel to Stratford and Pinesville.
   - Buses go from Hastings to Blissville.
   - From Mapletown, buses go to Williamsburg.
   - From Blissville, buses go to Pinesville.
   - Buses go from Williamsburg to Stratford.
   - From Stratford, buses go to Brackport.

   Using the Longwinded Bus Company, how would you travel:
   a. from Stratford to Blissville?
   b. from Morgantown to Mapletown?
   c. from Williamsburg to Oakwood?
   d. from Pinesville to Oakwood?

e. from Hastings to Williamsburg?
f. from Mapletown to Brackport?
g. from Stratford to Pinesville?
h. from Brackport to Williamsburg?
i. from Pinesville to Mapletown?
j. from Temple to Hastings?

23. Place six plants along the four walls of a room so that each of the walls has the same number of plants placed along it.

24. Consider a billiard table that is arranged in the form of a grid as follows. A ball that starts its path from one corner of the table at an angle of 45° will traverse diagonally across each square until it hits side. It will then reverse its direction and once again travel at an angle of 45° until it hits another sid This will continue until the ball hits a corner. An example of such a path is given below. In this cas the width of the table is 3 units, while its width is 2 units.

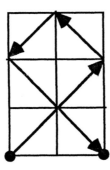

a. Draw a set of seven such tables, such that in each case the width is two units, and the lengths are 1, 2, 3, 4, 5, 6, and 7 units respectively. In each case, show the complete path that the ball would travel if it started from the bottom left corner, and was struck at an angle of 45° to the side.
b. State at least three patterns that you notice in the above set of pictures.
c. Using these pictures, where will the ball will end up for a table that has dimensions 27 x 2 units? 100 x 2 units? 1002 x 2 units? Explain how you obtained your answers.

25. A population of bacteria doubles every day. On the 30th day the population is 20 million. On what day was it 5 million?

26. Tyler used 2989 digits to number the pages of a book. How many pages does the book have? Justify your answer.

27. Sara, Cathy, and Tina have just finished playing three games. There was only one loser in each game. Sara lost the first game, Cathy lost the second game, and Tina lost the third game. After each game, the loser was required to double the money of the other two. After three rounds, each woman had $24. How much did each have at the start?

Extending the Activity

28. Suppose you are playing "Poison" and there are 6 tiles left on the table. If it is your turn, how many tiles should you take?

29. Suppose you are beginning a game of "Poison" and there are 29 tiles on the table. Do you want to play first or second? How many tiles should you take to be sure you will win?

30. Suppose you are playing "What's My Number?" Here is a list of the guesses and information obtained for each guess. What's the number?

Guess	Correct Digits	Correct Places
123	1	0
234	1	0
345	1	1
456	0	0
567	1	1
678	1	0
789	1	0

31. Suppose you are working with the Tower of Hanoi puzzle and you have 6 disks on the left peg and you want to move them to the right peg (the third peg is in the middle). What is your first move?

32. Suppose you have 11 disks on the left peg and you want to move them to the right peg. What is your first move?

33. Given the number of disks and the target peg, can you predict the first move? Explain your answer.

34. Write down an eight digit number consisting of the two 1's, two 2's, two 3's, and two 4's such that the 1's are separated by one digit, the 2's are separated by two digits and so on.

35. Pick any single digit number. Multiply this number by 273. Now multiply the answer by 407. What do you see? Try this with several different single digit numbers.
    a. Explain why you get such an answer each time.
    b. Suggest two different numbers (other than 273 and 407) that would work in the same way.

36. Visualize a 4 x 4 x 4 cube.
    a. How many smaller cubes is it made up of?
    b. If the large cube were painted on all the exposed sides, how many of the smaller cubes would have
        i.   all four sides painted?
        ii. exactly three sides painted?
        iii. exactly two sides painted?
        iv. exactly one side painted?
        v.   no side painted?
    c. What strategies did you use to answer the questions in a. and b. above?

Writing/Discussing

37. Looking for relationships between problems is an important part of doing mathematics. The solution to "Stacking Cereal Boxes" could have been very helpful in solving "Laying Blocks in a Patio" or vice versa. Explain the connections you see between these two problems.

38. Discuss the strategies that you used in constructing numbers in Activity 1.6.

39. Write a historical account of how your group solved either the "Valentine's Day Party" problem or the "Puzzle of the Hefty Hippos" problem. Then write an efficient explanation of the problem solution.

40. Discuss what you have learned about doing mathematics so far in this course. In particular, consider what you have learned about various problem-solving strategies, making and testing conjectures, and evaluating solution efforts. Include in your discussion your thoughts about how this course has been different from previous mathematics courses.

Chapter 2: Numeration

Chapter Overview:

Among the most important topics in elementary school mathematics are those concerned with systems of recording and naming numbers: numeration systems. In this chapter you will learn about the properties of a good numeration system by comparing and contrasting properties of several systems that have been used by various cultures throughout history. Also, in order to help you appreciate the issues involved when young children first begin to learn properties of our base ten (decimal) numeration system, your group will develop one of your own. Finally, you will investigate two special properties of numeration systems—place value and base—in order to help you better understand the roles these properties play in the base ten system we use.

Big Mathematical Ideas:

generalizing, problem-solving strategies, decomposing, mathematical structure, representing

NCTM Standards Links:

K - 4:   Mathematics as problem solving; Mathematics as communication; Mathematics as reasoning; Mathematical connections; Number sense & numeration

5 - 8:   Mathematics as problem solving; Mathematics as communication; Mathematics as reasoning; Mathematical connections; Number & number relationship; Number systems & number theory

Chapter Outline:

Activity 2.1—Early Numeration Systems

Read the historical/social/cultural notes in Chapter 2 of the *Resource Manual* to learn about different numeration systems. Then complete the following activity that explores some early numeration systems.

1. The use of tally marks to record numbers was a common numeration system used by primitive tribes. This system is as follows:

Primitive Numeral	Our System
/	1
//	2
///	3
////	4
/////	5
721	6
///////	7
////////	8
.	.
.	.
.	.

How would you write 13 with this system? 24? 56? 104?

2. The early Chinese-Japanese numeration system was a base ten system. The system was as follows:

Chinese-Japanese Numerals	Our System
⌣	1
≈	2
≋	3
凸	4
五	5
六	6
七	7
⌢	8
九	9
十	10
百	100
千	1000

Numbers were represented by numerals written in vertical columns. For example,

Chinese-Japanese Numeral						
五	(5)	一	(1)	五	(5)
十	(10)	百	(100)	千	(1000)
≈	(3)	≈	(2)	六	(6)
		十	(10)	百	(100)
		六	(6)	≈	(2)
				十	(10)
				五	(5)

Our System					
53	5(10) + 3	126	1(100) + 2(10) + 6	5,625	5(1000) + 6(100) + 2(10) + 5

How would you write 345 with this system? 1,039? 12,678?

Activity 2.2—The Hindu-Arabic Numeration System

The numeration system that we use is called the Hindu-Arabic numeration system. It has this name because both Hindus and Arabs contributed to this system. The Hindus developed an alphabet and used some letters to represent some of their digits in their numeration system. In about 600 A.D., this system developed a place value notation, and eventually, the system evolved to the system we use today. The Arabs' contribution to our numeration system lies primarily with their transmitting the information about it to other parts of the world.

The Hindu-Arabic numeration system has six basic characteristics. These will be defined and then there will be questions for you to answer.

Definition 1: A numeration system has a **base** if it reflects a process of repeated grouping by some number greater than one. This number is called the base of the system, and all numbers are written in terms of powers of the base.

What base does the Hindu-Arabic numeration system use? Justify your answer.

Definition 2: A numeration system is a **place value** system if the value of each digit is determined by its position in the numeral.

Give an example to illustrate why the Hindu-Arabic numeration system is a place value system.

Definition 3: A numeration system is **multiplicative** if each symbol in a numeral represents a different multiple of the face value of that symbol.

Give an example to illustrate why the Hindu-Arabic numeration system is multiplicative.

<u>Definition 4</u>: A numeration system is **additive** if the value of the set of symbols representing a number is the sum of the values of the individual symbols.

Give an example to illustrate why the Hindu-Arabic numeration system is additive.

<u>Definition 5</u>: A numeration system has a **zero** if there is a symbol to represent the number of elements in the empty set.

Explain the use of the zero in the numeral 906.

<u>Definition 6</u>: A numeration system is a **unique representation** system if each numeral refers to one and only one number.

What would be the disadvantages of a system in which some numerals did not represent unique numbers?

Discuss as a group the relationships among a number, a numeral, and the name of a number.

Activity 2.3—Comparing Numeration Systems

1. What are some advantages and disadvantages of the tally mark numeration system?

2. Explain how the Egyptian system is an additive system.

3. What advantages does the Egyptian system have over the tally mark system?

4. Explain how the Babylonian numeration system used the idea of place value. What does each place represent in this system?

5. Why does the absence of a symbol for zero make this system sometimes hard to use?

6. Explain how the Chinese-Japanese numeration system is a base ten system.

7. What are some advantages and disadvantages of the Chinese-Japanese numeration system?

8. The Roman numeration system was an additive system with subtractive and multiplicative features. Explain how these two features are illustrated in this system.

9. Does the Roman numeration system have a place value scheme? Explain your answer.

Activity 2.4—Mathematical and Non-mathematical Characteristics of Systems

1. How many separate digits does the Primitive (tally) system have? The Egyptian? The Babylonian? The Chinese-Japanese? The Roman? The Hindu-Arabic?

System	Number of digits
Primitive	
Egyptian	
Babylonian	
Chinese-Japanese	
Roman	
Hindu-Arabic	

2. Fill in the chart below for each of the numeration systems we have studied, noting whether or not the systems have the listed characteristics.

	Tally	Egyptian	Babylonian	Chinese-Japanese	Roman	Hindu-Arabic
Mathematical Characteristics						
Additive						
Multiplicative						
Has base						
Place Value						
Symbol for zero						
Non-mathematical Characteristics						
Unique representation						
Convenient, easy to use						
Economical in terms of number of distinct symbols						
Ease with which it can be learned						

Activity 2.5—Creating a Numeration System

In your group create your own numeration system different from the Hindu-Arabic system. Include several of the following aspects:

1. Provide a table of symbols basic to your system and the Hindu-Arabic equivalent of each symbol.

2. Have examples of larger numbers represented by the numerals of your system so that your method of recording is clear.

3. Give a rationale that supports the design of your system and indicate the characteristics your system has.

4. Indicate which of the basic operations (addition, subtraction, multiplication, division) are possible in your system, and give examples showing how such operations would be performed.

Activity 2.6—Exploring Place Value Through Trading Games

This activity involves playing two games called "310 (Fifty-two)" and "Give Away" using base four blocks. In preparation for playing the games you need to become familiar with names for the blocks on the table. The smallest block is called a unit. The next largest block is called a long, the next is a flat, and the largest block is called a cube.

Read the explanation of the first game and answer questions 1 and 2 before playing the game. Answer 3 and 4 after you have played the game.

310 (Fifty-Two)

Each person starts with no blocks. Take turns spinning the spinners and finding the sum or difference of the numbers on the two spinners. The sum or difference is the number of unit pieces you must add or return. You must trade smaller pieces for equivalent larger pieces to always have the fewest number of pieces. The first player to reach the equivalent of fifty-two unit pieces, without going over, is the winner. Record your totals after each transaction in the table below. As you play the game try to think about what mathematical concepts are present in this game.

# of cubes	# of flats	# of longs	# of units	total # in units

1. What is the fewest number of spins you would need to win a flat? What would they be?

2. What is the largest number of spins you would need to win a flat? Why?

3. What is the fewest number of unit pieces that are needed to play this game if you were going to package and sell the game for four players? Why? (Note: An adequate supply of cubes, flats, and longs will also be provided.)

4. What mathematical concepts are illustrated in this game?

Read the explanation of this game and answer questions 1-3 before playing. Answer questions 4 and 5 after playing the game.

Give Away

Each player starts with two flats. Take turns spinning the spinners and finding the sum or difference of the numbers on the two spinners. The sum or difference is the number of unit pieces you must add or return. The winner is the first player to return all the blocks by the exact spin of the spinners. Record your totals after each transaction in the table below.

# of cubes	# of flats	# of longs	# of units	total # in units

1. What is the fewest number of spins of the spinners you would need to give away all of your blocks? What would they be?

2. What is the largest number of spins you would need to give away all of your blocks? Why?

3. Answer questions 1 and 2 for this game when it takes seven units to make a long.

4. Using the same blocks that you are using, a student had recorded 132 in her table. If she traded in all of her blocks for units, how many would she have?

5. What mathematical concepts are illustrated in this game?

Activity 2.7—Converting from One Base to Another

1. Change these base ten numerals into numerals in the given base.

<u>Base 10</u>   <u>Base 2</u>   <u>Base 5</u>   <u>Base 6</u>

6

21

45

39

2. Change the numerals below to base ten numerals.

<u>Base N</u>   <u>Base 10</u>

11_{two}

35_{six}

104_{five}

17_{nine}

3. Find the largest number from each group. Be able to justify your answer.

   a. 5_{six} 11_{four} 101_{three}

   b. 122_{three} 112_{four} 76_{eight}

   c. ET_{twelve} 101_{eight} 11110_{two}

   d. 325_{twelve} 523_{six} 10122_{three}

Activity 2.8—Place Value and Different Bases

1. The Hindu-Arabic numeration system is a base ten and place value system. What does this mean?

2. How does a numeration system with base two and place value differ from the Hindu-Arabic system?

3. How would you change a base ten numeral to a base two numeral? Hint: Doing an example may help you develop a strategy.

4. How would you change a base two numeral to a base ten numeral?

Activity 2.9—Solving a Problem with a Different Base

The ACME Potato Chip Problem

The ACME Potato Chip Company received 6 freight cars supposedly full of potatoes in 100-lb. bags. It was learned that the automatic weighing machine was broken for awhile and that some of the freight cars were full of 90-lb. bags of potatoes. Ms. Jones said, "Let's load some sacks of potatoes from each freight car into our truck. Then in one weighing we will locate the freight cars containing sacks with the 90-lb. bags. Let's take 1 bag of potatoes from the first freight car, 2 from the second, 4 from the third, 8 from the fourth, 16 from the fifth, and 32 from the sixth. So we will have a total of 63 bags. If all the sacks weigh 100 lbs., the correct answer from the weighing should be 6300 lbs. more than the truck. Suppose the answer is 5870 lbs. more than the truck (i.e., the potatoes in the truck are 430 lbs. too light). Since each light sack differs from 100 lbs. by 10 lbs., there are 43 light sacks in the truck."

How could Ms. Jones determine which freight cars had bags of potatoes weighing 90 lbs. instead of 100 lbs.? Try to generalize this procedure.

Activity 2.10—Computations in Different Bases

1. Do the following computations in the base that is indicated.

312_{four} $TE3_{twelve}$ 100_{two} 156_{seven}

$+ 233_{four}$ $+ \quad 99_{twelve}$ $- \quad 11_{two}$ $- \quad 64_{seven}$

23_{four} 45_{six} 78_{nine}

$\times \quad 30_{four}$ $\times \quad 32_{six}$ $\times \quad 234_{nine}$

2. Illustrate (by drawing base ten blocks) the division of 57 by 2.

3. How would you divide 234_{five} by 12_{five}? Explain your answer in terms of flats, longs and units.

4. Find the whole number base indicated by the letter b.

  a. $67_{ten} = 61_b$

  b. $12_{ten} = 1100_b$

  c. $234_{ten} = 176_b$

5. Change the following base ten numerals to the indicated base and place your answers from left to right in the numbered square. If your work is correct, the answers should read the same horizontally and vertically.

  a. $486 =$_____ five

  b. $1064 =$_____ six

  c. $848 =$_____ seven

  d. $298 =$_____ six

a.			
b.			
c.			
d.			

Things to Know from Chapter 2

Words to Know
- additive
- base
- expanded notation
- face value
- multiplicative
- number
- numeral
- numeration system
- place value
- subtractive
- unique representation

Concepts to Know
- what it means for a numeration system to have a base
- what it means for a numeration system to have place value
- what it means for a numeration system to be multiplicative
- what it means for a numeration system to be additive
- what it means for a numeration system to have a zero
- what it means for a numeration system to have unique representation
- the relationships among a number, a numeral, and the name of a number
- the relationship between a number written in base ten and the same number written in another base

Procedures to Know
- representing a number in various numeration systems
- representing a number in various bases
- converting a numeral from base ten to another base
- converting a numeral from one base to base ten
- performing arithmetic operations with numerals in bases other than ten

Exercises & More Problems

Exercises
1. Complete the following table.

Hindu-Arabic	Babylonian	Egyptian	Mayan	Roman
72				
	《▾◀▾▾▾			
			⊜	
				MCMLXV
121				
		𝟫𝟫∩∩		

2. Consider the following table. The number in the lower row represents the number represented by each dot in that column. Thus, in the first table, the number represented is 128. After studying the table, state the numbers represented in the other two tables. Then, make up two of your own, using the same pattern of numbers in the bottom row.

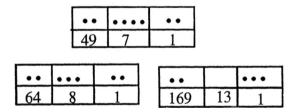

3. Explain each of the following characteristics of our base ten numeration system. Define what each characteristic means and illustrate its meaning using the rational number 254.71.
   a. it has place value
   b. it is multiplicative
   c. it is additive
   d. it has unique representation

4. What is the place value of 7 in the numeral 25746, 0 in the numeral 70822, and 2 in the numeral 342?

5. Write a number in which 5 has the place value thousand, 3 has the place value hundred, and 0 has the place value unit.

6. a. What is the place value of 7 in 23753_{eight}?
    b. Write a number in base seven in which the digit 3 represents 3 times 49.
    c. Write the following numbers using expanded notation: 356475, 1101001_{two}, $5T390_{\text{twelve}}$ (the letter T represents the number 10 in base ten), 21322_{five}

7. Convert the following numbers from the base they are written in to base ten.
    a. 7542_{nine} b. 21122_{three} c. 563_{eight}
    d. $E9323_{\text{twelve}}$ (E is used as a digit that represents the number 11 in base ten)

8. Convert the following numbers from base ten to the base indicated.
    a. 689 to base three
    b. 4955 to base eleven
    c. 201 to base five

9. Find x.
    a. $127_{\text{nine}} = 411_x$
    b. $321_{\text{four}} = 111_x$

10. Which of the following could be used to represent the number twenty-four?
    a. XXIV
    b. 44_{five}
    c. 20_{twelve}
    d. 1011_{two}
    e. all of the above
    f. a, b, and c

11. Describe how to do the following using cubes, flats, longs and/or units:

    $20_{\text{four}} - 13_{\text{four}}$

12. Describe how to do the following using cubes, flats, longs and/or units:

    $1220_{\text{four}} - 33_{\text{four}}$

13. How many cubes, flats, longs and/or units in base 3 would you need to represent the number 35? How many would you need in base 6?

14. Use the least number of quarters, nickels, and pennies necessary to make 87¢.

15. How would you write 324.132_{five} in expanded notation?

16. How would you write $(abcd.efg)_{\text{base n}}$ in expanded notation?

17. Numerals in Braille are written using a combination of dots, in a cell that is 2-dot (across) by 3-dot (down). All numerals are preceded by a backward L dot symbol. The following table shows the basic symbols used in Braille.

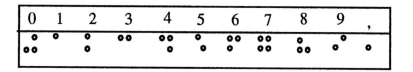

The following are examples of some numbers written in Braille numerals.

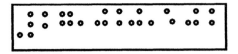

27,020,502

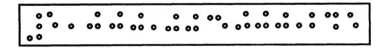

5,003,000,245

a. Write down the following Braille numerals in the Hindu-Arabic system.

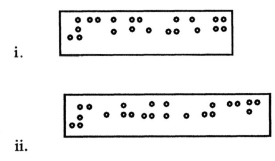

i.

ii.

b. Write down the following Hindu-Arabic numbers in Braille numerals

i. 60,203, 378

ii. 345,200

18. Complete the following addition table. The numerals are written in base four.

+			21
20		33	
	100		
	122		132

19. Complete the following addition table. The numerals are written in base six.

+			43
21		102	
	105		
	122		134

20. Write $9 \cdot 12^7 + 11 \cdot 12^4 + 10$ as a base twelve numeral.

21. Write $7 \cdot 11^5 + 6 \cdot 14^2 + 3$ as a base eleven numeral.

22. Perform the following operations as indicated
    a. $8475T_{eleven} + 94T48_{eleven}$
    b. $1101001_{two} + 1001001_{two}$
    c. $7437_{eight} - 5476_{eight}$
    d. $TE78_{twelve} - 9365_{twelve}$
    e. $3323_{four} \cdot 23_{four}$
    f. $645_{seven} \cdot 36_{seven}$

For #23-24, find the sum and state the base being used. Some helpful conversions are as follows: 3 tsp = 1 Tbsp, 16 Tbsp = 1 cup, 2 cups = 1 pint, 2 pints = 1 quart, 4 quarts = 1 gallon, 12 in = 1 ft, 3 ft = 1 yd, 1000 mm = 1 m, 1000 m = 1 km.

23.
```
    1 gal   3 qts   1 cup
    1 gal           3 cups
+           2 qts   1 cup
```

24.
```
    9 hrs   40 min   26 sec
    3 hrs   50 min   17 sec
+           47 min   33 sec
```

For #25-26, find the difference and state the base being used.

25.
```
    5 yd   2 ft   3 in
-   2 yd   2 ft   7 in
```

26.
```
    5 km   3 m   2 mm
-   2 km   4 m   9 mm
```

27. Explain the method you used to add and subtract in #23-26 above.

Convert the following measurements.

28. 512 in = _____yd_____ft_____in

29. 39.5 ft =_____yd_____ft_____in

30. 47 tsp =_____gal_____qts____cups____Tbsp_____tsp

31. 79 Tbsp =_____gal_____qts____cups____Tbsp_____tsp

32. Explain the method for each conversion in #28-31.

33. What do #28-31 have to do with doing computations in other bases?

34. Convert 5144 seconds into the nearest number of hours, minutes, and seconds.

Critical Thinking

35. A sultan arranged his wives in order of increasing seniority and presented each with a gold ring. Next, every third wife, starting with the second, was given a second ring. Of these wives with two rings, every third one starting with the second received a third ring, and so on in this manner. His most senior and most cherished wife was the only one to receive ten rings. How many wives did the sultan have? Try to generalize your solution.

36. Is it possible for a numeration system to be multiplicative but not have a base? Justify your answer.

37. Three boxes with lids are placed on a shelf. 3 dimes and 3 quarters are placed in the three boxes so that there are two coins inside each box. The boxes are labeled 50¢, 35¢, and 20¢, but none of the boxes are labeled correctly. What is the minimum number of coins that you need to pull out, and from which box, in order to label all the three boxes correctly?

38. a. Jack discovered, in climbing his beanstalk, that the giant had a numeration system based on "fee, fie, foe, fum." When the giant counted his golden eggs, Jack heard him count "fee, fie, foe, fum, fot, feefot, fiefot, foefot, fumfot, fotfot, feefotfot, ..." Jack believes that the giant has 20 eggs. What are the other nine numerals that the giant used to finish the counting?
    b. If possible, characterize even and odd numbers by looking at the units digit of a given number when it is expressed in base two. In base three. In base four. In base five. In the "fee, fie, foe, fum" system.
    c. Explain your rule for determining the even numbers in base two.

39. What is the largest six-digit base three number? Justify that this is the largest.

40. a. If all the letters of our alphabet were used as our single-digit numerals, what would be the base of this system?
    b. If a represented zero, b represented one, and so on, what would be the base ten numeral for the "alphabet" numeral zz? Justify your answer.

41. A time machine carried an adventurer far into the future. Although welcomed by the natives of Septuland, he began to question their honesty when they sent him 9 wives rather than the 12 that had been promised him, and only 19 free movie passes when they had promised him 25. If the Septuland natives were honest, what would explain the differences in interpreting numerals?

42. If the adventurer was promised the following number of articles by the natives, determine the number (from the base ten adventurer's point of view) that he would actually receive.
    a. 15 suits
    b. 12 milkshakes
    c. 113 CDs
    d. 225 bananas
    e. 24 rugs
    f. 66 neckties

43. What is the smallest number of whole-number gram weights needed to weigh any whole-number amount from 1 to 12 on a balance scale? What about from 1 to 37 grams? What is the most you can weigh using six weights in this way?

44. A national track association makes shot puts that weigh 1, 2, 3, 4, . . ., or 15 pounds. They keep them in storage houses all over the United States. You have been hired to travel around the country and make sure that the weights stamped on the shot puts are correct. Each shot put has a whole-number weight. You must check, for example, that no 4-pound shot put has been mistakenly stamped "3 pounds." What is the minimum number of weights you must carry in order to check each weight of shot put? What are these weights? Justify your answers.

Extending the Activity

45. Which number is larger, 5 or 8? Which numeral is larger?

46. a. Some children have trouble with reversals; that is, they confuse 13 and 31, 27 and 72, 59 and 95. What characteristics of the Hindu-Arabic numeration system might contribute to the children's confusion?
    b. What numerals might give ancient Roman children difficulties? Why? How about Egyptian children? Why?

47. A woman had 40 sacks of gold dust which ranged in weight from 1 to 40 ounces. (No two sacks weighed the same and there were no fractional weights.) One day, upon returning from a long trip, she suspected that a thief had pilfered some of the gold in whole number of ounces, so she hires you to weigh each sack. She provides you with a balance scale and a box of 40 weights, ranging from 1 ounce to 40 ounces.
    a. If you are allowed to place weights on only one side of the balance and only sacks on the other side, what is the minimum number of weights you'll take from the box in order to weigh the sacks of gold and decide which sacks (1-40) had some stolen (if any)? How many ounces does each of these weights weigh?
    b. If you are given the same task but are allowed to use both sides of the balance for weights or sacks, what is the minimum number of weights you'd need to use? How heavy is each weight?
    c. Using both sides for weights only, what is the minimum number of weights you'd need to use? How heavy is each weight?
    d. With the weights in a. above, every counting number 1 - 40 can be represented. To what base are these weights related? What about the weights in c?
    e. How does this problem relate to the ACME potato chip problem?

Writing/Discussing

48. Discuss what you consider to be the three most important features of a numeration system and why.

49. Discuss what you have learned about the Hindu-Arabic numeration system after working with base blocks.

50. Explain, using units, longs, flats and cubes, how to change a number from base six to base three without first converting it into base ten.

51. Describe a general procedure for changing a number represented in base n to base ten. Write another procedure for changing a base ten number to base n.

52. Write an algorithm for adding two numbers that are written in a base other than ten. Note: Do not change the numbers into base ten to add them.

Chapter 3: Operations with Natural Numbers, Whole Numbers & Integers

Chapter Overview:

A solid understanding of addition, subtraction, multiplication, and division is crucial to being able to do mathematics and these operations play central parts in the elementary school mathematics curriculum. In this chapter you will study the various models (representations) for these operations involving natural numbers, whole numbers, and integers and explore different computational techniques (called algorithms). Special attention will be placed on developing deep understanding of each of the four operations and the wide range of algorithms that have been developed for doing large number computations.

Big Mathematical Ideas:

mathematical structure, verifying, generalizing, using algorithms

NCTM Standards Links:

K - 4: Mathematics as problem solving; Mathematics as communication; Mathematics as reasoning; Mathematical connections; Concepts of whole number operations; Whole number computation

5 - 8: Mathematics as problem solving; Mathematics as communication; Mathematics as reasoning; Mathematical connections; Computation & estimation

Chapter Outline:

Activity 3.1: Exploring Sets of Numbers
Activity 3.2: Sets and Their Properties
Activity 3.3: Classifying Word Problems by Operation
Activity 3.4: Integer Addition and Subtraction
Activity 3.5: Integer Multiplication and Division
Activity 3.6: Scratch Addition Algorithm
Activity 3.7: Lattice Multiplication Algorithm
Activity 3.8: Cashiers' Algorithm
Activity 3.9: Austrian Subtraction Algorithm
Activity 3.10: Russian Peasant Algorithm
Activity 3.11: Using Algorithms to Solve Problems
Activity 3.12: Operation Applications
Things to Know
Exercises and More Problems

Activity 3.1—Exploring Sets of Numbers

We suggest that you read the explanations about the properties of sets discussed in this activity in Chapter 3 of the *Resource Manual* before beginning this activity.

1.   Identify the property for integers that is illustrated in each example.

a.	$4+0=4$	k.	commutative prop. for addition
b.	$5\cdot6=6\cdot5$	l.	additive inverse
c.	$5\cdot1=5$	m.	additive identity
d.	$(2\cdot7)\cdot5=2\cdot(7\cdot5)$	n.	multiplicative identity
e.	$6+3=3+6$	o.	associative prop. for mult.
f.	$7 + -7 =0$	p.	distributive property
g.	$5\cdot6=30$	q.	closure for addition
h.	$(3+4)+9=3+(4+9)$	r.	commutative prop. for mult.
i.	$9+7=16$	s.	associative prop. for addition
j.	$7(5+2)=7\cdot5+7\cdot2$	t.	closure for multiplication

a.____b.____c.____d.____e.____f.____g.____h.____i.____j.____

2.   The set of Natural numbers can be written as {1,2,3,4,...}. How does the set of Whole numbers differ from the set of Natural numbers?

3.   What is the relationship between these sets?

4.   What is the relationship between these sets and the set of Integers?

5.   Draw a picture that illustrates this relationship.

6.   What does it mean to say that the set of Integers is closed under addition? Under multiplication?

7.   Is the set of Integers closed under division? Justify your reasoning.

8. Is the set of Integers closed under subtraction? Justify your reasoning.

9. Is the set of Whole numbers closed under addition? Under multiplication? Under subtraction? Under division? Be able to justify your answers.

10. Is the set of Natural numbers closed under addition? Under multiplication? Under subtraction? Under division? Be able to justify your answers.

11. What conclusions can you make concerning the relationship between the sets of Natural numbers, Whole numbers, and Integers and the operations under which these sets are closed?

12. If a set of numbers has a Commutative Property for a certain operation this means that the order of the numbers can be changed, and performing the operation will still yield the same answer. Give an example showing that a commutative property for a certain operation and set of numbers is true, and another example showing that a commutative property in a different situation is not true.

13. Think of a name for this property that might be easier to remember.

14. If a set of numbers has an Associative Property for a certain operation this means that the way three or more numbers are grouped can be changed and performing the operation will still yield the same answer. Give an example showing that an associative property for a certain operation and set of numbers is true, and another example showing that an associative property in a different situation is not true.

15. Think of a name for this property that might be easier to remember.

16. Does the set of Integers have an identity element for addition? If yes, identify it. Does the set of Whole numbers? The set of Natural numbers?

17. Does the set of Integers have an identity element for multiplication? The set of Whole numbers? The set of Natural numbers?

18. Which of these sets of numbers have an additive inverse for every element of the set?

19. Which of these sets of numbers have a multiplicative inverse for every element of the set?

20. What do you think is the definition of an additive identity? A multiplicative identity?

21. What do you think is the definition of an additive inverse? A multiplicative inverse?

22. Why are the Commutative Properties for Addition and Multiplication so important for our use of the set of Integers? What if these properties were not true for the set of Integers?

23. What if the set of Integers was not closed under addition, subtraction and multiplication? Of what consequence is it that the set of Integers is not closed under division?

Activity 3.2—Sets and Their Properties

1. Below is a table showing the operation & for the set { □ , ○ , △ , ⌂ }.

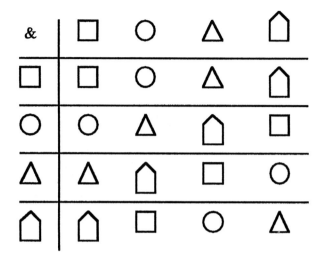

 a. Is this set closed under &? Why or why not?

 b. Does the set have a commutative property for &? Associative property for &? Justify your answers.

 c. Is there a & identity? If so, what element is the identity?

 d. Does each element have a & inverse? If so, identify the inverses.

2. * is an operation on the set of whole numbers where a * b means 2a - b. Answer questions a, b, c, and d above for the operation * over the set of whole numbers.

3.   Below are the six different ways in which two copies of an equilateral triangle with vertices 1, 2, and 3 can be placed, one covering the other. R1, R2, and R3 are rotations about the center of the triangle, while F1, F2, and F3 are flips (reflections) about one vertex.

$$R1 = \begin{vmatrix} 1 & 2 & 3 \\ 1 & 2 & 3 \end{vmatrix}$$

$$R2 = \begin{vmatrix} 1 & 2 & 3 \\ 2 & 3 & 1 \end{vmatrix}$$

$$R3 = \begin{vmatrix} 1 & 2 & 3 \\ 3 & 1 & 2 \end{vmatrix}$$

$$F1 = \begin{vmatrix} 1 & 2 & 3 \\ 1 & 3 & 2 \end{vmatrix}$$

$$F2 = \begin{vmatrix} 1 & 2 & 3 \\ 3 & 2 & 1 \end{vmatrix}$$

$$F3 = \begin{vmatrix} 1 & 2 & 3 \\ 2 & 1 & 3 \end{vmatrix}$$

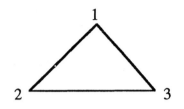

This chart shows the relationships between the rotations and flips using the operation that does the rotation or flip in the column first and then the one in the row.

	R1	R2	R3	F1	F2	F3
R1	R1	R2	R3	F1	F2	F3
R2	R2	R3	R1	F2	F3	F1
R3	R3	R1	R2	F3	F1	F2
F1	F1	F3	F2	R1	R3	R2
F2	F2	F1	F3	R2	R1	R3
F3	F3	F2	F1	R3	R2	R1

What properties (closure, commutative, associative, identity, inverse) are valid for this set of rotations and flips?

Activity 3.3—Classifying Word Problems by Operation

Group these story problem situations by operation. Then group them within the operation into sets of the same type of problem.

1. I have 8 marbles and Tom has 3. How many more do I have than Tom?

2. I have 2 apples and 3 oranges. How many pieces of fruit do I have altogether?

3. I have 3 shirts of different colors and 4 shorts of different colors. How many different outfits can I wear?

4. I have 45 pieces of candy and there are 9 children who will share the candy equally. How many pieces will each child receive?

5. I had 8 marbles. Now I have 2. How many did I lose?

6. I have 4 vases and I want to put 3 roses in each vase. How many roses do I need?

7. I had 8 marbles. Then I lost 5. How many do I have left?

8. I have 45 pieces of candy. I am going to give 5 pieces of candy to each child in a group. How many children will receive candy?

9. A marching band has 8 rows of band members, with 7 members in each row. How many people are in the band?

10. Penguin's Ice Cream shop has 6 flavors of ice cream and 8 different toppings. How many different one dip cones are possible?

11. The library has 80 books on dogs and there are 10 students who will check out the books, each taking the same number. How many books can each student take?

12. A company owns 7 old buses and 20 new buses. How many buses are there altogether?

13. Barb finished 14 of the homework problems and Jim finished 9. How many more did Barb complete than Jim?

14. A gardener planted 16 rows of tulip bulbs, with 8 bulbs in each row. How many bulbs did she plant altogether?

15. Bob was taking 6 classes. Then he dropped 2 because of time. How many classes was he still taking?

16. Joan has 5 sisters and she is giving each of them 3 tickets to a play. How many tickets does she need?

17. Donald Trump owned 14 cars. Now he has 7. How many did he sell?

18. An airline is advertising 66 discount tickets to persons buying pairs of tickets. How many people can buy a pair of tickets?

Activity 3.4—Integer Addition and Subtraction

1. Think of some situations in everyday life where we use negative numbers. Write down a list of some of these situations.

    Is it possible to represent these situations with positive numbers only? Are negative numbers really necessary?

2. Negative integers are often depicted in the following way on the integer-number line:

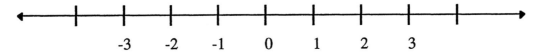

    Thus, -3 is the opposite of 3, and 9 is the opposite of -9, etcetera.

    a. Using this number line, how would you model addition involving negative integers? For example, how would you model 3 + (-2)? (-3) + 2? (-2) + (-3)?

    b. How would you model subtraction on this number line? For example, how would you represent 12 – (-7)? (-5) – 8? (-6) – (-6)?

3. For each of the following statements, write a mathematical expression that uses addition as the only operation. Then find the answer.

    a. A certain stock registered the following gains and losses in a week: First it rose by 7 points, then it dropped 13 points, then it gained 8 points, then it gained another 6 points, and finally lost 8 points. What was the net change in what the stock was worth during the week?

    b. In a certain city, the temperature was 40° Fahrenheit on Sunday. It rose by 12° F on Monday, dropped by 5° F the next day, dropped another 3° F the next, and finally rose by 9° F. What was the temperature on the final day of this record?

    c. In a football series, a team gained 5 yards, lost 7 yards, gained 5 yards, and finally lost 4 yards. What was the total loss or gain?

    d. In a Las Vegas casino, a gambler gained $ 200, lost $ 115, lost another $ 285, and gained $245. What was his total loss or gain?

4. Jennifer and Harry have overdraft protection at their bank. At the end of a month, Jennifer's account shows a balance of -875, while Harry's balance is -1575. Who has the bigger debt and by how much?

5. Tom's bank charges a service fee of $25 each time his account is overdrawn. At the beginning of a certain month, he had $ 1150 in his account. He wrote checks for $250, $348, and $628. He then deposited a check for $786, withdrew $350, wrote a check for $440, and finally deposited $500.

    a. If each check (or withdrawal or service fee) that Tom writes is written as a negative integer, and each deposit as a positive integer, write a statement representing Tom's transactions.

    b. What was his final balance?

Activity 3.5—Integer Multiplication and Division

We modeled addition and subtraction of integers using number line models. It is harder to construct such models for either multiplication or division. For example, we may represent 2 • (-3) in the following way on the number line.

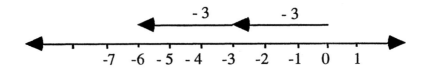

However, it is not possible to use this model to represent, say, (- 2) • 3, primarily because it does not make sense to think of this expression as 3 taken -2 times. Therefore, to be able to consider such multiplication, we will look at pattern models, such as the one given below.

$$3 \bullet 3 = 9$$
$$2 \bullet 3 = 6$$
$$1 \bullet 3 = 3$$
$$0 \bullet 3 = 0$$
$$-1 \bullet 3 = -3$$
$$-2 \bullet 3 = -6$$

Here, as numbers in the extreme left column decrease by 1 at each step, the numbers in the extreme right column decrease by 3 each time. Thus, we get (- 2) • 3 = - 6. We can look at similar patterns to consider multiplication of two negative integers.

1.   Construct a six-step pattern model to show (- 3) • (- 5) = 15.

2.   Susan is recording the results of a chemical reaction every ten minutes, starting at 1 p. m. The temperature of the reaction is being controlled so as to drop by 2° Fahrenheit every minute, and the temperature at 1 p. m. is 60° F.

   a.   Write down the temperatures for the first 5 minutes of the reaction.

   b.   When will the temperature have reached 0° F?

   c. Show Susan's temperature column for the reaction until 2:30 p. m.

Division on the set of integers can be defined as the reverse operation of multiplication. Thus 40 ÷ (- 5) = 8 because 8 • (- 5) = 40. This approach may also be regarded as the missing factor approach, because essentially we are considering ? • (-5) = 40 (or, (- 5) • ? = 40).

3.   How could you construct a pattern model for division by a certain integer? How would this pattern model be similar to the one you constructed in #1 for multiplication? How would it be different?

4.   Construct a eight-step pattern model for division by -4. Begin with 16 ÷ -4 and decrease the dividend by 4 each time.

5.   Two divers record their depths under the sea as - 50 ft, and - 44 ft.

   a.   What can be regarded as the 0 level for the divers?

   b.   What is their average depth?

6.   Justin's business account shows a balance of - 2400 (in dollars) after three business transactions. If he lost equal amounts in each of these transactions, what was his loss in each of them?

Activity 3.6—Scratch Addition Algorithm

Your instructor will lead you in doing a computation using an algorithm for addition called "scratch addition". This algorithm allows one to do complicated additions by doing a series of additions involving only two single digits.

$$4\ 2\ 3_{\text{five}}$$

$$3\ 2\ 0_{\text{five}}$$

$$+\ \ 1\ 4\ 4_{\text{five}}$$

Compute the following addition using the scratch algorithm.

$$2\ 5\ 6_{\text{seven}}$$

$$4\ 4\ 0_{\text{seven}}$$

$$+\ \ 2\ 3_{\text{seven}}$$

Why does the scratch algorithm work?

Activity 3.7—Lattice Multiplication Algorithm

One algorithm for multiplication is called "lattice multiplication". Your instructor will lead you in doing the computation for 14 • 23 using this algorithm.

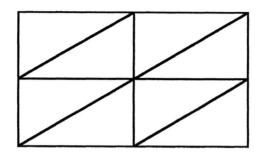

Find the product of 345 • 56 using lattice multiplication.

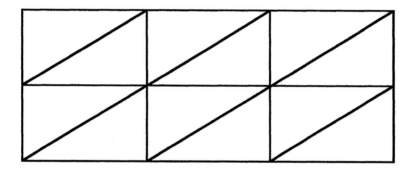

Why does lattice multiplication work?

Activity 3.8—Cashiers' Algorithm

The following is an example of the cashiers' algorithm. Suppose you buy $23 of school supplies and give the cashier a $50 bill. While handing you the change the cashier, using the cashiers' algorithm, would say "23, 24, 25, 30, 40, 50." How much change did you receive?

Now you are the cashier: The customer owes you $62 and gives you a $100 bill. What will you say to the customer, and how much money will you give back?

Why does the cashiers' algorithm work?

Activity 3.9—Austrian Subtraction Algorithm

The Austrian subtraction algorithm consists of the following steps:

```
   5   2   7                  5   2   17        (add 10 to top and bottom)
 - 4   9   8       ───▶     - 4   10  8
 _____                _____
```

```
   5   12  17               (add 100 to top and bottom)
 - 5   10  8
 _____
       2   9
```

Use the Austrian subtraction algorithm to find 721 - 348.

Why does the Austrian subtraction algorithm work?

Activity 3.10—Russian Peasant Algorithm

One algorithm for multiplication is the Russian peasant algorithm. This algorithm is illustrated below through the computation of $27 \cdot 51$.

Halving		Doubling
27	•	51
13	•	102
~~6~~	•	~~204~~
3	•	408
1	•	816

Notice that the numbers in the first column are halved (disregarding any remainder), and that the numbers in the second column are doubled. When 1 is reached in the halving column, the process is stopped. Next each row with an even number in the halving column is ignored (crossed out) and the remaining numbers in the doubling column are added. Thus, $27 \cdot 51 = 51 + 102 + 408 + 816 = 1377$.

Use the Russian peasant algorithm to find $74 \cdot 18$.

Why does the Russian peasant algorithm work?

Activity 3.11—Using Algorithms to Solve Problems

1. The numerals below are base six representations, and in each case the addends have three digits. Recreate each problem and its solution. Under the given conditions, is there more than one possible arrangement of digits?

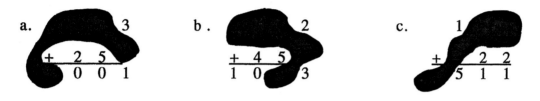

a.
```
      3
  + 2 5
    0 0 1
```

b.
```
      2
  + 4 5
  1 0  3
```

c.
```
    1
  +   2 2
    5 1 1
```

2. Find the missing digits for this base ten numeral.

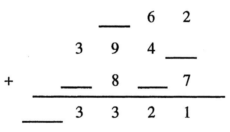

```
            __  6   2
        3   9   4  __
  +   __ 8  __   7
  _____
    __  3   3   2   1
```

3. What strategies did you use to find the missing digits?

4.   What are the values of S, M, and O? Each letter represents a unique digit.

```
      S   E   N   D
  +   M   O   R   E
  ─────────────────
  M   O   N   E   Y
```

5.   Are these the only values for S, M, and O? Why or why not?

Activity 3.12—Operation Applications

1. Insert the arithmetic symbols +, -, x, and ÷ between the 6s in each line to make the eight different equations true. In each case the arithmetic operations should be performed in order from left to right without regard to the order of operation rules.

$$5 = \quad 6 \quad 6 \quad 6 \quad 6$$

$$8 = \quad 6 \quad 6 \quad 6 \quad 6$$

$$13 = \quad 6 \quad 6 \quad 6 \quad 6$$

$$42 = \quad 6 \quad 6 \quad 6 \quad 6$$

$$48 = \quad 6 \quad 6 \quad 6 \quad 6$$

$$66 = \quad 6 \quad 6 \quad 6 \quad 6$$

$$108 = \quad 6 \quad 6 \quad 6 \quad 6$$

$$180 = \quad 6 \quad 6 \quad 6 \quad 6$$

2. Eighteen students were seated in a circle. They were evenly spaced and numbered in order. Which student was directly opposite (a) student #1? (b) student #5? (c) student #18?

3. Another group of students was seated in the same way as above. Student #5 was directly opposite student #26. How many students were in the group?

4. A large group of students is standing in a circle evenly spaced. The 7th student is directly opposite the 791st student. How many students are there altogether?

5.   Choose any number. Multiply by 2. Add 5. Multiply by 5. Subtract 25. Divide by 10. Why did you get the answer that you did? Will this always work?

6.   Choose any number. Multiply by 3. Add 8. Add your original number. Divide by 4. Subtract your original number. Why did you get the answer that you did? Will this always work?

7.   Choose any number. Add the number that is one larger than your original number. Add 11. Divide by 2. Subtract your original number. Why did you get the answer that you did? Will this always work?

8.   Make up an algorithm so that the final result will always be 7, no matter what number is chosen.

Things to Know from Chapter 3

Words to Know
- addition
- algorithm
- associativity
- closure
- commutativity
- distributivity
- division—repeated subtraction, sharing
- identity
- integers
- inverse
- multiplication—repeated addition, cross product, array
- natural numbers
- negative
- operation
- positive
- subtraction—comparison, take away, missing addend
- whole numbers

Concepts to Know
- what it means for a set of numbers to be closed under an operation
- what it means for a set of numbers to have commutativity under an operation
- what it means for a set of numbers to have associativity under an operation
- what it means for a set of numbers to have an identity under an operation
- what it means for each element of a set of numbers to have an inverse under an operation
- what it means for a set of numbers to have distributivity for two operations
- relationships among the sets of natural numbers, whole numbers and integers
- why particular algorithms work

Procedures to Know
- determining what properties hold for a set of numbers
- classifying word problems by operation type
- performing arithmetic operations with integers
- determining why particular algorithms work

Exercises & More Problems

Exercises

1. Use numbers to illustrate the following properties of integers:
   a. associative property of addition
   b. commutative property of multiplication
   c. identity property for addition
   d. multiplicative inverse property

2. Define operation @ on the set of whole numbers by $x @ y = 3x - 2y$.
   a. Is @ commutative? Explain.
   b. Is @ associative? Explain.
   c. Is the set of whole numbers closed under @? Explain.
   d. Does the set of whole numbers have an identity element under @? Explain.

3. Given below is an addition chart for the set {a, b, c}.

+	a	b	c
a	a	b	c
b	b	c	a
c	c	a	b

   a. Does this set have an additive identity? Explain.
   b. Is addition commutative on this set? Explain.
   c. Does b have an inverse? Explain.

4. Given the table below, answer the following:

@	a	b	c
a	b	c	a
b	a	b	c
c	c	a	b

   a. Is the set {a, b} closed under @? Explain.
   b. Is the set {a, b, c} closed under @? Explain.
   c. Does the operation @ have an identity element? Explain.
   d. Is @ commutative? Explain.
   e. Does c have an inverse? Explain.

5. Give an example that illustrates whether or not division on the set of whole numbers is distributive over subtraction.

6. Place parentheses, as needed, to make the following statements true.
   a. $3 + 9 - 4 + 2 = 4$
   b. $3 + 9 - 4 + 2 = 10$
   c. $7 \times 2 + 5 = 49$
   d. $7 + 6 - 4 \times 2 = 5$
   e. $3 \times 5 + 2 = 21$

7. Create a word problem situation illustrating the following:
    a. addition
    b. missing addend subtraction
    c. cross product multiplication
    d. sharing division
    e. array multiplication

8. Create a word problem situation illustrating the following:
    a. comparison subtraction
    b. take away subtraction
    c. repeated addition multiplication
    d. repeated subtraction division

9. For each of these word problem situations, identify the operation type (a - I). The operation types may be used more than once.

    a. addition   b. comparison subtraction   c. take away subtraction
    d. missing addend subtraction   e. repeated addition multiplication
    f. cross product multiplication   g. array multiplication
    h. repeated subtraction division   i. sharing division

    _____ I have 8 oranges and Jane has 5. How many more do I have than Jane?
    _____ I have 3 sweaters of different colors and 5 pairs of pants of different colors. How many different outfits can I wear from these clothes?
    _____ I have 72 pencils. I am going to give 3 pencils to each student in my class. How many students are in the class?
    _____ Rebekah got 10 problems correct on the quiz and Jill got 7 correct. How many more did Rebekah get correct than Jill?
    _____ Moses drove 75 miles in the morning and 120 miles in the afternoon. How many miles did Moses drive?

10. Which of the following are integers? If they are, identify as positive, negative, or neither.
    a. 13   b. -4   c. .5   d. 0   e. -1/4   f. 2   g. 5.75   h. 1

11. Illustrate the following sums:
    a. 4 + (-2)   b. -7 + 3   c. -6 + (-5)

12. Find the following sums using scratch addition.
    a.   6 3 4   b.   6 4 5
           1 5 8   3 4
              4 2   3 7 9
           3 9 2   4 8
        + 5 1 0   + 2 5 2

13. Find the following products using lattice multiplication.
    a. 543 • 61   b. 1802 • 435

14. Suppose you are a cashier and a customer gives you $30 when making the following purchase. Describe how you count out the money you return to the customer.
    a. $22   b. $21.50   c. $26.80

15. Use the Austrian subtraction algorithm to find:
    a. 631 - 287   b. 2423 - 1657

16. Use the Russian peasant algorithm to find:
    a. 13 • 59   b. 23 • 62

Exercises #17-22 are written with missing numbers. The geometric shapes used to represent these numbers are defined in the statement of the problem. Use the geometric shapes to describe the solution process for each problem.

17. Sam is making a long-distance telephone call that costs △ for the first minute and ▭ for each additional minute. If Sam talks for ◯ additional minutes, what is the cost of his call?

18. The student council operates a school store that sells pencils and notebooks. The council receives a profit of △ cents on each pencil and ▱ cents on each notebook they sell. During one week the store sold ◯ pencils and ◇ notebooks. How much profit did the council make that week ?

19. Michelle is planning a pizza party. △ people will be at the party. Michelle guesses that each person will eat ▭ pieces of pizza. If each pizza is to be cut into ◯ pieces, how many pizzas should Michelle order?

20. A gym class has ◇ students. △ teams are formed with ◯ players on each team. How many students have yet to be assigned to a team?

21. A carton of ◇ bottles of soda is priced at ▭ dollars including deposit. If Jill bought a single bottle at this rate, how much change should she receive from a ◯ dollar bill?

22. A punch is made from ◯ ounces of fruit juice and ◇ bottles of ginger ale. Each bottle of ginger ale contains ▭ ounces. How many △-ounce servings of punch will this recipe produce?

23. Express each of the numbers 1 through 10 using four 4's and any of the four basic operations.

24. Create three algebraic equations involving the four basic arithmetic operations, each of whose solution is a negative integer.

25. Create two word problems representing real situations that involve operations with integers.

Critical Thinking
26. a. If a set is closed under addition, must it also be closed under multiplication? Explain your answer or give a counterexample.
    b. If a set is closed under multiplication, must it also be closed under addition? Explain your answer or give a counterexample.

27. A given set contains the number 1. What other numbers must also be in the set if it is closed under addition? Explain.

28. An eighth-grade student claims she can prove that subtraction of integers is commutative. she points out that if a and b are integers, then a - b = a + -b. Since addition is commutative, so is subtraction. What is your response?

29. A student claims that if $x \neq 0$, the $|x| = -x$ is never true since absolute value is always positive. What is your response?

30. True or false:
    a. Every natural number is a whole number.
    b. Every natural number is an integer.
    c. Every whole number is a natural number.
    d. Every whole number is an integer.
    e. Every integer is a whole number.
    f. The set of additive inverses of the whole numbers is equal to the set of integers.
    g. The set of additive inverses of the integers is equal to the set of integers.

31. Find the following sums using scratch addition. The numerals are written in base six.

    a.
    ```
          2  3  4
          1  5  3
             4  2
          3  0  2
       +  5  1  0
    ```

    b.
    ```
          1  4  5
             3  4
          3  2  1
             4  0
       +  1  5  2
    ```

32. Find the following products using lattice multiplication. The numerals are written in base five.

    a. 342 • 41

    b. 1203 • 230

33. Complete the pyramid below so that each number represents the sum of the two numbers directly below it.

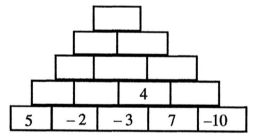

34. Complete the pyramid below so that each number represents the product of the two numbers directly below it.

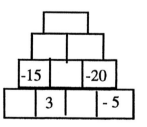

35. An elevator in an office building is at the fourth floor. It goes up 10 floors from there, then comes down 6 floors, then goes up 15 floors, comes down 3 floors, and goes up another 2 floors, from where it is 4 floors below the top of the building. How many floors does the building have?

36. Sara, Tyler, Diana, Joanna and Adam were standing for election for the posts of the President, the Vice President, and the Treasurer. Assuming that each of them was eligible for all the three posts, and that one and only one person could hold each of the posts, in how many ways can the three posts be filled? Describe the strategies you used to solve the problem.

Extending the Activity

37. a. Is the set of whole numbers closed under addition if 7 is removed from the set? Explain your answer.
    b. Is the set of whole numbers closed under multiplication if 7 is removed from the set? Explain your answer.
    c. Answer the same questions if the number to be removed is 6 instead of 7. Explain your answer.

38. Identify the property or properties illustrated in the statements below.
    a. $17 + 34 = 34 + 17$
    b. 7 times 5 is a whole number
    c. $25 \cdot 34 = 34 \cdot 25$
    d. $7 + 0 = 7$
    e. $3 \cdot 1/3 = 1$
    f. $(5 \cdot 3) \cdot 23 = (3 \cdot 5) \cdot 23 = 3 \cdot (5 \cdot 23)$
    g. $7 + 0 = 0 + 7$
    h. $5 + (-5) = 0$

39. Below is an illustration of another algorithm that can be used to find the product of two whole numbers.

$$
\begin{aligned}
54 \cdot 13 &= 54 \cdot (10 + 3) \\
&= 54 \cdot 10 + 54 \cdot 3 \\
&= (50 + 4) \cdot 10 + (50 + 4) \cdot 3 \\
&= 50 \cdot 10 + 4 \cdot 10 + 50 \cdot 3 + 4 \cdot 3 \\
&= 500 + 40 + 150 + 12 \\
&= 702
\end{aligned}
$$

    a. What property of numbers is used in the above algorithm?
    b. How is this algorithm similar to the standard algorithm for multiplication?
    c. Pick two 3-digit numbers, and find their product using this algorithm.
    d. What aspects of this algorithm make it easy to use?

40. Explain why the standard algorithm for division works. For example,

```
          2  9
  1 2 | 3  4  8
      - 2  4
        1  0  8
      - 1  0  8
               0
```

41. A third-grade teacher prepared her students for division this way:

20 ÷ 4

```
      20
  -    4        *
      16
  -    4        *
      12
  -    4        *
       8
  -    4        *
       4
  -    4        *
       0            Thus, 20 ÷ 4 = 5
```

How would her students find 42 ÷ 6? Why does this algorithm work?

42. Make up your own algorithms for each of the four operations.

Writing/Discussing

43. Discuss why you think we use the algorithms that we do for addition, subtraction, multiplication, and division.

44. Pick one algorithm for an operation that you think has advantages over other algorithms for the same operation and discuss what the advantages are.

45. Generalization is a key idea in these activities. Discuss what generalization is and why you think it is considered a key idea.

46. Read the article by Corwin (1989) that is listed in the bibliography in Chapter 3 of the *Resource Manual*. Discuss your thoughts about the article.

47. Write an explanation of the most efficient way to solve a problem like #4 in Activity 3.11.

Chapter 4: Number Theory

Chapter Overview:

Number theory is a branch of mathematics that involves the study of numbers and, in particular, the natural numbers. In this chapter you will be introduced to prime and composite numbers and investigate the concepts of divisibility, greatest common divisor, and least common multiple—concepts that are fundamental to understanding operations on fractions. An especially interesting aspect of this chapter is that you will see that there are some quite challenging and valuable problems involving what appears at first glance to be a very simple branch of mathematics. A final important feature of this chapter is that you will begin to learn how to construct mathematical proofs.

Big Mathematical Ideas:

> conjecturing, decomposing, verifying, problem-solving strategies, and representing

NCTM Standards Links:

> **K - 4:** Mathematics as problem solving; Mathematics as communication; Mathematics as reasoning; Mathematical connections; Number sense & numeration; Concepts of whole number operations; Patterns & relationships
>
> **5 - 8:** Mathematics as problem solving; Mathematics as communication; Mathematics as reasoning; Mathematical connections; Number systems & number theory; Patterns & functions

Chapter Outline:

Activity 4.1—The Locker Problem

Students at an elementary school decided to try an experiment. When recess is over, each student will walk into the school one at a time. The first student will open all of the first 100 locker doors. The second student will close all of the locker doors with even numbers. The third student will change all the locker doors with numbers that are multiples of three. (Change means closing locker doors that are open and opening lockers that are closed.) The fourth student will change the position of all locker doors numbered with multiples of four; the fifth student will change the position of the lockers that are multiples of five, and so on. After 100 students have entered the school, which locker doors will be open?

Activity 4.2—Searching for Patterns of Factors

Complete this grid to show the factors of each number from 1 through 50. What patterns do you see in the grid?

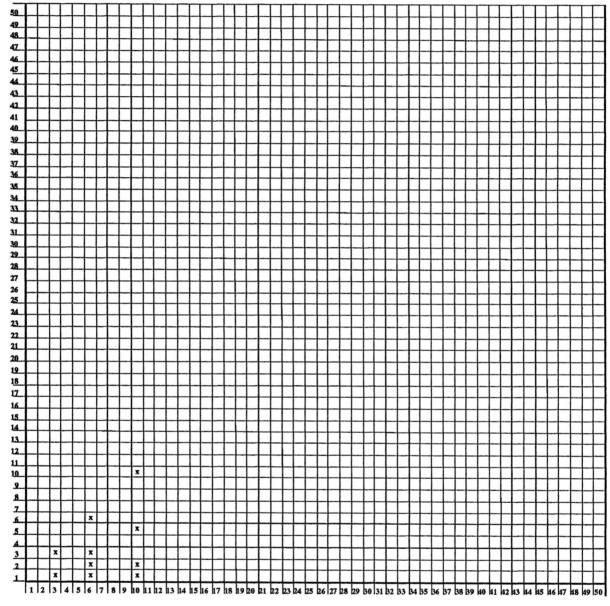

NUMBERS

Numbers that have exactly two factors are known as "prime numbers." Except for the number 1, numbers that are not prime are called "composite numbers" and can always be broken down into a product that consists entirely of prime numbers. This product is known as the "prime factorization" of the number. For example, the prime factorization of 6 is 2 x 3 and the prime factorization of 60 is 2 x 2 x 3 x 5.

Complete the table below.

Number	List of all factors	# of factors	"prime" or prime factorization
2			
3			
4			
5			
6			
7			
8			
9			
10			
11			
12			
13			
14			
15			
16			
17			
18			
19			
20			
21			
22			
23			
24			
25			

Activity 4.3—Factor Feat: A Game of Factors

	2	3	4	5	6	7	8	9	10
11	12	13	14	15	16	17	18	19	20
21	22	23	24	25	26	27	28	29	30
31	32	33	34	35	36	37	38	39	40
41	42	43	44	45	46	47	48	49	50
51	52	53	54	55	56	57	58	59	60
61	62	63	64	65	66	67	68	69	70
71	72	73	74	75	76	77	78	79	80
81	82	83	84	85	86	87	88	89	90
91	92	93	94	95	96	97	98	99	100

Rules: Play with a partner. Players alternate taking turns picking numbers and marking it (one player use a circle and the other use an x). When a player has marked a number, also mark all the factors of that number that have not already been marked. The winner is the player with the **largest sum of marked numbers** when the game is over (when either time is called or all the numbers have been marked).

Activity 4.4—Classifying Numbers According to Prime Factorization

1. Examine the numbers with exactly 3 and 5 factors. Name three numbers greater than 50 with exactly 3 factors.

2. Name two numbers greater than 50 with exactly 5 factors.

3. Predict the smallest integer that has exactly 7 factors.

4. Write a conjecture about the numbers that have exactly 3 factors.

5. Here is a conjecture about some of the numbers that have exactly 5 factors. Conjecture: Every number with prime factorization p^4 has exactly 5 factors. Does this seem true? Why or why not?

6. Do you think this conjecture is true for k^4, where k is any number? Justify your answer.

7. Predict three numbers greater than 50 with exactly 6 factors.

8. Write a conjecture about the numbers with exactly 6 factors.

9. Without writing out the list of factors for 225, explain why 225 (15 x 15) has an odd number of factors, but more than 3 factors.

10. Now write out all the factors of 225.

11. Explain why 289 (17 x 17) has exactly 3 factors.

12. What are all the factors of 289?

13. Use your conjectures to fill in the following chart.

Number	Prime Factorization	Odd or Even # of Factors	Exact # of Factors
529	23 x 23		
126	2 x 3 x 3 x 7		
441	3 x 3 x 7 x 7		
169	13 x 13		
11025	3 x 3 x 5 x 5 x 7 x 7		
841	29 x 29		

14. Write a conjecture about the numbers that have exactly 7 factors.

15. Write a conjecture about the numbers that have an odd number of factors.

16. Write a conjecture about numbers that have exactly 2 factors.

17. Write a conjecture about numbers that have exactly 4 factors.

18. Test your conjecture on the examples in the chart below. Note: p and q stand for prime numbers.

Number	Prime Factorization	Exactly 4 factors?
34	2 x 17	
546	2 x 3 x 91	
95	5 x 19	
	p x q	
45	5 x 9	
	p x p x q	
8	2 x 2 x 2	
27	3 x 3 x 3	
	p x p x p	

19. How would you prove that there are exactly two representations of numbers with 4 factors?

Activity 4.5—E-Primes

Let E = { 1, 2, 4, 6, 8, ...}. In this set there are some numbers that can only be written as a product of 1 and the number itself, but cannot be written as the product of two other elements of the set. An element of E will be called **E-prime** if it can only be expressed as a product of 1 and itself. For example, 6 is E-prime since 6 = 1 x 6; 6 = 2 x 3 but 3 is not in E. An even number will be called **E-composite** if it is not E-prime. Note: 1 is not E-prime.

1. Determine the first ten E-primes.

2. Can every E-composite number be factored into a product of E-primes? Justify your reasoning.

3. List several even numbers that have only <u>one</u> factorization into E-primes.

4. Find an even number whose E-prime factorization is not unique, that is, an even number that can be factored into products of E-primes in at least two different ways.

5. Determine a test to decide whether an even number is E-prime.

Activity 4.6—Twin Primes and Prime Triples

1. Consider the following triplets of numbers:

    5, 6, 7   11, 12, 13   17, 18, 19   29, 30, 31

    The first and third numbers in each triplet are called *twin primes* because they form a pair of consecutive prime numbers.

    a. What do these triplets have in common?

    b. Make a conjecture about twin primes in general.

    c. Verify that this conjecture is valid.

2. *Prime triples* are three prime numbers of the form p - 2, p, p + 2. There is exactly one prime triple. Find it and justify why there are no others.

Activity 4.7—Divisibility Tests

Use this page to record your work about divisibility tests.

Activity 4.8—Divisibility in Different Bases

1. Determine a divisibility test for 3 in a base twelve system. Justify your test.

2. Determine a divisibility test for 5 in a base six system. Justify your test.

3. Determine a divisibility test for 2 in a base five system. Justify your test.

Activity 4.9—Factors and Multiples

1. Find the largest common factor of both 180 and 693.

2. Find the largest common factor of 360, 336, and 1260.

3. What strategies did you use to find these factors?

4. What is the name given for the largest common factor of several numbers?

5. Write a generalization describing how to find the largest common factor for any group of numbers.

6. Find the smallest number that will be divisible by both 80 and 36.

7. Find the smallest number that will be divisible by 126, 525, and 300.

8. What strategies did you use to find these numbers?

9. What is the name given for the smallest number divisible by several numbers?

10. Write a generalization describing how to find the smallest number divisible by a group of numbers.

Activity 4.10—A Different Way of Counting

Nicole and Bob had been cooped up in the house all day because of rain and were very bored. To keep them busy, their mother gave them a problem to do. They were promised a special treat if they could give her the right answer. The problem was as follows:

Nicole was born 969 days after Bob. If Bob was born on a Wednesday, on what day of the week was Nicole born?

Nicole: Okay, let me make a chart. We'll have Monday, Tuesday, Wednesday, . . . Sunday. Then, we can start counting.

So, she wrote down:

M	T	W	Th	F	S	Sun

Then she counted:

			Th	F	S	Sun
			1	2	3	4
5	6	7	8	9	. . .	

Bob: Wait, Nicole, I think we can do this faster!

Nicole: (after a pause) Oh, I see what you mean! Hmm, (thinks for a few minutes) I was born on a Sunday!

Try to figure out how Bob and Nicole worked this problem out so fast. Find a way to work out similar problems starting from any day of the week, and for any number of days thereafter.

Activity 4.11—Operations with Modular Arithmetic

1. How can addition and subtraction be represented on a clock? For example, if you have a 5-hour clock, and it is 2 o'clock now, what time will it be in 7 hours? What time was it 8 hours ago?

2. Write a procedure for finding the time, given that you start at time a and let b hours elapse.

3. How is arithmetic on the 5-hour clock similar to arithmetic mod 5? How is it different?

4. Fill in these tables for addition and multiplication in mod 4.

+	0	1	2	3
0				
1				
2				
3				

x	0	1	2	3
0				
1				
2				
3				

5. Use the tables to find:

    a. $2 - 3 =$

    b. $3 - 1 =$

    c. $0 - 2 =$

    d. $3 \div 2 =$

    e. $2 \div 3 =$

    f. $0 \div 2 =$

6. Are there any restrictions on subtracting or dividing in mod arithmetic? How does 5d. relate to dividing by zero over the set of integers?

Activity 4.12—Mystery Numeration System

The numeration system proposed below has a number theoretic basis. Complete the table by discovering the pattern. Hint: Look at the representation of prime numbers first. Then look at the representation of composite numbers.

	Mystery System		Mystery System
one	0	eleven	10000
two	1	twelve	12
three	10	thirteen	100000
four	2	fourteen	1001
five	100	fifteen	110
six	11	sixteen	
seven	1000	seventeen	
eight	3	eighteen	
nine	20	nineteen	
ten	101	twenty	

1. What are the advantages and disadvantages of the Mystery System?

2. For small values (e.g., 1-25), is each numeral in the Mystery System associated with a unique number? Justify your answer.

3. For large values (e.g., 2^{10}), is each numeral in the Mystery System associated with a unique number? Justify your answer.

4. Is each number associated with a unique numeral in the Mystery System?

Activity 4.13—Figurate Numbers

1. **Triangular numbers** are numbers that can be represented by dots in an equilateral triangle. The first four triangular numbers are illustrated below. T_n denotes the nth triangular number.

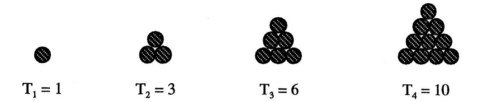

$T_1 = 1$ $\qquad$ $T_2 = 3$ $\qquad$ $T_3 = 6$ $\qquad$ $T_4 = 10$

   Find a generalization that gives the nth triangular number.

2. **Square numbers** are numbers that can be represented by dots in a square arrangement or array. The first four square numbers are illustrated below. S_n denotes the nth square number.

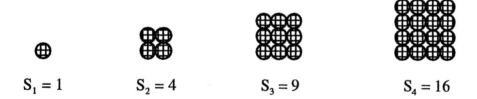

$S_1 = 1$ $\qquad$ $S_2 = 4$ $\qquad$ $S_3 = 9$ $\qquad$ $S_4 = 16$

   Find a generalization that gives the nth square number.

3. **Oblong numbers** are numbers that can be represented by dots in a rectangular array having one dimension one unit longer than the other. The first four oblong numbers are illustrated below. O_n denotes the nth oblong number.

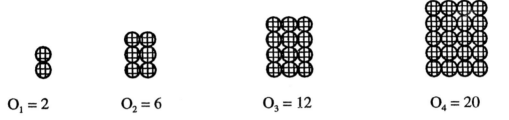

$O_1 = 2$ $O_2 = 6$ $O_3 = 12$ $O_4 = 20$

Find a generalization that gives the nth oblong number.

4. **Pentagonal numbers** are numbers that can be represented by dots in a pentagonal array. The first four pentagonal numbers are illustrated below. P_n denotes the nth pentagonal number.

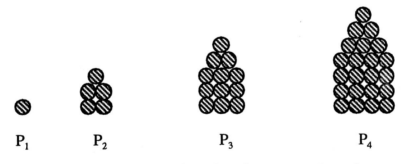

P_1 P_2 P_3 P_4

Find a generalization that gives the nth pentagonal number.

Activity 4.14—Number Ideas: Proofs Without Words

The following illustrations depicts an example of what some mathematicians call "a proof without words."

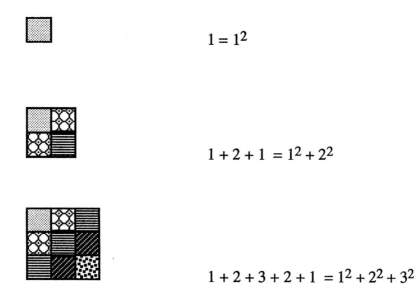

$1 = 1^2$

$1 + 2 + 1 = 1^2 + 2^2$

$1 + 2 + 3 + 2 + 1 = 1^2 + 2^2 + 3^2$

1. Sketch the next illustration in this pattern.

2. Generalize the result above. Then use the generalization to find the sum of the first n natural numbers.

Activity 4.15—The Fibonacci Sequence

The Fibonacci sequence is one of the most fascinating sequences of numbers that has ever been studied by mathematicians. The sequence was first suggested by Leonardo of Pisa, also called Fibonacci (whom we also encountered in Chapter 3 in the historical/social/cultural notes in the resource manual), in about 1202 in a book entitled *Liber Abaci*. In it, he proposed a problem about rabbits. The problem is as follows:

> A pair of rabbits, one month old, produce a new pair every month. starting from the second month. If each new pair of rabbits does the same, and assuming that none of the rabbits ever die, calculate the number of rabbits at the beginning of each month.

1. Work this problem out for the first six months. What do you notice about the numbers?

2. Now write down the first 20 numbers in this sequence.

A sequence of numbers that follows this pattern is called the Fibonacci sequence. One of the fascinating aspects of this sequence is that it appears in an amazing variety of creations, both natural and artificial. It appears in pine cones, sunflowers, the keys of a piano, the reproduction patterns of bees, pineapples, data sorting, and Roman poetry.

A Fibonacci sequence is also extremely interesting because of the innumerable patterns of numbers hidden in the sequence. We will consider some of these patterns in the following questions.

3. Consider the list of numbers in the Fibonacci sequence you have written down.

   a. Which terms in the sequence are divisible by 2? Describe any patterns that you see.

   b. Which terms in the sequence are divisible by 3? Describe any patterns that you see.

   c. Which terms in the sequence are divisible by 5? Describe any patterns that you see.

d. Which terms in the sequence are divisible by 13? Describe any patterns that you see.

e. Which terms in the sequence do you think will be divisible by 55?

4. Consider the following pattern.

$$1 + 1 \qquad\qquad\qquad = \qquad 2$$
$$1 + 1 + 2 \qquad\qquad = \qquad 4$$
$$1 + 1 + 2 + 3 \qquad\quad = \qquad 7$$
$$1 + 1 + 2 + 3 + 5 \qquad = \qquad 12$$

a. Describe the pattern that you notice here.

b. Write down the next five steps in this sequence without actually performing the addition.

5. The Fibonacci sequence can start with an arbitrary first and second term. For example, we could choose 2 and 5 as the initial numbers. Then the sequence will be as follows:

$$2, 5, 7, 12, 19, 31, 50, \ldots$$

Check and see if the patterns defined above hold true in this sequence as well.

6. Study the Fibonacci sequence and find another pattern. Check to see if your pattern still holds when you start with two different numbers.

Activity 4.16—Pascal's Triangle

Consider the pattern of numbers given below.

```
                    1
                 1     1
              1     2     1
           1     3     3     1
        1     4     6     4     1
     1     5    10    10     5     1
  1     6    15    20    15     6     1
                    .
                    .
                    .
```

1.   How do you get each successive row of this triangle?

2.   Add two more rows to the triangle.

This pattern of numbers is called Pascal's triangle, after the great seventeenth century French mathematician Blaise Pascal. The pattern was known and in use much before Pascal's time, but he is credited with making ingenious use of it in the theory of probability. The triangle may be continued indefinitely. In this activity, however, we will only look at some of the interesting number patterns hidden here, without delving into probability.

3.   Find the sum of the numbers in each row. How is this sum related to that particular row?

Consider the diagonal patterns marked below.

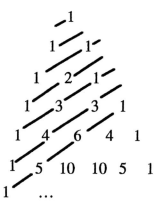

4. Find the sum of the numbers lying along each diagonal. What do you find?

5. Find and describe two other patterns in Pascal's triangle.

Things to Know from Chapter 4

Words to Know
- composite
- congruence modulo m
- divisibility
- divisibility test
- divisor
- even
- factor
- Fibonacci Sequence
- figurate number
- greatest common factor
- least common multiple
- modular arithmetic
- multiple
- odd
- Pascal's Triangle
- prime
- prime factorization
- proof

Concepts to Know
- what it means for a number to be prime
- what it means for a number to be composite
- what it means for a number to be even
- what it means for a number to be odd
- what it means for a number to be divisible by another number
- what it means for a number to be a factor of another number
- what it means for a number to be a multiple of a number
- what it means for a number to be a common factor of two or more numbers
- what it means for a number to be a common multiple of two or more numbers
- what it means to count modulo m
- what it means to prove something

Procedures to Know
- finding all the factors of a number
- writing the prime factorization of a number
- classifying a number by the number of its factors
- testing whether one number is divisible by another number
- finding the greatest common factor of two or more numbers
- finding the least common multiple of two or more numbers
- performing arithmetic operations in modulo m
- representing figurate numbers symbolically
- proving an idea geometrically

Exercises & More Problems

Exercises

1. Write the prime factorization of the following:
   a. 210   b. 136   c. 54   d. 1000   e. 2000

2. Write the prime factorization of the following:
   a. 28   b. 72   c. 91

3. Find the prime factorization of 110 and 204. Describe the process that you used to find the prime factorization.

4. Identify the following as prime, composite, or neither:
   a. 39   b. 1   c. 59   d. 119   e. 113   f. 0   g. -3

5. Classify the following numbers as prime or composite. Explain your answer.
   a. 7   b. 16   c. 28   d. 29   e. 32   f. 43   g. 57
   h. 102   i. 116   j. 125   k. 143

6. Classify the following numbers as even or odd. Explain your answer.
   a. 7   b. 16   c. 28   d. 29   e. 32   f. 43   g. 56
   h. 102   i. 118   j. 125   k. 143

7. Simplify each of the following fractions. Then write a brief description of the method you used.

   a. 12/28   b. 90/105   c. $\dfrac{2 \cdot 5^3 \cdot 7 \cdot 11}{3 \cdot 5 \cdot 7^2}$

8. List five numbers that have:
   a. exactly 2 factors   b. exactly 3 factors   c. exactly 4 factors

9. Consider the integer 310. Does this integer have more than 6 factors, exactly 6 factors, or less than 6 factors? How do you know? Explain.

10. True or false:
    a. 3 is a factor of 9   b. 9 is a factor of 3   c. 9 is a multiple of 3

11. If 21 is a factor of n, what are other factors of n?

12. Determine whether the following are divisible by 3. Explain your answers.
    a. 234,567   b. 19,582   c. 111,111

13. Decide whether or not the following are true using divisibility ideas. Explain your answers.
    a. 325,608 is divisible by 24   b. 1,732,800 is divisible by 40
    c. 13,075 is divisible by 45   d. 677,916 is divisible by 36

14. Pick any ten numbers, each of which has at least four digits. Test each of them for divisibility by each of the numbers for which divisibility tests are given in Chapter 4 of the *Resource Manual.* Check your answers by actual division.

15. Find the greatest common factors for each of the following groups of numbers.
    a. 924 and 1012   b. 864, 624, and 819
    c. 1056 and 2480   d. 488, 720, 968, and 704

16. Find the least common multiple of each of the group of numbers in #16.

17. Complete the following addition table in mod 4.

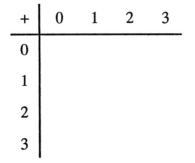

    a. What is the additive inverse of 3 (mod 4)?
    b. What is the additive inverse of 2 (mod 4)?
    c. What is the identity under addition in mod 4?

18. Complete the following multiplication table in mod 4.

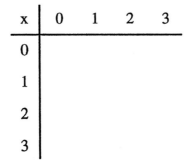

    a. Does 2 have a multiplicative inverse mod 4? If so, what is it? Explain.
    b. Does 3 have a multiplicative inverse mod 4? If so, what is it? Explain.

19. Perform the following operations modulo the number indicated in the parentheses.
    a. 3 + 9 (mod 11)   b. 1 ÷ 3 (mod 4)   c. 5 • 7 (mod 8)
    d. 8 + 3 (mod 9)   e. 2 − 5 (mod 8)   f. 3 + 5 (mod 6)
    g. 2 ÷ 5 (mod 6)   h. 5 − 7 (mod 9)   i. 3 ÷ 2 (mod 5)
    j. 1 + 4 (mod 5)   k. 3 • 6 (mod 7)   l. 4 • 5 (mod 10)
    m. 3 − 2 (mod 4)   n. 1 − 5 (mod 7)   o. 8 • 9 (mod 11)
    p. 4 ÷ 6 (mod 8)

20. Find the additive inverses of the following. Explain your answers.
    a. 3 (mod 5)   b. 4 (mod 6)   c. 2 (mod 7)

21. Find the multiplicative inverses of the following. Explain your answers.
    a. 5 (mod 7)   b. 6 (mod 9)   c. 3 (mod 4)

22. For integers a, b, c and k, suppose that ac = bc (mod k). Show by an example that we need not have a = b (mod k).

Critical Thinking

23. How many factors does p^{13} have, where p is a prime number? Explain.

24. Use the prime factorization of the given numbers to answer the following:
    a. The number 2352 is the product of two consecutive numbers. Find them.
    b. The number 65025 is the product of the squares of two consecutive odd numbers. Find them.
    c. The number 15525 is the product of three consecutive odd numbers. Find them.

25. The primes 2 and 3 are consecutive integers. Is there another pair of consecutive integers both of which are prime? Explain.

26. A number is said to be *perfect* if the sum of all its proper factors is equal to the number. One such number occurs within the first ten counting numbers. Find it.

27. Which of the following numbers is perfect?

    a. 28   b. 51   c. 256   d. 496

28. A number has 2, 3, and 5 as divisors. If it has exactly five other divisors, find the number.

29. Construct a number with exactly five divisors. Make a generalization about any number with an odd number of divisors.

30. Find the smallest, positive integer with exactly six divisors. Justify why this is the smallest, and why it has exactly six factors.

31. A prime is said to be a *superprime* if all the numbers obtained by deleting digits from the right of the number are also prime. For example, the prime number 7331 is a superprime because the numbers 733, 73 and 7, obtained by removing digits on the right of 7331, are all prime.

    a. What digits cannot appear in a prime that is a superprime?
    b. Of the digits that can appear, which cannot appear as the leftmost digits?
    c. Of the digits that can appear, which cannot appear as any except the leftmost digits?
    d. Write down all the two-digit superprimes.

32. A trainer in an athletic department was asked to arrange the towels in the locker room in stacks of equal size. When she separated the towels into stacks of 4, one was left over. When she tried stacks of 5, one was left over. The same was true for stacks of 6. However, she was successful in arranging the towels in stacks of 7 each. What is the smallest possible number of towels in the locker room?

33. If the GCD (x, y) = 1, what is the GCD (x^2, y^2)? Explain.

34. For any two positive integers, a and b, it is always true that LCM (a, b) is divisible by GCD (a, b). Justify why this is true.

35. Devise a divisibility test for 12.

36. Fill in the blanks with the largest digit (0 - 9) that makes each statement true.
    a. 9874___ is divisible by 2
    b. 69___14 is divisible by 3
    c. 9631___ is divisible by 8

37. True or false:
    a. If a number is divisible by 2 and by 4, then it is divisible by 8.
    b. If a number is divisible by 8, then it is divisible by 2 and 4.

38. By selling cookies at 24¢ each, Jose made enough money to buy several cans of soda pop costing 45¢ each. If he had no money left over after buying the soda, what is the least number of cookies he could have sold? What number theory idea could you use to answer this question?

39. Adam was to plant evergreens in a rectangular array. He has 144 trees. Find all possible numbers of rows if each row is to have the same number of trees.

40. Rebekah was practicing addition by adding the numbers along each full week on the calendar. After a while, Rebekah saw the following pattern for finding the sum of the numbers (that represented the dates) in a week: Take the first number. Add 3. Multiply by 7. Does Rebekah's pattern work? Explain your answer.

41. Three teachers—Allison, Barbara, and Chelsea—go to the local library on a regular schedule. Allison goes every 15 days, Barbara goes every 8 days, and Chelsea goes every 25 days. If they are all at the library today, how many days from now will they all be back again? What number theory idea can be used to answer this question?

42. In the following expression, put appropriate mathematical symbols in appropriate places to make the expression true. Find as many ways as you can to do so.

    1   2   3   4   5   6   7   8   9   =   100

    (Remember, you can also leave the space blank to make a number that has more than 1 digit. For example, if you put nothing between 7 and 8, the number reads as 78.)

43. Here is a proof of the result that there are an infinite number of primes. The proof can be found in many books. It is an example of a proof by indirect reasoning. In this kind of a proof, we assume a statement that is opposite in meaning to the result that we would like to prove. Based on this assumption, we logically derive a series of statements until we arrive at a contradiction. This contradiction shows that the assumption we made was not true, and hence its opposite, that is the result that we wanted to prove is true.

    Result: There is an infinite number of primes.

    Proof: Suppose there is only a finite number of primes, say, 2, 3, 5, 7, ..., p, where p is the greatest prime. Now, let us consider the number, N = (2 • 3 • 5 • ... • p) + 1. This number N is greater than 1. (Why?) Suppose N were composite. Then it would be divisible by a prime number. But none of 2, 3, 5, ..., p can divide N. (Why?) So N cannot be composite. Then N has to be prime. But this cannot be true, because N is bigger than any of 2, 3, 5,..., p. Thus, we get a contradiction. Hence, our initial assumption that there are only a finite number of prime numbers cannot be true. Therefore, there must be an infinite number of primes.

    Supply the missing details in this proof.

44. A student predicted (before actually checking) that the number 58 would have more than 2 factors and less than 5 factors. How do you explain this prediction?

45. A student asks you if zero is considered a factor of any number. What is your reply?

46. A student argues that there are infinitely many primes because "there is no end to numbers." How do you respond?

47. How do you see factors, divisors, multiples, primes, and composites in activities you do in your everyday life?

48. The United States Census Clock has flashing light signs to indicate gains and losses in the population. Here are the time periods of these flashes in seconds: Birth, 10; Death, 16; Immigrant, 81; Emigrant, 900. In other words, every 10 seconds there is a birth, every 16 seconds a death, etc. Assume that these lights all started flashing at the same moment.

   a. If you saw the birth and emigrant signs light up at the same time, how many seconds would pass before they would both light together again?
   b. Suppose you saw the immigrant and emigrant signs both light at the same time. What is the shortest time before they will both be lighted together again?
   c. It is possible for the birth and death signs to light together every 80 seconds. Why?
   d. What is the increase in population during a one-hour period?

49. A recipe for a large batch of cookies calls for 5 eggs. Before baking several batches of cookies, there are a number of cartons of a dozen eggs and 3 additional eggs. After baking there is one egg left over. How many eggs were there to begin with?

50. Rapti went to the Post Office to buy an assortment of stamps. She told the clerk that she wanted 9-cent stamps, four times as many 13-cent stamps as 9-cent stamps, and some 3-cent stamps. She gave the clerk $5.00 and said that she wanted no change. Can her request be met?

51. A game is played with 5 containers into which marbles are dropped one at a time. For example, the first marble is dropped into container 1, the second into container 2, the third into container 3, the fourth into container 4, the fifth into container 5, the sixth into container 1, the seventh into container 2, etc. If you started the game with 49 marbles, which container would be the one into which the last marble would be dropped?

52. Suppose you wanted to avoid dropping the last marble into the third container. What possible number of marbles can you start with using a range of 20 and 192? Try to generalize your answer.

53. a. Explain why the following statement is true.

   Any number in which a digit (except 0) appears exactly thrice (or in an exact multiple of 3) is always divisible by 3. For example, 123123123, or 773133713313.

   b. Make a similar deduction for another single digit number.

54. A palindrome is a number that reads the same forward and backward.
   a. Is every four-digit palindrome divisible by 11? Explain your answer.
   b. Is every five-digit palindrome divisible by 11? Explain your answer.
   c. Is every six-digit palindrome divisible by 11? Explain your answer.
   d. Is every seven-digit palindrome divisible by 11? Explain your answer.
   e. Make a generalization based on the above results.

55. Write a six-digit number by first writing down a three-digit number and then repeating it. For example, your number will look like 365365, or 859859. Now divide this number successively by 7, 11, and 13. Try this with several different numbers. What do you get in each case? Explain why you get this answer.

56. Find the remainder for each of the following without dividing the integers. Explain your strategies. What ideas from number theory did you use?
    a. $3245 \div 5$ b. $289 \div 3$ c. $11^4 \div 3$
    d. $5^{32} \div 3$ e. $2^{102} \div 5$ f. $2^{96} \div 7$

57. In a chocolate box, the number of chocolates is such that if they are divided among seven children equally, there are two left over. If they are divided equally among five children, then there are three left over. What is the least number of chocolates that the box can contain?

58. Three pirates have a chest full of gold pieces, that are to be divided equally among them. Before the division takes place, one of the pirates secretly counts the number of pieces, and finds that if he forms three equal piles, then one is left over. Not being a generous man, he adds the extra piece to one pile, takes the pile and leaves. Later, the second pirate goes to the chest, divides the gold pieces into three equal piles, and finds a piece left over. He adds this piece to one of the piles, takes the pile and leaves. The third pirate then comes and does likewise. Later, the three pirates meet and divide the remaining gold pieces into three equal piles. How many gold pieces were there in the original pile?

59. When Gauss was a child, one of his mathematics teachers, in a bid to keep the children in the class busy for some time, asked them to find the sum of the first 100 natural numbers. However, Gauss came up with the answer in only a few minutes. He did so by rearranging the first 100 numbers in a way that immediately suggested the answer.

    a. Try to do the same. Describe the method you used.
    b. Use the method you described to find the sum of the first n natural numbers (where n is any natural number).

60. Moses was playing with a calculator and noticed that for
    $1 \cdot 2 \cdot 3 \cdot 4 \cdot 5 = 120$, $2 \cdot 3 \cdot 4 \cdot 5 \cdot 6 = 720$, $3 \cdot 4 \cdot 5 \cdot 6 \cdot 7 = 2520$
    the GCD $(120, 720, 2520) = 120$. Imagine Moses's excitement upon looking at
    $8 \cdot 9 \cdot 10 \cdot 11 \cdot 12$, $9 \cdot 10 \cdot 11 \cdot 12 \cdot 13$, $10 \cdot 11 \cdot 12 \cdot 13 \cdot 14$,
    and $11 \cdot 12 \cdot 13 \cdot 14 \cdot 15$, and discovering that the GCD for all these seven products is 120. Was Moses just lucky or can any numbers constructed in this way be added to the list and have the GCD for the entire list remain 120? (Hint: Recall any class discussions you may have had about factors of consecutive integers.)

Extending the Activity
61. a. Consider the integers from 26 to 50. Predict and record the integers that have the greatest number of factors.
    b. Predict and record the integers that have the least number of factors.

62. Organize the information for the integers 26-50 in a table like that in Activity 4-2.

63. a. If a number is divisible by 4, is it always divisible by 12. Justify your answer.
    b. If a number is divisible by 12, is it always divisible by 4. Justify your answer.

64. a. Diana used the following procedure to find all the factors of an integer, n: first she wrote down 1 & n since their product is n; then she found the next largest factor (after 1) and its companion factor so that the product of these two is n. She continued on in the same manner. In order to find all the factors of this integer, what is the largest number Diana must test? Explain.

    b. Suppose Diana wanted to test whether an integer, p, was prime. What is the largest prime she must test? Explain.

65. How are mod 7 and base 7 alike? How are they different?

66. Make the addition and multiplication tables for mod 6.

67. Write 3 subtraction and 3 division problems in mod 6 and find the answers from these tables.

68. What properties [closure, commutative, associative, identity] are valid for addition mod 6? For multiplication mod 6? For addition mod n? For multiplication mod n?

69. Think of the square numbers in the following way:

   What relationship do you see between the triangular numbers and the square numbers?

70. Use the following pictures to state and prove a result about the sum of successive odd integers.

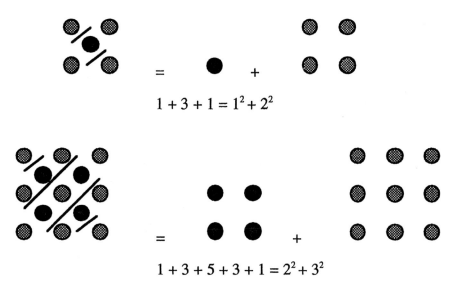

$$1 + 3 + 1 = 1^2 + 2^2$$

$$1 + 3 + 5 + 3 + 1 = 2^2 + 3^2$$

71. Consider the following series of pictures:

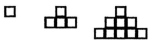

    a. Sketch the next two figures in the above pattern.
    b. What number pattern is suggested by this picture pattern?

    c. How many little squares will be there in the 10th picture in this sequence?
    d. How many little squares will be there in the 100th picture in this sequence?
    e. How many little squares will be there in the nth picture in this sequence (where n is any natural number)?

72. Consider the following series of pictures:

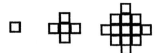

    a. Sketch the next two figures in the above pattern.
    b. What number pattern is suggested by this picture pattern?
    c. How many little squares will be there in the 10th picture in this sequence?
    d. How many little squares will be there in the 100th picture in this sequence?
    e. How many little squares will be there in the nth picture in this sequence (where n is any natural number)?

73. Generate twelve terms of the Fibonacci sequence that begins with 1, 1, 2, ... Observe the following pattern:
$$1^2 + 1^2 = 1 \cdot 2$$
$$1^2 + 1^2 + 2^2 = 2 \cdot 3$$
$$1^2 + 1^2 + 2^2 + 3^2 = 3 \cdot 5$$
Use the terms of the sequence to predict what $1^2 + 1^2 + 2^2 + 3^2 + \ldots + 144^2$ is without performing the computation. Then use your calculator to check your prediction.

74. Extend the Pascal's triangle in Activity 4.16 to have 10 rows. Then predict the sums along the next three diagonals (after the ones marked in the triangle in the activity) in the triangle.

75. a. Create Pascal's triangle with seven rows. Draw a circle around one number and the six numbers immediately surrounding it. Find the sum of the encircled seven numbers.
    b. Draw several more circles as in part a. and find the sum of the encircled seven numbers.
    c. Explain how the sums of the encircled numbers are related to one of the numbers outside the circle.

76. Write out 16 terms of the Fibonacci sequence beginning 1, 1, 2, ...
    a. Look at the fourth term in the sequence. Is it odd or even?
    b. Is the sixth term odd or even? the eighth term? Look for and describe a pattern that relates the term of the sequence with evenness or oddness.
    c. Predict which of the following terms are even and which are odd: the 20th term, 41st term, 250th term.
    d. Look for and describe a pattern that relates the term of the sequence and divisibility by 3.

77. Prove or disprove: The sum of any ten consecutive Fibonacci numbers is a multiple of 11.

Writing/Discussing
78. Make a concept map for factors and explain the connections you made.

79. Write an explanation of the Locker Problem solution.

80. Make up and explain a divisibility test for 6 in base six. Generalize and explain your observations.

81. Discuss the statement that factoring and finding a product are reverse processes.

82. Explain why the Sieve of Eratosthenes works, in general, in identifying prime numbers.

83. Make a second concept map about factors. Write a reflection comparing your first and second maps and explain your present understanding of number theory ideas.

Chapter 5: Probability & Statistics

Chapter Overview:

A great many events in the world around us involve uncertainty and chance. It is easy to find examples from business, education, law, medicine, and everyday experience. Two examples come readily to mind: (1) the weather forecaster on TV says, "There is a 70% chance of rain tomorrow"; (2) with only a very small portion of votes counted, newscasters are able to project winners of political elections and final percentages of votes with considerable accuracy. How was the 70% figure obtained? How can newscasters attain such accuracy with so little information? The branches of mathematics called probability and statistics were developed to help us deal with situations involving uncertainty and chance in a precise and objective manner. In this chapter you will conduct several experiments where you will explore basic principals underlying probability and statistics.

Big Mathematical Ideas:

> Data & chance, independence/dependence, representation, mathematical model

NCTM Standards Links:

> *K - 4:* Mathematics as problem solving; Mathematics as communication; Mathematics as reasoning; Mathematical connections; Statistics & probability

> *5 - 8:* Mathematics as problem solving; Mathematics as communication; Mathematics as reasoning; Mathematical connections; Statistics; Probability

Chapter Outline:

Activity 5.1—Probability Experiment I: A Spinner Experiment

Examine the spinner given to your group. Read through the following questions. Discuss and then obtain consensus about your predictions.

1. Would you be just as likely to obtain a red as you would a blue? If not, which color is more likely to occur? Why?

2. What do you think the chances are of spinning a red in one spin?

3. What do you think the chances are of getting a blue in one spin?

Record below what happens as you experiment by making 25 spins. Keep in mind that you are testing your conjectures. Reflect on the results and state any generalizations. Also discuss how experimental results may or may not change with 100 spins.

Activity 5.2—Probability Experiment II: What's in the Bag?

DO NOT LOOK in the bag your group has been given. It contains a total of 10 objects in 4 different colors. You have 15 minutes to try and determine the four colors and find the number of tiles of each color. Do this by drawing an object, recording its color, and RETURNING it to the bag. Repeat this process as many times as you wish without peeking inside the bag.

When your group has consensus, write down your prediction of the color combination. State in writing why and how you knew you had enough information to make the prediction.

Prediction:

Explanation:

Activity 5.3—Probability Experiment III: An Experiment with Dice

The study of probability developed from games such as those that are played using dice. Many games are played by rolling two dice and finding the sum of numbers shown on the top face. In this activity, your group will develop and use strategies to predict some probabilities. Roll the dice to gain some empirical data and then determine the probabilities listed below. Be prepared to explain your reasoning.

1. List all possible sums of the two dice (these sums are called the outcomes of the rolls of the dice). List the probability of rolling each sum.

2. Find the probability of rolling a 7 or a 11 on the first roll—an automatic win in the popular game of Craps.

3. Find the probability of not rolling a 7 or a 11 on the first roll.

4. Find the probability of rolling a 1.

5. Find the probability of rolling a sum of 2, 3, or 12 on the first roll—an automatic loss in Craps.

6. Which sum that is most likely to occur? Least likely to occur?

7. Two experiments are conducted in which tokens are drawn from a bag. In both experiments there are 10 tokens in the bag and each token has a different number written on it.

   Experiment I: A person reaches into the bag a draws out a token and records the number on it. The token is then placed back into the bag and the person draws out another token and again records the number on it.

   For experiment I, what is the probability that the sum of the 2 tokens drawn from the bag is 12?

   Experiment II: A person reaches into the bag a draws out a token and records the number on it. The token is not put back into the bag. The person then draws out another token and again records the number on it.

   For experiment II, what is the probability that the sum of the 2 tokens drawn from the bag is 12?

8. Think of other situations in which the probability of occurrence of an event is affected by previous events.

Activity 5.4—Are These Dice Games Fair?

For Game 1 and Game 2, read through the game rules; then, BEFORE YOU PLAY THE GAME, discuss with your partner and make a prediction whether or not you think each game is fair—that is, whether both players have an equal chance of winning. Play 3 rounds of each game. Record your results in a table. Keep track of who wins, "odd" or "even".

<u>GAME 1</u>: Rules
1. Choose one player to be "odd" and the other player to be "even".
2. Roll the dice and find the difference of the two numbers.
3. When the difference is an odd number, the "odd" player scores one point. When the difference is an even number, the "even" player scores one point. Remember, 0 is an even number.
4. Play the game for two minutes.
5. The winner is the person with the most points at the end of two minutes.

Prediction and Reasoning:

When you have finished, discuss with your partner and answer the following questions :

1. Do you feel more strongly about your prediction? If so, why? Do you feel less convinced about your prediction? If so, why?

2. Do you want to modify your prediction? How and why?

3. List possible strategies you could use to verify your predictions. Why would they work?

<u>GAME 2</u>: Rules
1. Choose one player to be "odd" and the other to be "even".
2. Roll the dice and find the product of the two numbers.
3. When the product is odd, the "odd" player scores one point. When the product is even, the "even" player scores one point.
4. Play the game for two minutes.
5. The winner is the person with the most points at the end of two minutes.

Prediction and Reasoning:

When you have finished, discuss with your partner and answer the following questions :

1. Do you feel more strongly about your prediction? If so, why? Do you feel less convinced about your prediction? If so, why?

2. Do you want to modify your prediction? How and why?

3. List possible strategies you could use to verify your predictions. Why would they work?

Activity 5.5—Basic Probability Notions

> The *sample space* associated with an experiment is the set of all possible outcomes (i.e., the set of all possible things that can happen) of the experiment.
>
> In an experiment, an *event* E is a subset of the sample space of the experiment. An event E is said to occur if the outcome of an experiment corresponds to one of the elements of E.

1. An urn is a vase whose contents are not readily visible. Your urn contains three blue marbles and two orange marbles. One marble is randomly selected, its color noted and it is not replaced. A second marble is then selected and its color noted.

    a. Draw a diagram or list the sample space showing all possible outcomes.

    b. What is the probability that

        • both marbles selected are orange? Justify your answer.

        • neither marble selected is orange? Justify your answer.

        • at least one of the marbles selected is orange? Justify your answer.

c. How would the probabilities in b. differ, if at all, if an actual experiment was conducted and you determined the probabilities based on your experiment data?

2. Jamaica is a first-year college student who is only beginning to organize her laundry. Specifically, she is still throwing her socks into the drawer without pairing them. One morning when Jamaica overslept, she hurriedly grabbed two socks from the drawer without looking. Jamaica knows that she has in her sock drawer 4 white socks, 2 blue socks, 2 black socks and 2 tan socks.

   a. If Jamaica first pulls out a tan sock, what is the probability that she will select another tan sock on the next try? Explain your reasoning.

   b. If Jamaica first pulls out a tan sock, what is the probability that she will <u>not</u> select another tan sock? Explain your reasoning.

   c. What are her chances of pulling out either a white sock or a blue sock on the first selection? Explain your reasoning.

   d. What are the chances that Jamaica pulls out a pair of matching socks if she makes two selections? Explain your reasoning.

Activity 5.6—Basic Counting Principles

Whenever we want to determine the probability or chances that a certain event will occur, we need to determine how many outcomes are favorable out of the total number of possible outcomes. It is not very difficult to count the number of possible outcomes when there are relatively few; for example, if we flip 3 coins, it is easy to simply list all 8 possible outcomes in some systematic way. Likewise, because the total possible outcomes is relatively small, it is not very difficult to list all possible outcomes of rolling a pair of dice. However, for many experiments this is not the case; there are simply too many outcomes to list conveniently. In this activity you will explore ways to count all possible outcomes of an experiment. To introduce these ways to count, let's consider some situations involving the need to determine all the ways to do something.

Situation I

Suppose that in 1996 there were approximately 50,000 automobiles of a certain make sold in the United States and that each of these cars was equipped with the same type of lock. Of course, the locks on these cars were not all "keyed" alike (note: two cars are "keyed" alike if one key will work in both locks).

The primary question is: Are there enough different arrangements of the tumblers in a lock to have a different key for each of the 50,000 cars?

Note: The tumblers in an ordinary lock are small metal cylinders whose height is adjusted by the depth of the notches cut into the key. If the correct key is inserted into the lock, the tops of the tumblers are aligned in such a way that the cylinder can be turned and the lock opened (or car ignition started). Of course, there also are more complex types of locks than these.

1. Suppose keys for the cars were designed with 6 notch positions and 6 depths of notch at each position.

   a. How many different keys could be made?

   b. What if there were 5 notch positions and 7 depths of notch at each position?

   c. What if there were 7 notch positions and 5 depths of notch at each position?

   d. Which type of lock would be best to install in the 50,000 cars mentioned above? Explain.

2. Several years ago in Tulsa, Oklahoma, two service station mechanics answered a call to start a white Ford Mustang parked on a particular city street. The owner came to the mechanics' garage and he gave them the keys to his car and also noted that he had been unable to start the car. Unknown to the mechanics, there were two white Ford Mustangs of the same year parked in the same block and, unfortunately, not seeing two identical cars, they got into the wrong one. Because the car started up without any trouble, they decided to test drive it before reporting back to the man who had given them the keys. As they were driving off, the real owner of the car returned and called the police. The police stopped the vehicle after it had gone only a few blocks and arrested the two unsuspecting mechanics. It turned out that the key the first man had given to the mechanics worked in the locks of both cars. The police officer in charge said, "It's just one of those one-in-a-million deals that I seem to get every night or so." Was it a "one-in-a-million" deal? How might you go about determining how likely it would be for one key to fit the locks of 2 different, but identical looking cars.

"Two Identical Cars Land Mechanic in Jail." Reported in the Daily Herald-Telephone (Bloomington, Indiana), November 6, 1975, p. 14.

3. Do we really need 3-digit area codes for long distance phone calls in the United States? Could we suffice with 2-digit area codes? (*Note:* Assume that the population of the U.S. is more than 250 million and that there are over 200 million telephones now in use. Also, note that you may not use 0 or 1 as a first digit in the area code or the local telephone number.)

4. Suppose that a multiple-choice quiz is given with 5 possible responses for each item. How many different answer sheets can there be for a two-item quiz. For a 5-item quiz?

5. A combination lock will open when a correct choice of 3 numbers is made. The numbers range from 1 through 50. How many different combinations are possible? (Is this the best name for this type of lock?)

6. Summarize the general counting method that you have used to solve the problems above (#1 - 5).

Situation II

Anagrams are "words" that use exactly the same letters but in different orders. For example, there are 2 anagrams for the letters N and O: NO and ON. (Both arrangements form standard words in the English language.) There are 6 anagrams for the letters A, E, and R: AER, ARE, EAR, ERA, RAE, REA.

1. How many anagrams are there for the letters E, N, O, and P? (Try to figure out how many there are without actually writing out all the possible arrangements.)

2. How many anagrams are there for the letters A, E, L, P, S, and T? (PLATES, STAPLE, PETALS, PASTEL, and PLEATS are a few of the possibilities)

3. How many anagrams are possible using the letters in the word BANANA?

4. If an apple, orange, pear, and avocado are placed in a row, how many arrangements of these fruits are there?

5. If the coach of a softball team wants the pitcher to bat last and the best hitter to bat in the clean-up position (i.e., 4th), how many different batting orders are possible?

6. a. The answer to questions 1 and 4 are the same. Find a 3rd problem that has the same answer.

   b. How would you describe a method for solving problems having the same basic features as problems 1 - 5?

Situation III

There are 10 teams in North Central Basketball Conference (NCBC). The top 3 teams will automatically be invited to the national championship tournament.

1. Assuming that there are no ties, in how many different ways can the top 3 positions of the NCBC standings be filled at the end of the season?

2. There are 10 floats entered in a July 4th contest. The best 5 are to be selected and lined up for the Hooterville Independence Day parade.

   a. How many different parades of floats can there be? What does it mean for two parades to be different?

   b. If a different parade began every half hour, 24 hours a day, how long would it be before the last parade started out? (Assume that the floats can appear in as many parades as needed.)

3. An airport bus has stopped to pick up 10 passengers to take them into the city. Four of the passengers already have their tickets, the others have to purchase theirs. If the passengers with tickets are allowed to board the bus first, in how many ways can the 10 passengers board the bus?

4. At a school cafeteria daily lunch plates are prepared for the students consisting of 1 main dish, 2 vegetable dishes, and a dessert. The lunch plates are chosen from a menu consisting of 10 main dishes, 8 vegetables, and 13 desserts. How many different lunch plates can be prepared before the students must repeat a plate?

5. Describe a method for solving problems having the same basic features as problems 1 - 4.

Situation IV

At State University, a group of 7 students wishes to select a committee of 4 to negotiate student activity fees with the Dean of Students.

1. How many committees can be selected from the group of 7?

2. Five students intend to play a round-robin tennis tournament among themselves. How many matches will there be?

3. How many 3-element subsets are there in a 6-element set?

4. A certain state's standard license plate contains a 2-digit number, followed by a letter of the alphabet, followed by a 4-digit number. The leading digit of the license plate cannot be 0. How many different license plates can be made? Would this arrangement of letters and numerals be sufficient for your state?

5. Create a "how many possible ordered arrangements"-type problem that would have meaning for elementary school students.

6. Create a "how many possible (unordered) sets"-type problem that would have meaning for elementary school students.

Activity 5.7—Basic Ideas of Statistics

Measures of Central Tendency

The following table shows the number of employees for a certain company and their corresponding salaried positions. During negotiations, management asserts that the average salary of the workers is $45,673. The Union asserts that the average salary is only $36,600. Who is telling the truth?

Position	Number of Employees	Salary
President	1	$200,000
Vice-President: Marketing	1	$120,000
Vice-President: Sales	1	$150,000
Vice-President: Financial	1	$140,000
Office Employees	10	$32,500
Salespersons	16	$36,600
Warehouse Staff	7	$22,000
Computer Analysts	4	$49,500

1. Determine the following statistics for the data above:

   Mean salary (total money paid in salary divided by the number of employees)

   Range of salaries (maximum salary - minimum salary)

   Median salary (salary that is exactly in the middle when the salaries are ranked smallest to largest)

   First quartile salary (salary below which one-quarter of the salaries lie)

   Second quartile salary (salary below which one-half of the salaries lie)

   Third quartile salary (salary below which three-quarters of the salaries lie)

   Interquartile range of salaries (the set of salaries falling between the first and third quartiles)

2. Why did each of the negotiators choose their respective statistic as an average? Which is the more appropriate average? Why?

3. Explain why the median and the third quartile are the same in this example.

4. Suppose a single position paying $180,000 were created at the company. Which average salary, the mean or the median would be increased more by the inclusion of this new salary? Explain your reasoning.

5. A useful and relatively easy way to represent a summary of a set of data is to construct a **box-and-whisker plot**. Box-and-whisker plots are a graphical representation of what statisticians call a 5-number summary of a set of data. The five numbers included in this summary are: the smallest value, the largest value, and the 3 quartile values (the first quartile, the second quartile, and the third quartile). In a box-and-whisker plot the center half of the data, from the first to the third quartile, is represented by a box with the second quartile depicted by a bar inside the box. A line extends from the first quartile to the minimum value, and another line from the third quartile to the maximum value. A box-and-whisker plot for the following 12 quiz scores (10 points was the maximum score) is shown below: 8, 4, 9, 10, 10, 5, 7, 3, 8, 2, 9, 7.

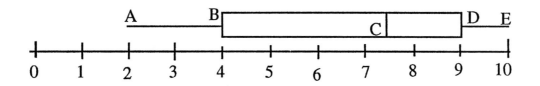

A -- lowest score;   B -- 1st quartile;   C -- 2nd quartile
D -- 3rd quartile;   E -- highest score

a. What is the 2nd quartile score for the 12 quizzes?

b. What is the interquartile range for the 12 quizzes?

c. What might a box-and-whisker plot be especially good for?

6. Create and sketch below a box-and-whisker plot using the original data for salaries for the employees of the company. Then create and sketch below a second box-and-whisker plots from the updated list which result from including the salary position described in #4 above. Compare the two plots. Will you change your reasoning in your answer to #3? Why or why not?

Activity 5.8—Exploring Unpaired Data: More on Box-and-Whisker Plots

The speeds (in mph) of a sample of 25 cars were checked by radar on an expressway.

Speed of Twenty-five Cars

57	53	53	71	73
54	69	56	58	49
56	53	52	82	62
61	60	71	75	60
57	61	58	78	64

1. Sketch a box-and-whisker plot for the data given above.

2. Answer each of the following questions. About what percent of the speeds are:

   a. below the median?

   b. below the lower quartile?

   c. above the lower quartile?

   d. in the box?

   e. on each whisker?

3 Is one whisker longer than the other? What do you think this means?

4. Why isn't the median in the center of the box?

5. If a police officer is writing tickets to each driver in the sample whose speed is more than 70 mph, about what percent of the drivers will be ticketed?

6. Why is the data set of the speed of twenty-five cars considered unpaired data?

7. Develop a scenario where these data are part of a set of paired data. What other information might you need?

8. Write a description summarizing the information in the box-and-whiskers plot.

Activity 5.9—Exploring Unpaired Data: Histograms

In preparation for this activity, you should take time to read the following discussion of histograms carefully. After you feel you understand the discussion, go on to the activity.

Histograms

A graph is really nothing more than a picture of information, that is, a picture of a set of data. Have you noticed that newspapers and many magazines typically resort to using graphs to provide their readers with a way to get a clear, accurate sense of what might be a very confusing amount of information otherwise. A histogram is one particularly good type of graph to use to represent a large amount of information in a clear and unambiguous manner. Suppose a newspaper such as *U.S.A. Today* wants to do a story on how the U.S. population is distributed by age. A reporter might get the necessary data from the U.S. Bureau of the Census and then decide to present the data in an easy to understand form.

The table below shows an abbreviated version of the data the reporter might have obtained from the Census Bureau.

Resident U.S. Population by Age: 1990
(in thousands)

Age	Frequency
Under 1 yr.	4,011
1 year old	3,969
2 years old	3,806
.	.
.	.
.	.
20 years old	4, 080
21 years old	3,969
.	.
.	.
.	.
40 years old	3,829
41 years old	3,716
.	.
.	.
60 years old	2,124
61 years old	2,100
.	.
.	.
.	.
80 years old	970
81 years old	883
.	.
.	.
.	.
90 to 95 years old	812
96 to 99 years old	214
100 years & older	44
TOTAL	252,175

Source: US Bureau of the Census, Current Population Reports, P25-1095 as reported in the American Almanac: Statistical Abstracts of the United States, 1993 (adapted from Pierce, D., Wright, E., & Rowland, L., *Mathematics for Life*, Upper Saddle River, NJ: Prentice Hall, 1997.)

Notice how difficult it is to look quickly at the table and make sense of it (especially if you had to look at the table with all 90 or more rows of numbers, instead of the abbreviated table shown above.) One way to simplify the task of digesting large amounts of information such as this is to construct a histogram of the data. One possible histogram for the Bureau of the Census data is shown in the following graph.

1990 U.S. Population

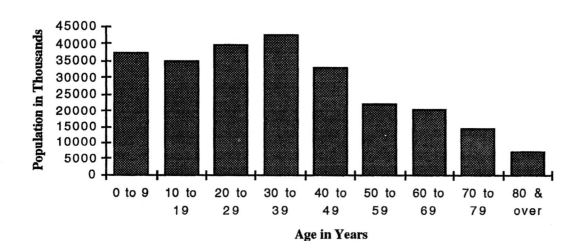

Activity: Displaying Unpaired Data with a Histogram

This activity involves the study of a collection of data and how that data might be represented using a histogram. The table below displays information about the amount of money spent by each state in the United States on public school education.

Average Number of Dollars Spent per Pupil on Public Elementary & Secondary Schools, 1988

State	Dollars	State	Dollars	State	Dollars
Alabama	2752	Kentucky	3355	North Dakota	3353
Alaska	7038	Louisiana	3211	Ohio	4019
Arizona	3265	Maine	4276	Oklahoma	3051
Arkansas	2410	Maryland	4871	Oregon	4574
California	3994	Massachusetts	5396	Pennsylvania	5063
Colorado	4359	Michigan	4122	Rhode Island	5456
Connecticut	6141	Minnesota	4513	South Carolina	3075
Delaware	4994	Mississippi	2760	South Dakota	3159
DC	5643	Missouri	3566	Tennessee	3189
Florida	4389	Montana	4061	Texas	3462
Georgia	2939	Nebraska	3641	Utah	2658
Hawaii	3894	Nevada	3829	Vermont	4949
Idaho	2814	New Hampshire	3990	Virginia	4145
Illinois	4217	New Jersey	6910	Washington	4083
Indiana	3616	New Mexico	3880	West Virginia	3895
Iowa	3846	New York	6864	Wisconsin	4991
Kansas	4262	North Carolina	3911	Wyoming	6885

Source: *Statistical Abstracts of the United States,* 1989.

1. In order to make it easier to make sense of the data shown in the table it would be useful to organize it into appropriate intervals. Discuss the table in your group and decide what intervals your group will use. Plot your chosen intervals and corresponding frequencies in a histogram. (Be sure to label it appropriately.)

2. Discuss and record observations made by your group about the graph. That is, what does the graph reveal about this data? List at least 3 questions that could be answered using the graph.

3. Discuss and make predictions about what differences there will be in the histogram if you change the intervals.

4. Change the intervals and record below any new information the graph may reveal about this data. Specify below your new interval choices; are they smaller or larger than in #1? How does changing the intervals affect data interpretation? Were the predictions you made in #3 correct? Why or why not?

5. Consider only the states east of the Mississippi River. Omit the District of Columbia and divide the other states into two groups, the NORTHEAST and the SOUTHEAST. The NORTHEAST states are Connecticut, Illinois, Indiana, Maine, Massachusetts, Michigan, Minnesota, New Hampshire, New Jersey, New York, Ohio, Pennsylvania, Rhode Island, Vermont and Wisconsin. The SOUTHEAST states are Alabama, Delaware, Florida, Georgia, Kentucky, Louisiana, Maryland, Mississippi, North Carolina, South Carolina, Tennessee, Virginia and West Virginia.

   Sketch histograms for the data from both the SOUTHEAST and the NORTHEAST.

   Discuss and record the comparison of the two distributions. What inferences can you make from the data?

Activity 5.10—Exploring Paired Data: Scatter Plots

Scatter Plots

There are many real-life situations that involve finding relationships between two sets of data. For example, you might want to see if there is a relationship between the number of hours you and your classmates spend studying for a test and your tests scores. Typically, if you wanted to determine if a relationship exists, you would organize the data as a set of ordered pairs. For example, the ordered pair (2, 65) might represent a student who studied for 2 hours and made a 65% on the test. The graph of such a set of all ordered pairs of hours studied and test score is called a **scatter plot**. In this example, the horizontal axis would show the number of hours studied and the vertical axis would show the percent score on the test.

---

1. Use the information provided in the table below to plot the ordered pairs given in the table as a scatter plot graph. (Be sure to label the graph.) Then use what you now know about scatter plots to complete the activities that follow the table.

Student	Number of Study Hours	Score on Test (maximum = 100)	Student	Number of Study Hours	Score on Test (maximum = 100)
Merissa	0	41	Jean	5	75
Howard	1	41	Ramona	6	66
Jacqui	2	51	Hank	6	64
Dyanne	3	57	Helene	6	91
Garner	3	47	Chris	7	85
Pete	4	48	Shondel	7	68
Susie	4	65	Art	8	90
Rachel	5	54	Ruth	8	78
Kirsten	5	70	Maria	9	94
Nathan	5	57	Fred	9	89

Use what you now know about scatter plots to complete the following activity.

Manatees live in the coastal waters near Florida and surrounding regions. They are very playful and friendly and seem to enjoy being near humans. There are not many of them, however, and conservationists have been concerned about the diminishing number. During the mid-1970's, the number of manatees who died and whose bodies washed up on the beach increased dramatically. The dead manatees were marked as if they had been scraped by a propeller. The Florida Department of Natural Resources investigated the power boats in the area and found the following data:

Manatees Killed by Boats, 1977-1987

Year	Boats (thousands)	Manatees killed	Year	Boats (thousands)	Manatees killed
1977	447	13	1983	526	15
1978	460	21	1984	559	34
1979	481	24	1985	585	33
1980	498	16	1986	614	33
1981	513	24	1987	645	39
1982	512	20			

1. Describe the relationship between the deaths of the manatees and the number of power boats in the area.

2. Use the pattern to estimate the number of manatees killed for 550 thousand power boat registrations.

3. Display the data with a scatter plot. Be sure to label the graph.

4. Should the data points in the scatter plot be connected by a line? Explain why or why not.

5. What would be a reasonable estimation of the number of manatees killed in the year 1995? Explain your answer.

Activity 5.11—Statistics and Sampling

Sampling Example 1.

On Feb. 18, 1993, just after President Clinton took office, a television station in Sacramento, California asked viewers to respond to the question: "Do you support the President's economic plan?" The next day the results of a properly conducted study asking the same question were published in the newspaper.

	Television Poll	Survey
Yes	*42%*	*75%*
No	*58%*	*18%*
Not Sure	*0%*	*7%*

Sampling Example 2.

In 1975 [advice columnist] Ann Landers asked "If you had it to do over again, would you have children?" Nearly 10,000 parents responded, with nearly 70% saying they would not. Many accompanied their responses by heart-rending tales of the cruelties inflicted on them by their children. . . . A nationwide random sample commissioned in reaction to the attention paid to Ann Lander's results found that 91% of the parents would have children.

[Both examples are reprinted from Pierce, D., Wright, E., & Roland, L., *Mathematics for Life*, Upper Saddle River, NJ: Prentice Hall, 1997, page 222.]

1. What can the discrepancies between the results of the television poll and the survey in the first example be attributed to?

2. Why do you think Ann Lander's question yielded such different results from those of the random sample?

Market Research

1. Market research is sometimes based on persons in samples chosen from telephone directories and contacted by telephone.

    a. What groups of people do you think will be underrepresented by such a sampling procedure?

    b. How could the sample be changed to include households that will be underrepresented?

    c. Using the sample frame of households chosen from telephone directories, discuss how general (or not) the results might be.

    d. List other ways that a sample may be chosen that will leave some groups of people underrepresented. Explain your reasoning.

2. A university employs 2000 male and 500 female faculty members. The equal employment opportunity officer polls a random sample of 200 male and 200 female faculty members.

    a. What is the chance that a particular female faculty member will be polled? Explain.

    b. What is the chance that a particular male faculty member will be polled? Explain.

    c. Explain why this is a probability sample.

    d. Each member of the sample is asked, "In your opinion, are female faculty members in general, paid less than males with similar positions and qualifications?"

    180 of the 200 females say "Yes."
     60 of the 200 males say "Yes."

    So 240 of the sample of 400 said, "Yes," and the report states that, "based on a sample, we conclude that 60% of the total faculty feel that female members are underpaid relative to males." Is this a valid conclusion? Explain why or why not.

3. The method of collecting data can influence the accuracy of sample results. The following methods have been used to collect data on television viewing in a sample household:

   a. The *diary method*. The household is asked to keep a diary of all programs watched and who watched them for a week, then mail in the diary at the end of the week.

   b. The *roster-recall method*. An interviewer shows the subject a list of programs for the preceding week and asks which programs were seen.

   c. The *telephone-coincidental method*. The household is telephoned at a specific time and asked if the television is on, which program is being watched, and who is watching it.

   d. The *automatic recorder method*. A device is attached to the set and records what hours the set is on and which channel it is turned to. At the end of the week, this record is removed from the recorder.

   For each method, discuss and record its advantages and disadvantages, especially any possible sources of error associated with each method. Method a. is most commonly used. Do you agree with that choice? Explain.

Searching for Misleading Data

Use a magazine(s) or newspaper section to find at least two examples of graphs or other data representations that you could argue is biased, misleading or otherwise manipulative. Then find at least one that you would argue is not biased and has accurate results representative of a population. Record your reasoning for each of your samples and be prepared to discuss your ideas.

Things to Know from Chapter 5

Words to Know

- box-and-whisker plot
- combination
- conditional probability
- counting principles
- data (unpaired, paired)
- event (dependent, independent, mutually exclusive, random)
- experiment (trial)
- fair
- favorable outcome
- frequency
- histogram
- interval
- mean (arithmetic average)
- median
- mode
- percentiles
- permutation
- probability
- quartile (first, second, third, interquartile range)
- sample space
- sampling (representativeness)
- scatter plot
- statistics

Concepts to Know

- what probability means, including conditional probability
- why probability is always a number, p, such that $0 \leq p \leq 1$
- what an event is (independent, dependent, mutually exclusive, random)
- what it means for an event to be fair
- why the counting principles are valid
- what are measures of central tendency and what can we learn from them
- what type of data are unpaired and what type of data are paired
- why one might use: box-and-whisker plot; histogram, scatter plot
- how sampling procedures can affect the data collected
- what representative means

Procedures to Know

- determining the probability of an event occurring
- determining the sample space for an event
- knowing when and how to use the counting principles
- finding mean, median, mode for a data set
- making box-and-whisker plot, histogram, scatter plot
- interpreting information from a plot, table
- determining intervals, percentiles, quartiles for various plots

Exercises & More Problems

Exercises
1. How many elements are there in the sample space for each of the following experiments? Justify your answers.
    a. Tossing 3 dice   b. Writing all 3-letter "words" with a vowel as the middle letter
    c. Drawing 2 cards from a standard deck   d. Answering 5 True-False questions

2. Suppose that a college dormitory keeps records by gender (F, M) and year in school (Fr., So., Jr., Sr., Grad). How many classifications are needed for the records? Why?

3. Suppose there are five sandwiches and four drinks that you like at a local fast food establishment. From how many sandwich-drink combinations can you choose? What if there were also a choice of three desserts, then how many sandwich-drink-dessert combinations are there? Explain your reasoning.

4. Draw a tree diagram to represent the following sequence of experiments. Experiment I is performed twice. The three outcomes of experiment I are equally likely.

5. Draw a tree diagram to represent the following sequence of experiments. Experiment I is performed. Outcome *a* occurs with probability .3 and outcome *b* occurs with probability .7. Then experiment II is performed. Its outcome *c* occurs with probability .6 and its outcome *d* occurs with probability .4.
    a. What is the probability of having outcomes *a* and *d* occur?
    b. What is the probability of having outcomes *a* or *d* occur?

6. An experiment consists of selecting the last digit of a student identification number. Assume that each of the ten digits is equally likely to appear as a last digit.
    a. List the sample space (i.e., the set of all possible outcomes).
    b. What is the probability that the digit is less than 5? Explain.
    c. What is the probability that the digit is odd? Explain.
    d. What is the probability that the digit is not 2? Explain.

7. A penny, a nickel, a dime, and a quarter are tossed. What is the probability of at least 3 heads?

8. An electric clock is stopped by a power failure. What is the probability that the second hand is stopped between the 5 and 6? Explain.

9. The graph below shows how the value of a car depreciates each year. This graph will allow
    us to find the trade-in value of a car for each of 5 years. The percentages given in the graph
    are based on the selling price of the new car.

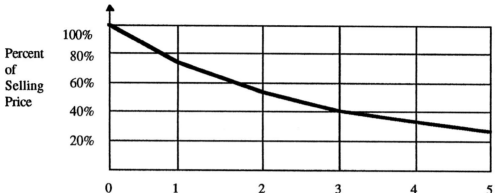

a. What is the approximate trade-in value of a $12,000 car after 1 year? Explain.
b. How much has a $20,000 car depreciated after 5 years? Explain.
c. What is the approximate trade-in value of a $20,000 car after 4 years?
d. Dani wants to trade in her car before it loses half its value. When should she do this?
    Explain.

The following table gives the percent of people 25 years or older in the United States and the
number of years of school they have completed. Use this table to answer exercises 10 - 15.

Percent of Population Completing School

	0-4 years	5-7 years	8 years	9-11 years	12 years	13-15 years	16 or more years
1970	5.5	10.0	12.8	19.4	31.1	10.6	10.7
1980	3.6	6.7	8.0	15.3	34.6	15.7	16.2
1987	2.4	4.5	5.8	11.7	38.7	17.1	19.9

Source: *Statistical Abstracts of the United States*, 1989

10. In 1987, what percent of the people in the U.S. had at least a high school education? Explain.

11   In 1970, what percent of the people 25 and older had not completed a high school education?
     Explain.

12. If a random sample of 3000 people was selected in 1987, approximately how many people in
     the sample would you expect to find had not completed a high school education?

13. In 1970, what percent of the people who started college had finished? Explain.

14. In 1987, what percent of the people who had started college had finished? Explain.

15. What trends can you observe from the data? What kind of sample might have produced this
     data?

16. An ice cream store offers 31 flavors. How many double scoop cones are possible if the person eating the cone cares which scoop is on top?

17. An ice cream store offers 31 flavors. How many double scoop cones are possible if the person eating the cone doesn't care which scoop is on top?

18. In how many different orders can a row of ten people arrange themselves?

Critical Thinking
19. In bowling, how many different outcomes are possible on the first roll?

20. Make up a problem that involves the probability of independent events. Write the problem and then solve it.

21. Create a problem involving conditional probability. Solve the problem you have created.

22. Find or create a realistic set of unpaired data with at least 10 data points.
    a. List them in a table and then represent them with a box-and-whisker plot. Summarize the information provided in the plot and give your interpretation of the data.
    b. Compare and contrast box-and-whisker plots, histograms, and scatter plots as ways to represent sets of data.

23. The following are the amounts (rounded to the nearest dollar) paid by 25 students for textbooks during the fall term: 35, 42, 37, 60, 50, 42, 50, 16, 58, 39, 33, 39, 23, 53, 51, 48, 41, 49, 62, 40, 45, 37, 62, 30, 23.

    a. Make a histogram to represent the data. What scales did you use for the intervals and frequency?
    b. Make two interpretations about the data from the histogram.
    c. Change the representation to a box-and-whisker plot. Find the median, first quartile, and third quartile values.
    d. Explain why the value of the third quartile is not a whole number.

24. You are cooking some spaghetti when suddenly one piece falls on the floor and breaks into 3 pieces. You friend, Henrietta, likes to bet. (In fact, she will bet on almost anything!) Henrietta takes a quick look at the 3 broken pieces of spaghetti on the floor and says, "I'll bet you $5 that I can form a triangle with those broken pieces of spaghetti." What is your chance of winning the bet?

Extending the Activity

25. If the spinner shown is spun, find the probabilities of obtaining each of the following:

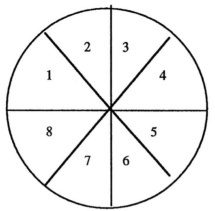

a. P (factor of 35)—remember that this means the probability of getting a factor of 35
b. P (multiple of 3)
c. P (even number)
d. P (6 or 2)
e. P (11)
f. P (composite number)
g. P (neither a prime nor a composite)

26. Paul, Norm, Fran, Kathy, and Dana are in a racquetball tournament. Individuals of the same sex have equal probabilities of winning, but each man is twice as likely to win as any woman.
    a. What is the probability that a woman wins the tournament?
    b. If Paul and Dana are married, what is the probability that one of them wins the tournament?

27. Four AAA batteries are chosen at random from a set of 16 batteries of which 6 are defective. Find the probability that:
    a. Exactly one of the 4 battery is selected is defective.
    b. None of the 4 is defective
    c. At least 1 is defective

28. From a pool of 20 smokers and 10 nonsmokers, a group of 10 is to be chosen for a medical study.
    a. In how many ways can this be done if it does not matter how many in the group are smokers and how many are nonsmokers?
    b. In how many ways can this be done if exactly 5 members of the group must be smokers and 5 must be nonsmokers?

29. a. An experiment consists of rolling a single die and observing the number showing on the top face. Give the sample space and the probability distribution for the experiment.
    b. An experiment consists of rolling a pair of dice and observing the product of the numbers showing on the top faces. Give the sample space and the probability distribution for the experiment.

30. A box of 200 transistors contains 10 defectives. An inspector draws 5 transistors at random and determines the number of defectives. The box is rejected if one or more of those selected are defective. Find the probability that the box is rejected.

31. Jamal Q. Student forgets to set his alarm with a probability of 0.2. If he sets the alarm it rings with a probability of 0.9. If the alarm rings, it will wake him on time for his 8:30 a.m. class with a probability of 0.8. If the alarm does not ring, he wakes in time for his 8:30 a.m. class with a probability of 0.3.
    a. Draw the tree diagram for this situation and give the appropriate probabilities on the branches.
    b. Find the probability that Jamal wakes in time for his 8:30 a.m. class tomorrow.

32. A pizza shop conducted a survey to find out which ingredients (extra cheese, green peppers or mushrooms) its customers wanted on their pizzas. Of the 100 respondents, 60 wanted extra cheese, 25 wanted green peppers, and 50 wanted mushrooms. In addition, 10 people wanted extra cheese and green peppers, 15 wanted green peppers and mushrooms, 25 wanted extra cheese and mushrooms. Finally, 5 people wanted extra cheese, green peppers and mushrooms.
    a. Draw a Venn diagram depicting the results of this survey. Include in it the number of people that fall into each of its regions.
    b. How many people wanted only mushrooms?
    c. How many people wanted green peppers and mushrooms but not extra cheese?

33. An urn contains 55 red and 45 green balls. A player draws a ball at random. If the green ball is drawn, the player wins $5 and the game ends. If a red ball is drawn, the player draws again from the remaining balls in the urn and wins $1 if a green ball is drawn.
    a. Draw the tree diagram for this game and give the appropriate probabilities for each branch.
    b. Make a probability distribution for the earnings and the probabilities.
    c. Find the expected winnings for the game.

34. A survey of 100 college faculty who exercise regularly found that 45 jog, 30 swim, 20 cycle, 6 jog and swim, 1 jogs and cycles, 5 swim and cycle, and 1 does all three. How many of the faculty members do not do any of these three activities? How many just jog?

35. An experiment consists of tossing a coin 8 times and observing the sequence of heads and tails.
    a. How many different outcomes are possible?
    b. How many different outcomes have exactly 3 heads?
    c. How many different outcomes have at least 2 heads?
    d. How many different outcomes have 4 heads or 5 heads?
    e. Explain a different way you could figure out an answer for c.

36. A letter is selected at random from the word "MISSISSIPPI."
    a. What is the sample space for this experiment?
    b. Describe the event "the letter chosen is a vowel" as a subset of the sample space.

37. A town is selected at random from the 60 towns in a particular geographical region.
    a. What is the probability that it is one of the 9 largest cities in this region?
    b. What is the probability that it is one of the 12 towns in the southern part of this region?

38. An exam contains five "true or false" questions. What is the probability that a student guessing at the answers will get three or more answers correct?

39. Two friends are playing a new game involving flipping two standard coins. Eric wins a point if the coins match (i.e., if the coins come up with two heads or two tails). Shelley wins a point if the coins do not match. Answer each of the following questions:
    a. Who is more likely to win, Eric or Shelley? Explain your answer.
    b. Is this a fair game? Explain your answer.

40. What is the probability of drawing a heart from a deck of 52 cards?
    What is the probability of drawing two hearts in a row, if:
    a. The first card is replaced before the second card is drawn?
    b. The first card is not replaced before the second card is drawn?

41. In a family with 3 children, what is the probability that at least one child is a girl? (What assumptions did you have to make to answer this question?)

42. What is the largest number of pieces into which you can cut a pizza with ten slices? (even though the slices may be of different sizes and shapes)

43. How many chess matches are needed in a round-robin tournament with ten players (where each player in the tournament plays against each of the other players)?

44. How many chess matches are needed in an elimination tournament with ten players (where a player is eliminated if he loses)?

45. How many handshakes does it take for a roomful of ten strangers to introduce themselves to each other?

46. Using what you now know about paired data, look back at your answer for #7 the "speed of 25 cars activity" of Activity 5.8. If you think you need to, revise it.

47. Find or create a realistic set of paired data with at least 10 data points. List them in a table.
    a. Summarize the information in your table in a bar graph (see Glossary).
    b. Summarize the information in your table in a scatter plot.
    c. Is there any information provided by the bar graph that you cannot get from the scatter plot? Is there any information provided by the scatter plot that you cannot get from the bar graph?

Analyze the data in the table below. Use this table to solve problems 48 - 53.

Final Medal Standings for the Top 20 Countries—1988 Olympics

Country	Number of Medals
USSR	132
East Germany	102
United States	94
West Germany	40
Bulgaria	35
South Korea	33
China	28
Romania	24
Great Britain	24
Hungary	23
France	16
Poland	16
Italy	14
Japan	14
Australia	14
New Zealand	13
Yugoslavia	12
Sweden	11
Canada	10
Kenya	9

48. Represent the data in a histogram. What scales will you use for the intervals and frequency?

49. List two interpretations that you can make by looking at the histogram.

50. Represent the data in a box-and-whisker plot. Determine the following values: median, first quartile, third quartile.

51. An *outlier* is a value that is widely separated from the rest of a group of data. Use the following rule to determine which, if any, of the data points in your list are outliers: An outlier is any value that is more than 1.5 interquartile ranges above the third quartile value or more than 1.5 interquartile ranges below the first quartile value. The interquartile range is the difference between the third quartile and first quartile values.

52. Eliminate any outliers from the data set above and determine the following values: median, first quartile, third quartile.

53. What number represents the best answer to the question, "What is the average number of medals won by the top 20 countries?" Explain.

Writing/Discussing

54. Think about events that may occur in your life.

    a. List 3 events that are certain to occur and explain why they are certain.
    b. List 3 events that are impossible to occur (i.e., cannot occur) and explain why they are impossible.
    c. List 3 events that are highly likely and explain why they are highly likely.
    d. List 3 events that are unlikely and explain why they are unlikely.

55. Think about the "Spinner" and "What's in the Bag?" experiments in Activity 5.1 and Activity 5.2. You made predictions and/or obtained experimental results. How close do you think your predictions were? What is a reasonable definition of probability?

56. Consider the "Dice" experiment. Describe a general method for finding out the probability of one event or another event occurring at the same time.

57. Explain the relationship between an outcome, an event, and the sample space for a particular experiment.

58. James tossed a coin 15 times and claimed that it turned up heads every time.

    a. Is this possible? Explain your answer.
    b. Is it likely? Explain your answer.
    c. What is likely to happen on the 16th toss of the coin? Explain your answer.

59. Give a reasonable argument why probabilities are never less than 0 and never great than 1.

60. Write a general statement explaining the process of determining combinations.

61. The article shown on the next page appeared in *USA Today*. Read the article and then create a graph or a chart that you feel would display the information conveyed as well or better than just using words.

A's in tough courses beat SATs, ACTs

How to get
into college
of your
choice, 4D;
Wednesday:
Financial aid

By Pat Ordovensky

USA TODAY

High school grades and the courses in which they're earned, are the most important factors in deciding who gets into college, say USA admissions directors. Scores on college admissions exams—the SAT and ACT—rank third in importance among items on a student's application. Choosier colleges say a student's essay has greater weight than test scores.

So finds a USA TODAY survey of 472 admissions directors, selected randomly from four-year colleges.

The findings echo recent public statements by admissions officers that the SAT and ACT are losing value in predicting college success—that A's in tough high school courses are more relevant.

"Almost everyone keys on academic progress over 3 1/2 years" in deciding which applicants to admit, says Richard Steele, Duke University admissions director. "The combination of high grades and a quality high school program is the best predictor of success."

For the survey, USA TODAY talked to large private universities with well-known names and small state colleges that specialize in training teachers. Among them are 27 highly selective schools—from Harvard and Princeton to Stanford and Cal Tech—that accept an average of only 31 percent of their applicants. We found:

• Almost 9 of 10 (88 percent) say grades are "very important" in admissions; 67 percent say rigor of high school courses; 52 say SAT/ACT scores; 45 percent say class rank.

• 58 percent of all schools and 52 percent of the choosiest say grades are the "most important" of all factors. Second is tough high school courses, mentioned by 16 percent of all schools, 28 percent of the choosiest.

• SAT and ACT scores are "most important" at 7 percent of the campuses but none of the selective schools.

• 17 percent of all schools but 60 percent of the choosiest say an applicant's essay is a "very important" factor.

• All schools responding have an average $1.5 million of their own money to help students who can't afford the tuition. At the selective schools, an average of $9 million is available.

• 89 percent of the selective schools used a waiting list this year for qualified applicants who didn't make the final cut. Average number of names on the list: 396.

Brown University admissions director James Rogers, an author of the new book *50 College Admissions Directors Speak to Parents*, writes that experienced admissions officers "can review a transcript and predict the student's test scores."

And although women consistently score lower than men on SAT/ACT, 52 percent of this year's freshmen are women.

Other factors—recommendations, interviews—enter in, says Steele, because with talented applicants, "you don't eliminate large numbers if you stop at academic performance."

On less selective campuses, grades carry even more weight.

At 15 percent of the colleges responding, because of state law or school policy, SAT/ACT scores are deciding factors.

Three of every 10 schools surveyed (29 percent) say they're required to accept students meeting certain academic criteria. More than half (54 percent) say criteria include test scores.

The University of Arizona, for example, is required to accept any Arizona high school graduate who meets four requirements: a 2.5 (C-plus) grade average, 11 college prep courses, standing in top half of class, a 930 SAT score or 21 on the ACT.

Forty percent of Arizona's students are from out-of-state, says admissions director Jerry Lucido, but they need at least a 3.0 (B) high school average, a 1010 on the SAT or 23 ACT score.

At Michigan, North Carolina, Vermont and other public universities where more than twice as many non-residents apply as can be accepted, officials also say standards are much tougher for students who don't live in their states.

Among other factors considered important in the admission processes, the USA TODAY survey finds:

• **Minority status:** Almost two-thirds (62 percent) of all schools and 96 percent of selective colleges say they're actively recruiting minority students who meet academic standards. That means minority status makes a difference between otherwise equal applications.

Of schools in the survey, this year's freshman class has an average 9 percent minorities—3 percent black.

• **Recommendations:** 70 percent of all schools, 96 percent of the most selective, say recommendations from teachers and guidance counselors are important. More than half (52 percent) of the choosy schools say they're very important.

Other recommendations, from the community leaders, clergymen and such, are important to 52 percent of all schools. 75 percent of the choosiest.

But "choose your references carefully," says Steele. "More is not better . . . . Last year, an applicant gave us 23 unsolicited letters of recommendation. We were not impressed."

• **Interviews:** Many highly selective schools use alumni across the USA to interview applicants in their area. At Duke, alumni reports weigh the same as teacher's recommendations.

Almost half (45 percent) of the surveyed schools and 64 percent of the choosiest say an interview is important.

• **Essay:** It's important to 92 percent of the selective schools but only half (50 percent) of all schools.

It offers a clue to a student's "quality of thinking," says Steele. "Few kids can write their way in, but it can help."

Errors—factual and grammatical—hurt. At Boston University a few years ago, an applicant was rejected because his essay had too much Whiteout.

• **Geography:** Most selective schools pride themselves on having students from all parts of the USA. A student from Montana applying to Harvard, for example, gets an edge over a New Englander.

At Duke, "we don't get many from the Dakotas," says Steele. "We snap to when one walks into the office."

More typical of all schools is Arizona where, Lucido says, "We're not shooting for geographic balance. We give no geographic preference."

• **Alumni ties:** Admission directors at selective schools say candidly that children of Alumni get special preference and children of generous alumni are even more special.

An alumni relationship is important to 44 percent of all schools, 80 percent of the most selective.

At Duke, 20 percent of all applicants are accepted. But for "alumni-connected" candidates the rate is over 40 percent.

Chapter 6: Fraction Models & Operations

Chapter Overview:

Many real-world situations require the use of fractions. The primary purpose of this chapter is to extend your sense of fractions and your understanding of operations on fractions. Because a deep understanding of fractions is essential for anyone who will teach fraction concepts and procedures to children, the first several activities involve considerations of various ways to interpret and model (that is, represent) fractions. Then, in addition to activities aimed at helping you develop better fraction sense, the chapter moves on to investigations involving fraction computations and everyday applications of fractions.

Big Mathematical Ideas:

> problem-solving strategies, conjecturing, verifying, decomposing, generalizing, using language & symbolism, mathematical structure

NCTM Standards Links:

> *K - 4:* Mathematics as problem solving; Mathematics as communication; Mathematics as reasoning; Mathematical connections; Number sense and numeration; Fractions & decimals
>
> *5 - 8:* Mathematics as problem solving; Mathematics as communication; Mathematics as reasoning; Mathematical connections; Number & number relationships

Chapter Outline:

Activity 6.1—Introducing the Region Model

For this activity, your instructor will give you five envelopes with three pieces of a square in each envelope. Your task is to reassemble the five squares following these rules:

1. No talking is allowed.
2. You may <u>give</u> a piece to another student, but you may not <u>take</u> a piece from another student.
3. After all the squares are completed, assign a fraction value to each piece. An assembled square is the unit. Talking is allowed during this time. You should not write on any of the pieces.
4. Record the value of each piece below and explain how you obtained this value.

#1 =   #2 =

#3 =   #4 =

#5 =   #6 =

#7 =   #8 =

#9 =   #10 =

#11 =   #12 =

#13 =   #14 =

#15 =

Activity 6.2—Introducing the Linear Model

Prove, using Cuisenaire Rods, that the yellow rod is half as long as the orange. This relationship can be written as 1/2 o = y. Find the other pairs of halves and record them. Then do the same for thirds, fourths, fifths, and so on, up to tenths. Record your findings. Then write the expressions the other way; for instance, 2y = 1o. Find at least 4 pairs for each fractional relationship.

Activity 6.3—Introducing the Set Model

In an adult condominium complex, 2/3 of the men are married to 3/5 of the women. What part of the residents are married?

Activity 6.4—Exploring Fraction Ideas through the Region Model

1. Cut out the strips and other shapes on page 170. Do <u>not</u> cut out the shapes on page 171.

2. Take the two strips of paper and tear one into two pieces and one into three pieces.

3. Compare your strips with your group members' strips and note the similarities and differences.

4. What directions need to be given so that each person ends up with strips equal in size after tearing?

5. Use the squares, rectangles, hexagons and circles that you cut out to divide the shapes into halves and thirds, following the steps below. In each case, use a cut out shape for folding, cutting or drawing, and then record your work on an identical shape on page 171.

   a. First, divide the shape by folding it, along lines of symmetry, into congruent pieces.
   b. Second, divide the shape by cutting (not on lines of symmetry) into congruent pieces. Verify that you have divided the shape into halves (or thirds) by placing the pieces on top of each other.
   c. Third, divide the shape by drawing line segments that separate it into equal-area, non-congruent parts.

6. How many ways were you able to fold a square in half? A rectangle? A hexagon? A circle? A square in thirds? A rectangle in thirds? A hexagon in thirds? A circle in thirds?

7. A square can be folded in half many different ways. Find ways that are different from the ways you folded it. Can you make a generalization about this folding process? Will it work for rectangles, hexagons and circles also?

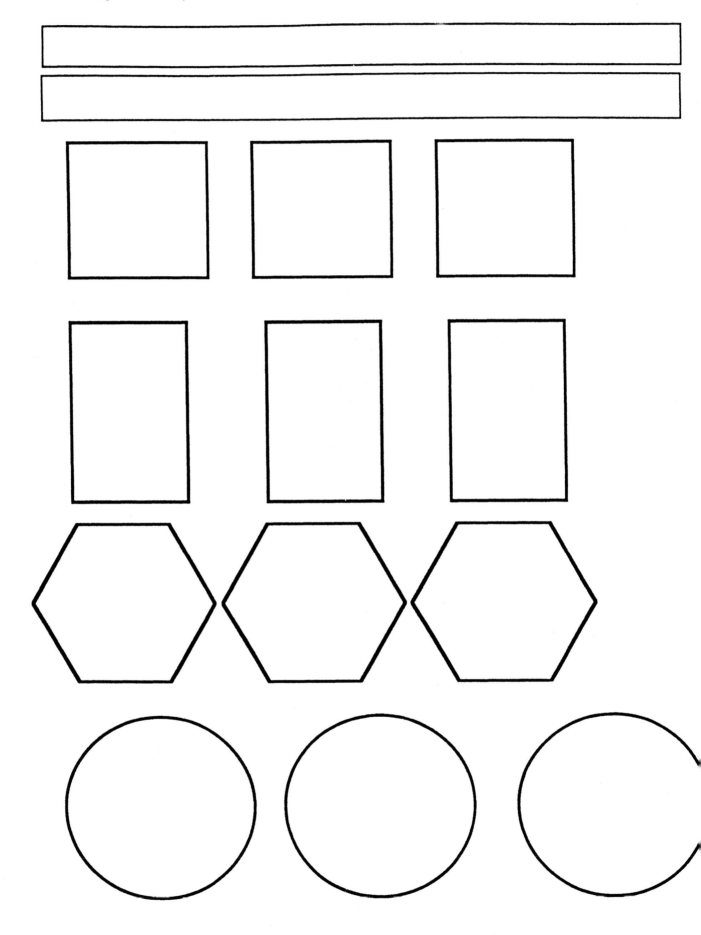

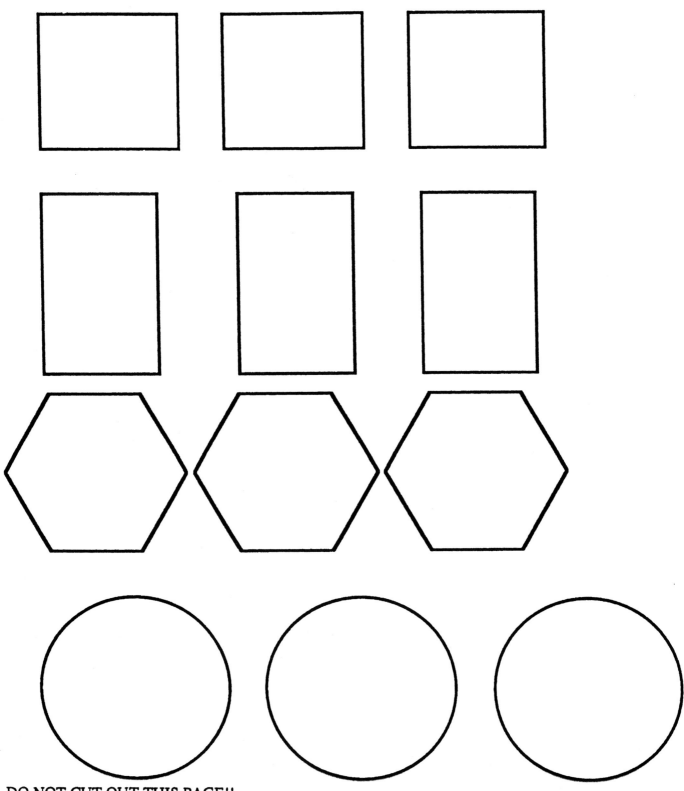

DO NOT CUT OUT THIS PAGE!!

Activity 6.5—Fractions on the Square: A Game using the Region Model

Play this game with another group member. Each player, in turn, spins two spinners (or throws two dice) and decides which is the larger of the two fractions appearing on the spinners (or whether the fractions are equivalent). If the player is correct, he or she can shade in, on one of the squares, a region equivalent to the fraction. The winner is the first player to completely shade in all squares on her or his sheet.

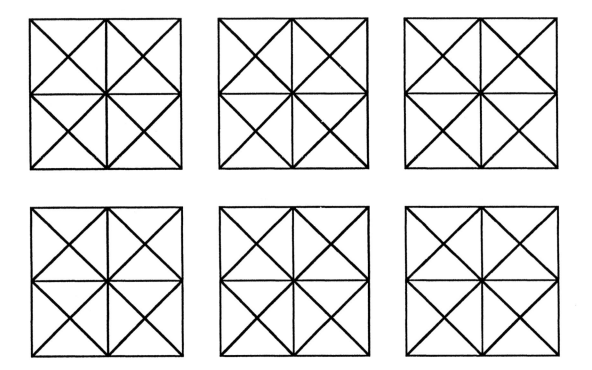

Activity 6.6—Fraction Puzzles using the Region Model

Build the following figures using pattern blocks and then sketch your figure.

1. Build a triangle that is 1/3 green and 2/3 red.

2. Build a triangle that is 2/3 red, 1/9 green, and 2/9 blue.

3. Build a parallelogram that is 3/4 blue and 1/4 green.

4. Build a parallelogram that is 2/3 blue and 1/3 green.

5. Build a trapezoid that is 1/2 red and 1/2 blue.

Activity 6.7—Looking for Patterns with the Linear Model

There are four different ways to make arrangements, called trains, equivalent in length to the light green rod: light green, red-white, white-red, and white-white-white.

Do the same for the other rods. Find a pattern that allows you to predict how many different ways there are to make trains for any length rod.

Activity 6.8—Exploring Fraction Ideas through the Linear Model

Cut out and use strips #1, 2, 3, and 4 from page 177 for this activity.

1. Suppose that strip #1 is 1 unit long. Use it to model 2/3. Illustrate the process you used and shade the answer.

2. Do the same for 3/4 and 3/2 using #1 strips from more than one group member.

3. Make a number line using strip #1 as 1 unit and place the numbers 2/3, 3/4, 3/2 in the appropriate locations.

4. If strip #1 represents 1 unit, what does strip #2 represent? strip #3? strip #4?

5. Model 2/3 with strip #2. Note that this is 2/3 unit, not 2/3 of strip #2. Illustrate with a diagram the process you used and shade the answer. Represent the process with mathematical symbols.

6. Model 3/4 with a strip other than #1. Illustrate the process you used and shade the answer. Represent the process with mathematical symbols.

7.   Model 4/5 with two different strips. Illustrate the process you used and shade the answer. Represent the process with mathematical symbols.

8.   Make a generalization concerning the following: Given a fraction, how can you represent it two different ways with strips of paper?

9.   If you have a 1 pound bar of chocolate, how much is 3/4 of it?

10. If you have a 3 pound bar of chocolate, how much is 1/4 of it?

11. Explain why your answers are the same.

12. For each of the following, model the operation with a strip of paper, illustrate with a diagram the process you used, and shade your answer.

a. 3 x 1/4

b. 1/4 x 3

c. 1/3 x 1/4

d. 1/4 x 1/3

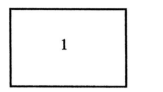

Activity 6.9—Exploring the Density of the Set of Real Numbers

1. Use two pieces of paper taped together end-to-end to make a number line. The place where the two pages meet can serve as the origin. Using strip #1 as length 1, mark on the number line all the integers that you can. Use one of the strips of paper to mark all the halves. Justify the process that you used to find these. Do the same for thirds and fourths.

2. Is it possible to use this same procedure to find other fractions on the number line?

3. If you were asked to mark all the sixths, what steps would you take to do this using strips of paper?

4. Describe where you would place 1/6 on the number line and why you would place it there.

5. Is it possible to use a certain number of sixths to represent the same number as 1/2? If so, how many?

6. Is it possible to use a certain number of thirds to represent the same number as 1/2? If so, how many?

7. If you have a fraction of the form 1/n, when will it be possible to use a certain number of 1/n's to represent the same number as 1/2?

8. How many sixths do you need to represent the number 2? How many thirds? How many fourths?

9. Do you think that every number has more than one representation? Justify your reasoning.

10. Now look at your number line. Consider the part from 1 to 3/2. Is there a number between 1 and 3/2? What is it?

11. Now look at the part of the number line from 3/2 to 5/3. Is there a number between these two numbers? What is it?

12. Make a conjecture concerning the existence of a number between any two numbers.

Activity 6.10—Exploring Fraction Ideas through the Set Model

Using 12 color tiles, model the following and illustrate your answer.

1.   2/3

2.   3/4

3.   1/2

4.   5/6

5.   1/2 • 2/3

6.   3/4 • 1/3

Can you illustrate division of fractions with these tiles? Why or why not?

Activity 6.11—Solving Problems using the Set Model

1. I'm thinking of a number. One half is a third of my number. What is my number?

2. A balance scale was in perfect balance when Horace placed a box of candy on one pan of the balance and 3/4 of the same sized candy box together with a 3/4 pound weight on the other pan. How much did the full box of candy weigh?

3. Every time Agnes goes to a flea market she buys another antique quilt. She has quite a collection of quilts, but she is reluctant to admit exactly how many she has.
    Alexander asked her directly, "How many quilts do you have now?"
    "Oh, I don't really have that many," Agnes replied evasively. "Actually, I have three quarters of their number plus 3/4 of a quilt."
    Alexander thought she must be kidding, but she was actually challenging him with a problem. How many quilts does Agnes have?

4. Samuel was riding in the back seat of the station wagon on the way home after a long and tiring day at the beach. He fell asleep halfway home. He didn't wake up until he still had half as far to go as he had already gone while asleep. How much of the entire trip home was Samuel asleep?

Activity 6.12—Classifying Problems by Operation: Revisiting Activity 3.3

Recall Activity 3.3 where you classified word problems into different categories for each of the four operations. In each of the blanks below, write the various classifications for each operation. For example, for subtraction there are the classifications of comparison, take away, and missing addend. Make up one word problem using fractions for each classification.

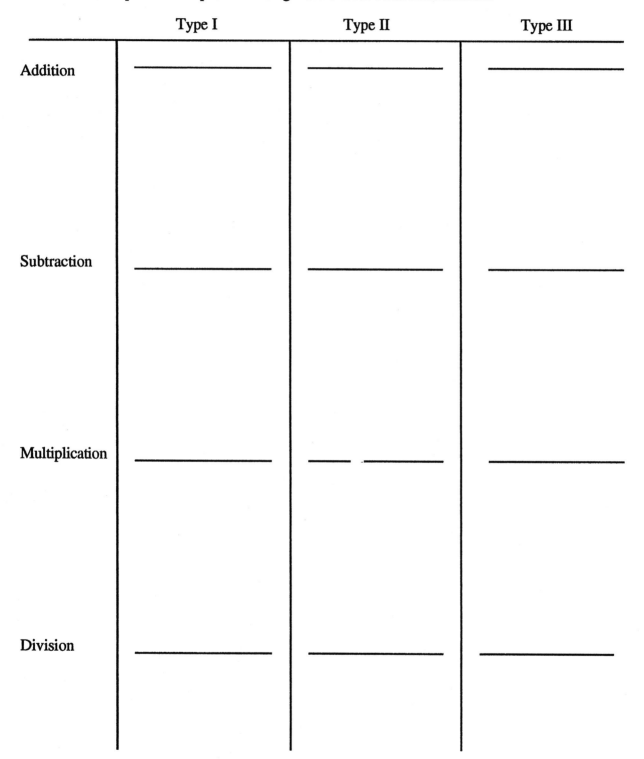

	Type I	Type II	Type III
Addition			
Subtraction			
Multiplication			
Division			

Activity 6.13—Illustrating Operations with Region, Linear and Set Models

Translate these into mathematical symbols, illustrate the problem, and solve it.

1.   Two-ninths of it is one-ninth. What is it?

2.   One-fifth of it is one-third. What is it?

3.   One-fourth of it is one-sixth. What is it?

Fold a strip of paper to illustrate the relationship in the diagram and record with mathematical symbols the action that is taking place.

4.

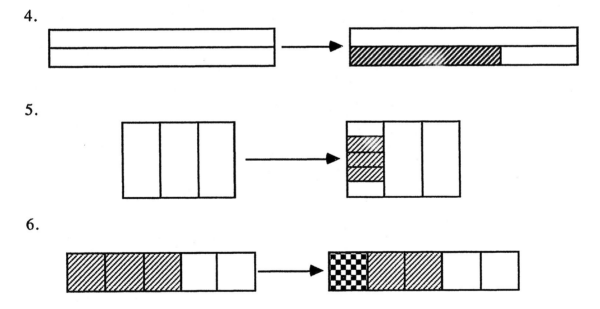

5.

6.

Model these with paper folding and draw an illustration.

7.   1/2 of 2/7

8.   2/7 of 1/2

Draw an illustration to represent the problem and solve.

9.   There are four bottles. Each bottle contains 2/5 of a liter. How many liters are there altogether in the bottles?

10. There are three bags of marbles, each with the same number of marbles. If 2/3 of the marbles are taken from each bag, what part of each bag remains? How many full bags of marbles could be made from the remaining marbles?

11. If a school cafeteria makes 44 pints of juice for lunch each day, and each lunch period group uses 11 pints, how many lunch period groups are there?

12. Now suppose that all the juice needs to be put into containers holding only 1/2 of a pint. How many containers will be needed?

Illustrate these problems and solve.

13. How many halves are contained in 3 units?

14. How many thirds are in 23? [Hint: Illustrate a simpler problem and use your conclusion to solve this problem.]

15. How many times is 2/7 contained in 4/7?

16. How many times is 3/11 contained in 9/11?

17. How many times is 4/11 contained in 9/11?

18. What conclusions can you make from the three previous problems?

19. How many times is 2/5 contained in 3/7? [Try to use what you learned in the above problems and the concept of fraction to explain the solution to this problem.]

Activity 6.14—Developing Fraction Sense with Linear Models

1. a, b, c represent whole numbers different from 0 and a > b > c. What can you say about:

   a. a/b   b. b/a   c. b/c

   d. c/b   e. a/c   f. c/a

2. Which is larger:

   a. a/c or b/c?   b. a/b or b/b?

   c. a/b or a/c?

3.

   a. If the fractions represented by the points D and E are multiplied, what point on the
      number line best represents the product?

   b. If the fractions represented by the points C and D are divided, what point on the number
      line best represents the quotient?

   c. If the fractions represented by the points B and F are multiplied, what point on the
      number line best represents the product?

   d. Suppose 20 is multipled by the number represented by E on the number line.
      Estimate the product.

   e. Suppose 20 is divided by the number represented by E on the number line.
      Estimate the quotient.

4.

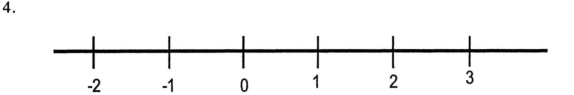

   a. Indicate, by using A, where 1/2 + 3/4 is on the number line.

   b. Indicate, by using B, where 1/2 - 3/4 is on the number line.

   c. Indicate, by using C, where 1/2 x 3/4 is on the number line.

   d. Indicate, by using D, where 1/2 ÷ 3/4 is on the number line.

5.   Use the ten digits to make the following numbers.

   a. the smallest positive fraction you can make using: two distinct digits, three distinct digits, four distinct digits, . . ., ten distinct digits

   b. the largest fraction, not equal to a whole number, you can make using: two distinct digits, three distinct digits, four distinct digits, . . ., ten distinct digits

   c. the fraction closest to, but not equal to, 2

   d. a number that is between 1/4 and 3/4

   e. a number that is between 7/8 and 1

   f. a number that is half as large as 1/6

   g. the number that is closest, but not equal to, 9/10 using four digits

   h. an estimate of 1/3 of $26.25

   i. an estimate of 1/4 of $27.50

Activity 6.15—Using the Region Model to Illustrate Multiplication

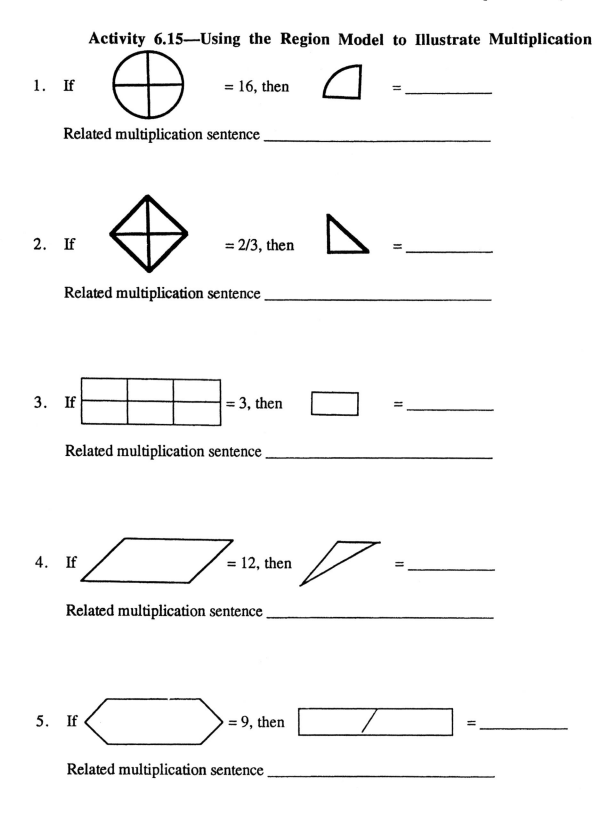

1. If ⊕ = 16, then ◺ = _____

    Related multiplication sentence _____

2. If ◈ = 2/3, then ◺ = _____

    Related multiplication sentence _____

3. If ▦ = 3, then ▭ = _____

    Related multiplication sentence _____

4. If ▱ = 12, then ◿ = _____

    Related multiplication sentence _____

5. If ⬡ = 9, then ▭ = _____

    Related multiplication sentence _____

Activity 6.16—Using the Region Model to Illustrate Division

Recall from Activity 6.4 the generalizations you made regarding dividing figures in half in infinitely many ways. For this activity your group will be investigating dividing figures into equal-area, noncongruent pieces.

1. Find a method of dividing this rectangle into two noncongruent pieces with equal area.

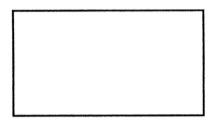

   Make a generalization about your method of division.

2. Now generalize the division for 3, 4, . . ., n noncongruent pieces with equal area.

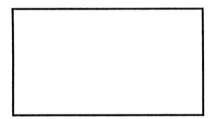 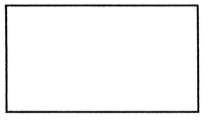

3. A square-topped cake that is a rectangular solid is frosted on all faces except the bottom. Cut it into five pieces so that each person gets the same amount of cake and the same amount of frosting. All cuts must be perpendicular to the top of the cake. Each person must get their cake in one piece.

Things to Know from Chapter 6

Words to Know
- density
- equivalent fractions
- fraction
- models of fractions (region, linear, set)
- number line
- simplest terms

Concepts to Know
- what is a fraction
- what is meant by equivalent fractions
- what the region, linear and set models of fractions represent
- what it means to put a fraction in simplest terms
- what it means to say that the real number line is dense

Procedures to Know
- recognizing equivalent fractions
- modeling fractions with region, linear and set models
- modeling operations with fractions
- simplifying fractions
- classifying word problems by operation category
- finding a number between two other numbers

Exercises & More Problems

Exercises

1. Combine the first 2/3 of "ten" with the last 2/3 of "Sam".

2. Combine the first 1/2 of "blue" with the last 3/4 of "send".

3. Combine the first 1/3 of "materials" with the last 3/4 of "this" and the first 1/4 of "fundamentals".

4. Take the first 2/3 of the first 1/3 of "different". Then take the second letter of the last 1/3 of "different". Take the second letter of the first 1/3 of "different". Now take the third letter of the first 4/9 of "challenge". Take the first 1/2 of the last 1/2 of the first 4/9 of "challenge". Finally, take the first 1/3 of the last 1/3 of "challenge". Reorder all the letters you have obtained to form a familiar word.

5. Make up two word puzzles, similar to the one in #4, that use multiplication of fraction ideas.

6. Shade in the appropriate region(s), or place at the appropriate place on the number line, so that the result shows the given fraction:

   a. $\dfrac{3}{4}$

   b. $\dfrac{2}{5}$

   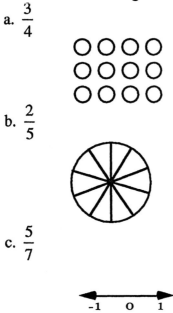

   c. $\dfrac{5}{7}$

7. a. Assume that each square below represents 1. What fraction is shaded in each? Write a multiplication sentence that would make sense in each picture below.

   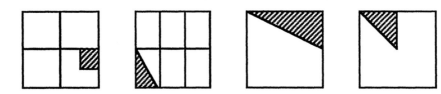

   b. Make up two other pictures like the ones above and write multiplication sentences for them.

8. Suppose there is a contest to decide on a design for the flag of a new republic. Draw four different designs that have the rectangular flag 1/4 blue, 1/4 red, and 1/2 yellow.

9. Write two fractions for each of the following that equal the given fraction:

    a. $\dfrac{3}{9}$ b. $\dfrac{-3}{5}$ c. $\dfrac{0}{2}$

10. Draw an area model to show that $\dfrac{2}{3} = \dfrac{6}{9}$

11. Compute each of the following:
    a. 2/7 + 8/11   b. -5/13 + 4/7   c. 2/5 - 7/9

12. Model the following situations by drawing an illustration:
    a. 1/3 of 3/5   b. 2/9 of 1/2

13. Determine which fraction does not equal the other two by reducing to simplest form:

    a. $\dfrac{7}{13}, \dfrac{28}{52}, \dfrac{35}{78}$ b. $\dfrac{-32}{63}, \dfrac{4}{-9}, \dfrac{-64}{144}$ c. $\dfrac{17}{21}, \dfrac{34}{63}, \dfrac{102}{126}$

14. Arrange each of the following in increasing order:

    a. $\dfrac{7}{11}, \dfrac{7}{14}, \dfrac{7}{9}$ b. $\dfrac{-3}{5}, \dfrac{-7}{8}, \dfrac{-8}{19}$

15. Find two rational numbers that are between the following two fractions:

    a. $\dfrac{7}{9}$ and $\dfrac{8}{9}$ b. $\dfrac{-9}{14}$ and $\dfrac{-8}{14}$ c. $\dfrac{13}{19}$ and $\dfrac{8}{11}$

16. Compute each of the following (simplify when necessary):

    a. $\dfrac{25}{42} \cdot \dfrac{28}{50}$ b. $7 \div \dfrac{1}{2}$ c. $\dfrac{\frac{7}{9}}{\frac{4}{18}}$

17. On the same number line determine where the following expressions should be placed:
    a. 3/2 + 3/4   b. 3/2 - 3/4   c. 3/2 x 3/4   d. 3/2 ÷ 3/4

18. Write a comparison subtraction problem involving the fractions 1/3 and 1/4, and solve the problem.

19. Illustrate how you could model, with a strip of paper, the quotient .2 ÷ .6. Explain.

20. Illustrate .9 ÷ .6 by drawing a model of base ten blocks. Explain your model and solution.

Critical Thinking

21. Under what conditions would one positive rational number with a greater numerator than another rational number, be greater in value?

22. Given a number. If one fourth is two thirds of that number. What is the number?

23. Illustrate the following situation and use that to solve the problem: Two-thirds of a number is three-fifths.

24. Illustrate how many times is 4/9 contained in 6/9.

25. What might be a reasonable estimate for 1/6 of 82? Explain how you determined that estimate.

26. Is taking one-third of a number the same as dividing the number by one-third? Explain

27. Diana bought a piece of cloth 48 inches wide and 1 yard long. It cost $10. She cut off one third and used it to make a tablecloth. From the remaining material she used a piece that was 12 inches wide and 12 inches long to make a scarf and a piece 2 feet by 1.5 feet to make the cover for a throw pillow. Her sister saw Diana's sewing efforts and said she really liked the material. She wanted to buy what was left to do some sewing of her own. Diana was willing to sell the leftover material for what she had paid for it. How much should she charge her sister? Find three different methods of doing this problem. Use paper folding for at least one of your methods.

28. After a cyclist has gone 2/3 of her route, she gets a puncture in a tire. Finishing on foot, she spends twice as long walking as she did riding. How many times as fast does she ride as walk?

29. Moses can eat 7 pizzas in 3 hours and Ryan can eat 9 pizzas in 7 hours. How many pizzas can Moses and Ryan eat together in 5 hours? Justify your answer.

30. Five maids can clean seven houses in three days. How long would it take eight maids to clean twenty houses if all the work was done at the same rate?

31. If you have a fraction of the form 1/n, when will it be possible to use a certain whole number of 1/n's to represent the same number as 1/2? Explain.

32. Adam put 1/2 of a cake in the freezer. Of the remaining half of the cake, Adam ate 1/5 and his dog ate the rest. What part of the whole cake did his dog eat?
    a. 1/2 - 1/5   b. 1/2 • 1/5   c. 1 - (1/2 • 1/5)
    d. 1/2 - 4/5   e. none of these

33. Rebekah is making bookmarks for the 5th grade class bazaar. She has a roll of 6 feet of ribbon. Each bookmark requires 4 3/4 inches of ribbon. How many (complete) bookmarks can she make? How much ribbon will she have left over?

34. Without computing common denominators, order these fractions from smallest to largest. Use estimation strategies and consider the relative sizes of the numerators and denominators.
    a. 11/16, 11/13, 11/22
    b. 23/16, 33/16, 3
    c. -1/5, -19/36, -17/30
    d. 5/6, 3/4, 7/8
    e. -1/6, -1/8, -1/7
    f. 2/5, 3/10, 4/10
    g. 0/7, 0/17, 3/17
    h. -2/3, 3/4, -4/7, 4/5

35. Suppose a/b and c/d are two fractions and a/b < c/d. Answer each of the following questions about a/b and c/d.
    a. If b = d, what do you know about a and c?
    b. If a = c, what do you know about b and d?
    c. If a = c and b = d, what do you know about the relationship among a, b, c, and d?

36. If the length of rod B is 2/3 unit, what is the length of rod A? Justify your answer.

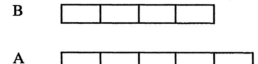

B

A

37. In a certain machine industry a marker is a worker who draws lines on a metal blank. The blank is cut along the lines to produce the desired shape. A marker was asked to distribute 7 equal-sized sheets of metal among 12 workers. Each worker was to get the same amount of metal. The marker could not use the simple solution of dividing each sheet into 12 equal parts, for this would result in too many tiny pieces. What was he to do? He thought a while and found a more convenient method. He wrote 7/12 as 1/3 + 1/4. Then he cut 3 of the sheets into fourths and 4 of the sheets into thirds and gave each worker one third of a sheet and one fourth of a sheet. How could he use his method to divide 5 sheets for 6 workers, 13 for 12, 13 for 36, and 26 for 21?

38. Suppose that $a > 1$, $0 < b < 1$, and $0 < c < 2$. Fill in each ☐ with $<$, $=$, $>$ or CT (can't tell).

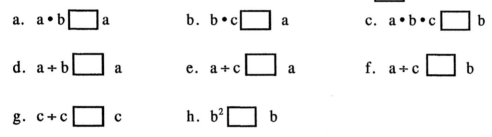

a. $a \cdot b$ ☐ a b. $b \cdot c$ ☐ a c. $a \cdot b \cdot c$ ☐ b

d. $a \div b$ ☐ a e. $a \div c$ ☐ a f. $a \div c$ ☐ b

g. $c \div c$ ☐ c h. b^2 ☐ b

39. Ms. Jones gave her students this interesting problem: "Place a fraction in each of the squares to make each equation true. However, you may not use a fraction equal to 2 in any of the squares."

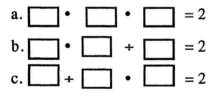

a. ☐ $\cdot$ ☐ $\cdot$ ☐ $= 2$

b. ☐ $\cdot$ ☐ $\div$ ☐ $= 2$

c. ☐ $\div$ ☐ $\cdot$ ☐ $= 2$

Jane said that the task was impossible. Mark said he could figure out the right fractions for each box! Hannah said she found several different solutions for each equation. Ms. Jones just smiled and said nothing. Who do you think is correct? Defend your choice with examples.

40. Decide whether each of the following statements is SOMETIMES, ALWAYS, or NEVER TRUE:
    a. If $x \neq 0$, $y \neq 0$ and $\dfrac{1}{x} < \dfrac{1}{y}$, then $x > y$.
    b. If $x > 0$, then $\dfrac{1}{x} < x$.
    c. If m, n, and p are whole numbers, $\dfrac{m + n}{p + n} = \dfrac{m}{p}$.

41. Explain, using an illustration, why $2/3 \div 2/5 = 2/3 \cdot 5/2$.

Extending the Activity

42. Use the idea of making trains with Cuisenaire Rods and apply it to prime and composite numbers. Hint: Look at the number of different single-color trains that can be made for each rod (switching the order of rods does not make a different train for this activity). For example, the train shown in Activity 6.7 has only 2 single-color trains—the train formed by the light green rod and the train formed by the three white rods. Write an explanation of how these trains can be used to illustrate prime and composite numbers.

Writing/Discussing

43. Make a concept map about fractions and explain the links and connections in the map.

44. Explain why the generalization from Activity 6.7 is valid. In other words, why does increasing the length of the rod by 1 cm double the number of trains?

45. Compare and contrast operations with integers and operations with rational numbers.

46. Explain why when you divide fractions you can invert the second fraction and multiply.

47. Is it important to learn about rational numbers through illustrations? Why? How has illustrating operations with rational numbers changed your understanding of rational numbers?

Chapter 7: Real Numbers: Rationals & Irrationals

Chapter Overview:

As technology (especially calculators) becomes more and more prevalent for everyday use, as well as for scientific purposes, so does the use of decimals (and percent). At the same time, ratio and proportion are also quite useful to solve a variety of real-world problems. In this chapter you will explore problems involving decimal, percent, ratio and proportion. Furthermore, to deepen your understanding of rational numbers (which is what the foregoing kinds of numbers are!), you will study the properties of rational numbers and be introduced to still another kind of number, the irrational numbers.

Big Mathematical Ideas:

> problem-solving strategies, conjecturing, verifying, decomposing, generalizing, representation, using language & symbolism, limit, mathematical structure

NCTM Standards Links:

> **K- 4 :** Mathematics as problem solving; Mathematics as communication; Mathematics as reasoning; Mathematical connections; Fractions & decimals
>
> **5 - 8:** Mathematics as problem solving; Mathematics as communication; Mathematics as reasoning; Mathematical connections; Number & number relationships

Chapter Outline:

Activity 7.1—Exploring Ratio and Proportion Ideas

1. In a classroom there are 15 women and 10 men.

    a. What is the ratio of women to men?

    b. Write another ratio that is equivalent to this one.

    c. What is the ratio of men to women?

    d. Write another ratio that is equivalent to this one.

    We can say that the ratios in a and b and in c and d form a **proportion**.

2. The ratio of men to women in a lecture hall is 12:5. If there are 36 men, how many women are there in the lecture hall?

    How did you solve this problem?

3. Discuss in your group and come up with a definition of the term "proportion."

Activity 7.2—Solving Problems using Proportions

1. During the softball season, Joan scores an average of two runs for every three runs scored by Amy. Joan scores 20 runs. How many runs does Amy score?

2. Charles is constructing a model of an early American steam locomotive using a scale of 1:24. If the length of the original locomotive is 12 meters, what is the length, in centimeters, of the model?

3. Triangles ABC and DEF are similar. The ratio of a given side of triangle ABC to the corresponding side in triangle DEF is 4/3. If the length AB is 8 cm, what is DE?

4. The point (3, 8) lies on a straight line that passes through the origin (0, 0) on a Cartesian grid. If the x-coordinate of another point on the line is 12, what is the y-coordinate of the second point?

5. The taxes on a piece of property valued at $40,000 are $800. At the same rate, what would the taxes be on a second piece of property valued at $25,000?

Activity 7.3—Graphing Proportion Problems

1. Graph the relationship between the scoring averages of Joan and Amy from #1 in Activity 7.2.

2. Write an equation that represents this graph. Explain what your equation means.

3. Choose two of the remaining proportion problems in Activity 7.2 and graph the relationships in the ratios. Write the equations that represent the graphs and explain what your equations mean.

Activity 7.4—Introducing Decimal Representation

1.   Write any rational number both as a fraction and as a decimal.

2.   How can you prove these are the same number?

3.   Model 2/5 both with a strip of paper and with base ten blocks. Draw a picture illustrating what you have modeled.

4.   Use base ten blocks to model these operations. Draw pictures of the steps involved in performing these operations.

   a. 2.346 + 1.27

   b. 3.3 - 2.875

   c. 2 x 2.35

   d. 4.84 ÷ 4

Activity 7.5—Explaining Decimal Point Placement

1. The rule for decimal point placement in sums and differences is as follows:

    Line up the decimal points of the numbers being added or subtracted. Add or subtract as integers. Place the decimal point for the sum or difference in line with other decimal points.

    Why is this rule valid?

2. The rule for decimal point placement in products is as follows:

    Multiply as with integers. Count the number of decimal places in both factors. Place the decimal point in the product by using the total number of decimal places in the two factors.

    Why is this rule valid?

3. The rule for decimal point placement in quotients is as follows:

    Multiply the divisor by a power of ten to make it an integer. Multiply the dividend by the same number. Place the decimal point in the quotient directly above the decimal point in the dividend. Divide as with integers.

    Why is this rule valid?

Activity 7.6—Modeling Operations with Decimals

Model these products and quotients with base ten blocks and then draw an illustration of the steps you used to model them. For each situation, specify which block represents 1.

1. $9.6 \div 3$

2. $.2 \cdot 1/3$

3. $.5 \cdot .5$

4. $.6 \div .2$

5. $.7 \div .3$

6. $.2 \div .6$

7. $2/3 \cdot 1/4$

8. $1.25 \cdot .4$

Activity 7.7—Converting Decimals to Fractions

1/2   1/3   1/4   1/5   1/6   1/7   1/8   1/9   1/10

1. Change each of these fractions to decimal representation.

2. In what ways can you categorize these decimals?

3. What is (are) the distinction(s) among the different categories?

4. What determines (besides dividing it out) which category a fraction will be in when expressed as a decimal? Justify your reasoning.

5. Convert these terminating decimals to fractions.

   a. .345

   b. 4.12

   c. -1.2359

6.   Describe, in general, how to convert a terminating decimal to a fraction. Why does this method work?

7.   Convert these repeating decimals to fractions. [Hint: Try to isolate the block of repeating digits so that you can convert this decimal to a fraction as you did above.]

a. $.\overline{3}$

b. $4.\overline{45}$

c. $1.0\overline{32}$

8.   Describe, in general, how to convert a repeating decimal to a fraction. Why does this method work?

9.   Can you use the same method to convert these decimals to fractions?

a.   .121121112 . . .

b.   3.515115111 . . .

10. How can you categorize decimals of this type?

11. What is the 100th digit after the decimal point in 1/22?

12. What is the 200th digit after the decimal point in 1/7?

13. What is the 50th digit after the decimal point in .121121112...?

14. What strategies did you use to find these digits?

Activity 7.8—Introducing Percent Representation

1. You go shopping with $60. You spend 1/4 on clothes, $30 for equipment for your home computer, and 10% of your original money on some food. How much do you have left?

2. A women bets $24 and gets back her original bet plus $48 more. She spends 25% of her winnings at a restaurant to celebrate, and 50% of her winnings to buy a present for her husband. Her paycheck was for $240, from which she made the original bet. How much money does she have left when she finally arrives home?

3. A man collects antique snuff boxes. He bought two, but found himself short of money and had to sell them quickly. He sold them for $600 each. On one he made 20% and on the other he lost 20%. Did he make or lose money on the whole deal? How much?

4. A collection of marbles has been divided into 3 different sets. The middle-sized set is two times the size of the smallest set, and the largest set is three times as large as the middle-sized set. What percent describes each part of the total marble collection?

Activity 7.9—Pay Those Taxes: A Game of Percents and Primes

Read all of the directions before starting to play.

The Game
Take turns spinning the two spinners. Use the two numbers you spin to form a two-digit number that represents the amount of money you have won this turn. For example, is you spun a 2 and a 4, you may choose to win $24 or $42. However, you must pay taxes according to the following schedule.

Tax Schedule
$0 - $30	pay 15% of your winnings
$31-$50	pay 25% of your winnings
$51- up	pay 35% of your winnings

Calculate your tax and deduct this from your winnings. Round off to the nearest dollar.

Primes
After the first round of play, you can buy a prime number whenever you have enough money. The prime numbers you can buy are 2, 3, 5, 7, or 11. The prime numbers cost $500 times their reciprocal. During the game, if a player chooses to use a number (obtained from the spinners) that is divisible by a prime that is owned by you, he or she must pay a commission of 50% of the winnings after taxes. If you need cash, you can sell your prime number back, for its cost minus 10% interest.

Bonus
If you spin a prime number greater than 20, you get a 20% bonus before taxes. But you must pay taxes on the new number.

Winner
The winner is the player with the most money when the game is stopped, after all players sell back their prime numbers.

Record Keeping
All players must keep a neat recording of their accounts. Anyone may check another player's accounts before the turn passes and charge a $10 fee for correcting any errors found.

Activity 7.10—Comparing Fractions, Decimals and Percents

In each row circle the item that does not belong. Justify your answer.

	A	B	C	D
1.	3/4	0.75	0.34	75%
2.	20% of 40	40% of 20	10% of 80	5% of 20
3.	1 cent	1%	1 centimeter	1° F
4.	3 1/4	0.325	3.25	325%
5.	50% of 18	18 (0.5)	1/2% of 18	18% of 50
6.	$100 at 6% for 2 years	$100 at 8% for 1 year	$100 at 2% for 4 years	$100 at 4% for 2 years
7.	percent change from 80 to 120	percent change from 66 to 99	percent change from 40 to 80	percent change from 48 to 72
8.	percent change from 100 to 90	percent change from 50 to 45	percent change from 200 to 180	percent change from 60 to 50

9. List four ratios such that three are equivalent to 10% and one is not.

Activity 7.11—Four in a Row: A Game of Decimals and Factors

Split your group into two teams, each with a calculator. In turn, each team chooses two factors (without using a calculator), one from the circular factor board below and one from the rectangular factor board. The other team multiples the two factors to find the product. The cell on the grid that contains the product is captured by the team that chose the two factors. The first team to capture four cells in a row (vertically, horizontally or diagonally) is the winning team. Play several games, using different group members' pages.

GRID

221.4	88.2	82.8	110.7
107.8	9	60.27	135.3
2.45	176.4	41.4	48.02
4.5	50.6	5.5	22.54

FACTOR BOARDS

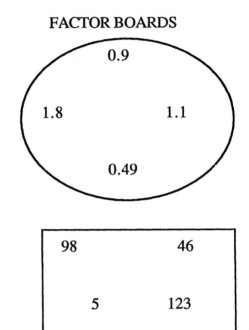

What mathematical ideas are used in this game?

Activity 7.12—Exploring Circles: Approximating an Irrational Number

1. Draw a circle, using a compass, with radius equal to the length of the red Cuisenaire rod.

   a. What is the diameter of this circle in centimeters? [The length of the white rod is 1 cm.]

   b. Find the circumference of the circle without using a formula. How did you find this?

2. Fill in the circumference and diameter information for the red rod and calculate the sum, difference, product and quotient of C and D.

Rod	Circumference (C)	Diameter (D)	C + D	C - D	C • D	C ÷ D
red						
light green						
purple						
yellow						
dark green						
black						

3. As the size of the rod (and the circle) increases, predict whether the numbers in each column increase, decrease, or remain the same.

   C   D

   C+ D   C - D

   C • D   C ÷ D

4.   Draw the other circles using the rods listed in the table. Then determine the circumference and diameter of each of the circles in centimeters and record in the table above.

5.   Calculate C + D, C - D, C • D, and C ÷ D for each of your circles and record these in the table above.

6.   Did your predictions hold? Why or why not?

7.   What number is being approximated by C ÷ D?

8.   Why is this an approximation?

9.   What could you do to get a better approximation?

Activity 7.13—Constructing Irrational Numbers

1. Construct a segment that is exactly $\sqrt{2}$ inches long.

2. Construct a segment that is exactly $\sqrt{13}$ inches long.

3.   Construct a segment that is exactly $\sqrt{7}$ inches long.

4.   Explain your strategies in drawing these segments.

Activity 7.14—Properties of Rational and Irrational Numbers

1. Justify whether or not the following properties are valid for the set of rational numbers.

    a. Closed under addition

    b. Closed under multiplication

    c. Commutative property for addition

    d. Commutative property for multiplication

    e. Associative property for addition

    f. Associative property for multiplication

    g. Identity element for addition

    h. Identity element for multiplication

    I. Inverse element for multiplication

2. Justify whether or not these properties are valid for the set of irrational numbers.

3.   The set of real numbers is the set of all rational numbers and all irrational numbers. Justify whether or not the above properties are valid for the set of real numbers.

4.   Illustrate the relationships among all the sets of numbers that you know.

Things to Know from Chapter 7

Words to Know
- associativity
- closure
- commutativity
- decimal (terminating; repeating; non-terminating, non-repeating)
- identity
- inverse
- irrational number
- percent
- pi (π)
- proportion
- ratio
- rational number
- real number

Concepts to Know
- what is a ratio
- what is a proportion
- what is a decimal
- why are decimal point placement rules valid
- why can some fractions be represented as terminating decimals while others cannot
- what is a percent
- what is a rational number
- what is an irrational number
- which group properties are valid for rational numbers, irrational numbers, real numbers

Procedures to Know
- representing quantities as ratios
- solving proportions
- representing numbers in decimal notation
- converting fractions to decimals and decimals to fractions
- representing quantities as percents
- performing operations with decimals and percents

Exercises & More Problems

Exercises

1. Illustrate what a base ten block model of 1/5 would look like.

2. Compute each of the following:
    a. 4.243 + 1.01   b. 1.32 - 2.1   c. -4.208 - 1.002

3. Compute each of the following:
    a. 4 • 3.021   c. 5.2 ÷ 3.2   d. -12.24 ÷ 2.04

4. Find a rational number, x, such that 7/36 < x < 5/24. Justify your answer.

5. Arrange these decimals in order from smallest to largest.

    a. 3.2, 3.$\overline{22}$, 3.2$\overline{3}$, 3.2$\overline{3}$, 3.23

    b. -1.454, -1.45$\overline{4}$, -1.45, -1.4$\overline{54}$, -1.$\overline{454}$

6. Arrange these decimals in order from largest to smallest.

    a. .002, .$\overline{02}$, .02$\overline{5}$, .00$\overline{2}$, .02

    b. -1.$\overline{19}$, -1.2$\overline{1}$, -1.19, -1.192, -1.$\overline{21}$

7. What strategies did you use to determine the order of several decimals?

8. Find a number between .84 and .85

9. Find a number between -2.3 and -2.29

10. Place the following decimals in order from least to greatest:
    a. 3.29, 3.231, 3.2957, 3.23057, 3.230525

    b. $-.7\overline{3}, -.737, -.7373, -737\overline{7}$

11. Which of the following are true:
    a. 7/8 > 6/7 > 15/28 > 6/10   b. -1.88 < -1.871 < -1.8701 < -1.8

    c. 3.2 < 3.2$\overline{2}$< 3.23 < 3.2$\overline{3}$ d. a and b
    e. b and c   f. a, b and c

12. Base ten blocks include units, longs, flats and cubes (1000 units).
    a. If 7 longs are used to represent the decimal 0.7, which block is equal to 1?
    b. Using the cube as 1, represent the following sum and its solution: 2.34 - 0.53.

13. Write the following fractions as terminating or repeating decimals:
    a. 7/8   b. 1/3   c. 11/12

14. Write the following terminating decimals as simplified fractions:
    a. -5.32   b. 4.022   c. 25.15

15. Write the following repeating decimals as fractions.

    a. $.4\overline{3}$ b. $.\overline{35}$

16. Determine which of the following represent irrational numbers:
    a. $\sqrt{29}$ b. $\sqrt{121}$ c. $(\sqrt{3})/2$

17. Determine two irrational numbers that exist between 3/4 and 1.

18. Is $\dfrac{\sqrt{48}}{\sqrt{108}}$ a rational number? Explain.

19. Draw a Venn diagram to indicate the relationships among the set of whole numbers, integers, rational numbers, natural numbers, irrational numbers, and real numbers.

Critical Thinking

20. Put numbers in the boxes that will give you the desired quotient.

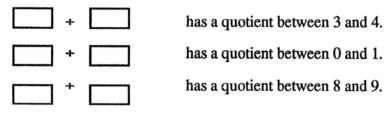

    ☐ ÷ ☐   has a quotient between 3 and 4.

    ☐ ÷ ☐   has a quotient between 0 and 1.

    ☐ ÷ ☐   has a quotient between 8 and 9.

21. Number suspects: 1/2, 3/4, 2/5, 3/5, 5/8, 7/10, 12/11.
    Clue 1: I am greater than .5.
    Clue 2: I am not equal to .75.
    Clue 3: If you multiply me by 2 you get a number that is less than 2.
    Clue 4: My denominator is a prime number.
    Who am I? _____

22. Make up a Number Mystery similar in structure to the one in #21. Name your own number suspects and write at least 4 clues.

23. If the ratio of boys to girls in a class is 3:8, will the ratio of boys to girls remain the same, become greater, or become smaller if 2 boys and 2 girls leave the class. Justify your answer.

24. How do you know that a number is irrational (what classifies it as such)?

25. How do repeating decimals affect the ordering of decimal values?

26. Explain the procedure used to convert repeating decimals to fractions.

27. When multiplying and dividing decimals why is it not important to line up the decimal points like when adding or subtracting?

28. Using some of the numbers .1, .2, .3, .4, .5, .6, .7, .8, and .9 and one or more of the four operations, represent each of the following:
    a. 1
    b. a number between .5 and 1
    c. a number between .4 and .5
    d. a number greater than 3
    e. a number between .1 and .2
    f. 0
    g. 1.5
    h. a number between -3 and -5

29. The answers to the computations below are estimates in which the decimal points have been left out. Place the decimal point where it belongs in each estimate. Justify your placement of the decimal point.
    a. 5.03 x 17.6 = 8 8 6
    b. 68.64 ÷ 4.4 = 1 5 6
    c. 6.23 x 17.91 x .131 = 1 4 6
    d. 16.55 x .008 = 1 3 2
    e. .726 ÷ .154 = 4 7 1
    f. 400.14 ÷ 85.5 = 4 6 8
    g. .198 ÷ .090 = 2 2
    h. .7265 ÷ .954 = 7 6 1 5
    i. 5.824 x .36 = 2 0 9 6 6 41.

30. Candy bars priced 50¢ each were not selling, so the price was reduced. Then they all sold in one day for a total of $31.93. What was the reduced price for each candy bar? Explain.

31. Explain why 3/7 cannot be written as a terminating decimal.

32. Rekekah ate 5 pieces of pizza and Moses ate 4 pieces. Rebekah says she ate 25% more than Moses, but Moses says he ate only 20% less than Rebekah. Who is correct? Justify your answer.

33. A collection of marbles has been divided into three different scts. The middle-sized set is 2 times the size of the smallest set, and the largest set is 3 times as large as the middle-sized set. What percent describes each part of the total marble collection?

34. Is it possible to have a square with area 5 cm²? Justify your answer.

35. Is it possible to have a square with area 11 cm²? Justify your answer.

36. Why do triangles help in analyzing irrational numbers (more specifically square roots) ?

37. If a 10 x 10 square of cubes is built (only 1 block high), glued together and suspended in the air, then the entire group of blocks is painted, what percent of the cubes will have the following?
    a. four faces painted   b. three faces painted   c. two faces painted

38. Answer the question in #4 for squares of cubes of the following dimensions.
    a. 9 x 9   b. 8 x 8   c. 7 x 7
    d. 12 x 12   e. n x n

Extending the Activity
39. Give three different examples that prevent you from thinking that all numbers are rational.

40. Which digit between the 50th and 60th digits after the decimal point in 1/17 is 9? Justify your answer.

Writing/Discussing
41. If the ratio of green marbles to red marbles in a collection is 4:7, explain how this ratio is different than saying that the green marbles are 4/7 of the collection.

42. Explain the procedure for changing a fraction to a decimal.

43. Explain why not all fractions can be changed to terminating decimals. Include in your explanation a discussion of how you can determine if a fraction can be changed into a terminating decimal.

44. Explain the procedure for changing a terminating decimal to a fraction.

45. Explain the procedure for changing a repeating decimal to a fraction.

46. Do you think it is possible, for every irrational number, to construct a length equal to that number in some unit like inches? Why or why not?

47. Explain the relationships among fractions, decimals, and percents.

48. Make a second concept map about fractions and explain the links and connections in the map. Then write a reflection comparing and contrasting your first and second concept maps.

Chapter 8: Patterns & Functions

Chapter Overview:

The concept of function is a central theme, a big idea, running through many areas of mathematics. In this chapter, the idea of function, which is a particular kind of relationship between to or more sets of objects, is introduced through explorations of patterns. Also emphasized will be different ways to represent functional relationships.

Big Mathematical Ideas:

> problem-solving strategies, functions & relations, representation, conjecturing, verifying, mathematical structure

NCTM Standards Links:

> *K - 4:* Mathematics as problem solving; Mathematics as communication; Mathematics as reasoning; Mathematical connections; Patterns & relationships
>
> *5 - 8:* Mathematics as problem solving; Mathematics as communication; Mathematics as reasoning; Mathematical connections; Patterns & functions

Chapter Outline:

Activity 8.1—Exploring Variables

The temperature of a cold winter day in Syracuse is measured for a 24-hr period. The table below gives the readings (time, temperature) for this winter day from 1:00 AM to midnight.

Time (hours)	Temperature (° F)	Time (hours)	Temperature (° F)	Time (hours)	Temperature (° F)
1	14	9	17	17	12
2	12	10	20	18	8
3	10	11	24	19	5
4	8	12	29	20	2
5	8	13	32	21	0
6	9	14	31	22	-1
7	10	15	27	23	-1
8	13	16	18	24	1

Use the data in the table to answer the following questions.

1. a. What was the temperature at noon?

    b. At which time(s) was the temperature 13° F?

2. a. How much does the temperature decrease between 2 p.m. and 6 p.m.?
        How does this increase compare to the decrease between 2 p.m. and 4 p.m.?
        Explain.

    b. What is the increase between 6 a.m. and noon?

3. During which time period was the temperature dropping fastest? Explain.

4. Plot the data pairs (time, temperature) using the data in the table below.

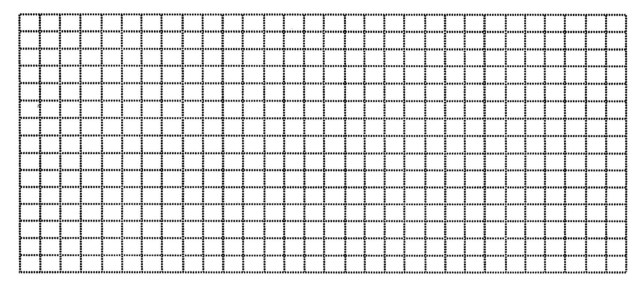

5. a. At what time was the temperature the highest?

   b. At what time was the temperature the lowest?

6. For each part a through d:
   i.   Write the value that correctly completes the statement.
   ii. Give the coordinate of the data point, (input, output), that supplies your answer.
   iii. Write the completed statement in words.

   a. T(7) = _____

   b. T(19) = _____

   c. T(___) = 0

d. T(___) = 29

7. Discuss the factors that affected the temperature during the day. Explain the temperature
    pattern of the day.

Activity 8.2—Investigating Variables Through Data in Tables

A movie theater found that by changing the price on a small bag of popcorn, they will change the number of bags they sell during a movie.

Cost ($)	# of bags sold during movie
$1.90	100
$1.95	95
$2.00	90
$2.05	85
$2.10	80
$2.15	75

1. What relationships do you notice between the cost and the amount of popcorn the theater sells?

2. Explain why these relationships seems reasonable (or unreasonable).

3. Is the information in the table above sufficient to determine the price that theaters should choose for a bag of popcorn? Explain your reasoning.

4. Suppose it costs the theater $1.25 to make and sell a small bag of popcorn. Make a third column in the table above that shows the amount of *profit* the theater makes for each selling price. Based on this, what would be the best price for the theaters to choose?

Since it seems that the number of bags sold depends on the cost of a bag, we could use *function notation* to describe the data in the above table. For example, to say that "If the cost is $2.10, the theater will sell 80 bags of popcorn," we could write *B($2.10) = 80*, where *B* represents the number of bags sold at the price (given in parentheses). Note that whenever you begin using a variable to represent something, you should let others know what that variable means. Since we have already stated what *B* stands for, you may continue to use it without needing to specify its meaning.

5. Use functional notation to represent each of the following sentences.

    a. When a bag of popcorn costs $1.90, 100 bags of popcorn will be sold.

    b. The theater only sells 75 bags when the cost is raised to $2.15.

6. Use functional notation to show the number of bags you think would be sold if the cost were raised to $2.40.

7. If we let *P* represent the *profit* earned, then write in words what *P($1.90) = $65* means.

8. Use functional notation to tell the theater the best possible cost if they wish to maximize profit.

9. What other factors besides cost could influence the number of bags of popcorn sold during a movie?

10. What are some possible consequences of making the cost of a bag of popcorn too *high*?

11. What are some possible consequences of making the cost of a bag of popcorn too *low*?

Activity 8.3—Investigating Variables Through Data in Graphs

In the desert, temperatures can range from extremely hot during the day to extremely cold at night. Below are some sample time and temperature data from a desert.

Time (hours)	Temperature (°F)
0 (midnight)	35
2	30
4	38
6	61
8	70
10	85
12 (noon)	98
14	96
16	88
18	66
20	48
22	40

Plot the above data in a line plot, with "Time" on the horizontal axis, and "Temperature" on the vertical axis. You may want to use graph paper, a spreadsheet, or a graphing calculator for your plot. Answer the questions below, stating the coordinates (when appropriate) that you used to find your answers. Coordinates should be given as ordered pairs (time, temperature).

1. Why is a line plot more appropriate than a bar graph for the given data?

2. What was the temperature at 4 p.m.?

3. At what times was the temperature in the 60s?

4. At what times was the temperature below 40°?

5. Was the temperature ever 73°? Explain your reasoning.

6.   What was the change in temperature between 8 and 10 p.m.?

7.   What was the *rate of change* (in degrees per hour) between 8 p.m. and 10 p.m.?

8.   What might the temperature have been at 7 a.m.?

9.   During which two hour time period was the temperature *rising* most rapidly?

10. During which two hour time period was the temperature *falling* most rapidly?

11. In terms of the appearance of the line plot, explain how you can tell when the temperature is *rising* most rapidly.

12. What might cause the drop in temperature that occurred between 4 p.m. and 6 p.m.?

13. Are the data in this table sufficient for determining the highest temperature in the desert for the day this data was collected? Why or why not?

Activity 8.4—Interpreting Graphs

1. In general, sales of a product depends on its price. The diagrams below show graphs of three possible relations between the price of a house and sales. No scales are given on the axes, but following the conventions that right and up represent positive values of price and sales respectively, you should be able to decide which graph seems most likely to match the relation between price and sales.

   a. For each diagram, explain why you think the graph does or does not fit the likely relation between price and sales.

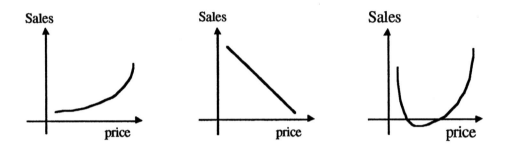

   b. List at least four factors other than price that are likely to affect the sales of a house.

   c. Pick a factor from your list that is a quantitative (numerical) variable. Sketch a graph similar to the ones above that shows the relation you would expect between that variable and house sales. Explain in words the relation shown by your graph. That is, tell what happens to house sales as the input variable increases, and give some possible reasons for this relation.

Identifying Graphs of Functions

Suppose you were to graph the height of water in a bathtub while it was filling, being used, and emptying? What would that graph look like? In each of the problems below, you are presented with a scenario and three possible graphs. For each scenario:

    a) Choose the graph you feel best represents that scenario. Be prepared to explain your selection.
    b) For each of the graphs you did *not* select, write an explanation of how that graph could have come about.

1. The height of water in a bathtub during the time that it is filling, being used, and emptying:

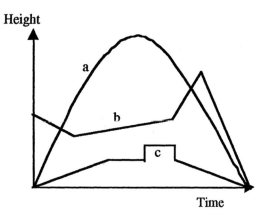

2. The daily temperature recorded in Chicago, Illinois, from January to December.

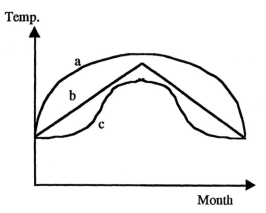

3. The fraction of the moon's surface that is visible over two months' time.

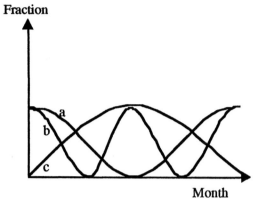

4. The number of apples you can buy with $5 as the cost of apples increases.

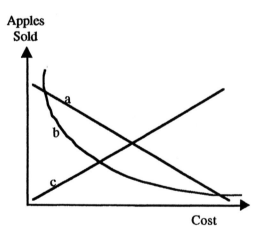

Activity 8.5—Investigating and Describing Numerical Patterns

For each input-output table below:
- Complete the table.
- Describe how the output number is related to the input number.
- Answer any included questions.

1.

Input	Output
1	3
2	6
3	9
4	12
5	
6	
	51

a. In words, describe how the output number is related to the input number.

b. If the input number were x, what would be the output number? _____

c. If the output number were n, what must be the input number? _____

2.

Input	Output
1	19
2	18
3	17
4	
10	
	6.5
0	

a. Describe the relationship:

b. If the input number were h, then the output number would be:

c. If the output number were j, then the input number was:

3.

Input	Output
1	1
6	11
20	39
13	25
5	
	41
	22

a. Describe the relationship:

b. If the input number were z, then the output number would be:

c. If the output number were d, then the input number was:

4.

Input	Output
3	12
7	56
1	2
0	0
25	
26	
	2256

a. Describe the relationship:

b. If the input number were x, then the output number would be:

c. If the output number were y, then the input number was:

5. Make up a table of your own, and describe a rule for that table. Be prepared to trade your table (but not your rule) with another group.

Input	Output

Activity 8.6—Investigating Numerical Situations

Suppose you are the director for the City Park Summer Program's soccer league. In this league, each team plays every other team once before the playoffs. So, the number of games to be scheduled (not including the playoff games) depends upon how many teams are allowed in the league. Your immediate task is to plan the soccer tournament.

1. To get a feel for the numbers involved, do some calculations. It will be helpful for you to record your findings in a table. It may also be helpful to think of ways to draw diagrams to model the problem situation.

2. Make a graph by plotting the data points from your table. If you have access to a spreadsheet or a graphing calculator, you may want to use it to create your graph. Does it make sense to connect the points together? Why or why not?

3. What type of relationship do you think there is between the number of teams and the number of games played?

4. How can you use the table and scatter plot to obtain more data points, without doing the types of calculations you did in #1?

5. If there are n teams in the league, find a formula for the number of games needed. Explain how you found this formula.

6. Use your formula to calculate the number of teams that can be in the league if the maximum number of games you can schedule is 120.

Activity 8.7—Identifying Rules and Functions

1. You can calculate the speed of a car by knowing the size of its tires and the revolutions per minute that the rotating tires make. Suppose the tires of a car cover about 2.5 meters of ground in one revolution and the tires are rotating at 500 revolutions per minute.

    a. What is the speed of the car?

    b. Write verbal and symbolic rules expressing the relation between time and distance.

    c. Calculate some specific data pairs, (time, distance), and record them in a table.

    d. Write the calculation required to find the distance traveled in 20 minutes. What is this distance?

    e. Sketch a graph showing the pattern of the relation between time and distance traveled. The input (independent) variable should be represented on the horizontal axis, and the output variable (dependent) should be on the vertical axis.

2. Regina has a part-time job working for a national company selling Internet subscriptions house to house. She is paid $100 per week plus $15 for each subscription she sells.

   a. Complete the table below, showing her weekly pay as a function of the number of subscriptions she sells.

Number of subscriptions sold	Weekly pay (dollars)
1	
2	
3	
6	
10	
12	
15	

   b. Using variables, write two symbolic rules, one for sales in terms of pay and one for the pay in terms of sales.

   c. Write the calculation required to answer each of the following questions about Regina's pay prospects. Then find the numerical result.

      i. How much does she earn if she sells 9 subscriptions in a week?

      ii. How much does she earn if she sells 0 subscriptions in a week?

      iii. Regina's goal is to earn $400 dollars next week. How many subscriptions does she need to sell if she wants to accomplish this goal?

Activity 8.8—Looking for an Optimal Solution

Below are the directions for making a box out of a sheet of paper. Follow these directions to create the box, then answer the questions that follow.

Making a Paper Box

Materials: You will need an eight-inch by ten-inch piece of paper, a ruler, scissors, and tape.

Directions:
•   Begin by tracing one-inch squares in each of the four corners of the paper, as shown:

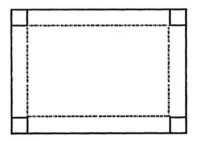

•   Next, cut out these four squares from the corners, and discard them. Finally, fold and crease along the indicated dotted lines, and tape the edges to form a box (with no lid).

1. What is the volume of the box you constructed? What is the outer surface area? Explain how you arrived at your answers.

2. What if, instead of cutting out squares that measured one inch on each side, you cut out squares that measure two inches on each side. What would be the resulting volume and surface area?

3. What is the largest size of square that you could cut from each corner? What would be the resulting volume and surface area?

4. What size square would you have to cut from each corner in order to maximize the volume? Explain how you went about finding your answer.

5. What size square would you have to cut from each corner in order to maximize the surface area? Explain how you went about finding your answer.

6. What if you cut out a square from each corner whose sides measured x inches. What would be the resulting volume and surface area?

7. Without actually measuring, what would be a *practical* way to compare the volumes of two of these paper boxes?

Shown below is an aerial view of Farmer MacDonald's barn. She wishes to put up a rectangular pen for her goats so that one side of the pen abuts one side of her barn, as shown:

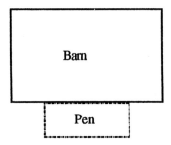

By using one side of the barn as one side of the pen, Farmer MacDonald realized that she will only need enough fence for the other three sides. Knowing that the long side of the barn measures 200 feet, and that Farmer MacDonald has 120 feet of fencing she can use, answer the questions below.

8. In the figure shown, the left and right sides of the pen must be the same length. What is the longest each of those two sides may be?

9. What is the longest that the front side of the pen may be? Explain how you arrived at your answer.

10. If MacDonald wanted a square pen that used all of the fencing, what would be the area of the ground within the pen?

11. Creating a rectangular pen as described above, what is the maximum area MacDonald can get by using all 120 feet of fencing? Be ready to explain how you went about finding this solution. How do you know that your solution represents the *maximum* area?

12. Creating a rectangular pen as described above, what is the minimum area MacDonald can get by using all 120 feet of fencing? Be ready to explain how you went about finding this solution. How do you know that your solution represents the *minimum* area?

13. What if she decided that instead of building the rectangular pen adjacent to the barn, she would build it in the middle of a field? Make a table that shows the relationship between the length of one side of the fence, and the area of the pen. What would be the minimum and maximum areas possible using all 120 feet of fencing?

Activity 8.9—Investigating Numerical Functions that Repeat

1. Get out a calculator. Pick a number (any number), and enter it on the calculator. Square it. Now, take the result and square it. Square the new result. Square it again. And again. Describe what is happening to the size of the number.

2. Square the result a few more times. What would happen if you could do this *forever*? What would the "long-term" behavior be?

3. So, you picked a number, repeatedly squared it, and described the long-term behavior. Try this again, but with a different "seed" (starting number). Is the long-term behavior the same?

4. See if you can get different long-term behaviors by starting with different seeds and repeatedly squaring the results. Try to classify all real numbers according to their long-term behavior in this process.

5. Suppose someone makes the statement that, whenever you square a number, the result will be a bigger number. Based on your explorations above, what could you say to that person?

6. Explore: What would happen if, instead of starting with a seed and repeatedly *squaring* the results, you instead *cubed* the results? In what ways would your results be the same as above? In what ways would the results be different?

More Iteration

This one is only a little more complicated, and the pattern may surprise you. You will need a calculator again. It may be helpful to know how to use the memory function of your calculator.

1. Pick a number.

2. Enter that number into the expression, $\frac{x}{2}+\frac{8}{x}$. (*Store* the result on your calculator.)

3. Write down the result.

4. Take this result (*recall* from your calculator), and reenter it into the same expression, $\frac{x}{2}+\frac{8}{x}$.

5. Repeat, writing your result at each stage.

Here is an example, assuming you started with the number 17.

Start with	End with
17	8.970588235
8.970588235	5.377097396
5.377097396	

Look at the list of numbers we have generated. What do you notice about the numbers?

1. Try the same exploration again, but with a different starting number. Keep track of the numbers you generate. Perform as many steps as it takes to begin seeing what you might call "predictable" long-term behavior. What relationships and patterns do you notice about the "seed" (starting number) and the "long-term" behavior of the list of numbers you generate?

2. Try the exploration again, but using the expression $\frac{x}{2}+\frac{1}{x}$. Begin with different seeds, each time generating a list of numbers. Describe the patterns and relationships you notice.

3. Notice that the "long-term" behavior seems to depend on the expression we use. When we changed from $\frac{x}{2}+\frac{8}{x}$ to $\frac{x}{2}+\frac{1}{x}$, the long-term behavior changed. Modify this expression again, and explore the expression you've created by trying different seeds and exploring the long-term behavior.

Activity 8.10—Investigating Real-Life Iteration: Savings Account Interest

To *iterate* something means to *repeat* it, which is exactly what you did when you repeatedly squared them.

"Iteration" is a good way to describe the way a bank calculates interest. Let's take a simple example of a bank that pays you 6% interest, compounded annually, on money in your savings account. "Compounded annually" means that once a year, the bank will calculate 6% of what you have in your account (actually, they figure out the *average* amount that has been in your account), and add that to your total. So, if you had $100 in your account for one year, how much would you have after the bank added interest?

Now, if you don't touch your savings account money for another year, the bank will *again* calculate 6% interest. But this time, they won't use $100 as the starting amount. Instead, they will give you interest on the $100 *plus last year's interest*. So, how much will you have in your account after the second year?

Suppose, now, that you just leave your savings account alone, allowing the interest to accumulate. Determine how much money you will have in your account (remember that you started the first year with $100) after each of the first 5 years.

Year	Total after that year
1	
2	
3	
4	
5	

1. How much will be in your account after 10 years? 20 years?

2. Generalize a way of finding the amount of money in your account after any number of years.

3. How many years would it take for your money to double?

4. What if the annual interest rate were 4%? How much would be in the account after 10 years (having started with $100)? After how many years would your money double?

5. Find a relationship between the annual interest rate and the number of years it takes for your money to double.

6. Points to Ponder:

What does it mean if a bank compounds interest semi-annually? Demonstrate that compounding interest semi-annually results in more interest than compounding annually. How do banks calculate interest? What is the difference between annual percentage *rate* and annual percentage *yield*?

Activity 8.11—Investigating Iteration: Geometry and Fractals

Begin with a line segment (this will be your "seed").

Now, *trisect* (cut into three equal parts) the segment:

Finally, create a equilateral triangle "bump" on the middle section, then erase that middle section:

Now, with our four new, shorter segments, we can *iterate* the same two steps as above, giving us this figure:

1. Using triangular graph paper, create the above figures, as well as the next three stages. Decide in advance on a segment length that will be easy to trisect, then trisect each smaller part, and so on.

2. Suppose the length of the original segment were 1 unit (we could call this "Stage 0"). Find the total length of each of the figures you drew.

Stage	Total length (in "units")
0	1
1	
2	
3	
4	
5	

3. Find a way to calculate the length after any stage. After how many stages would the path length be longer than 10 units? Longer than 100 units?

Iteration and Koch's Snowflake

Using simple iterative procedures, complex geometric and numeric patterns can arise.

Using triangular grid paper, construct an equilateral triangle with sides of 27 units. Orient your triangle so that the "top" vertex is near the top center of the paper.

For this activity, you will be measuring perimeters and areas of figures you construct. For our purposes, we will measure lengths in "units" where one unit is equivalent to the length of one side of one of the small triangles. We will measure area in "triangular units", equivalent to the area of one of the small triangles.

1. What are the perimeter (in units) and the area (in triangular units) of the triangle you constructed?

2. Now, as we did in the previous section, trisect each segment of your figure, and construct an equilateral "bump" on each middle section of the segments. These "bumps" should point outward, so that the resulting figure looks like a six-pointed star. What are the perimeter and area of this star?

3. Repeat the above steps by trisecting each of the smaller segments, constructing the bumps, etc. What are the new perimeter and area?

4. Repeat again, making note of the perimeter and area.

5. Complete the table below, listing the perimeters and areas for each stage so far, starting with stage 1 (the big triangle).

Stage	Perimeter (Units)	Area (Triangular Units)
1		
2		
3		
4		
5		
6		

6. Describe the "behavior" of the perimeter and area as you progress through the stages. Do you have enough information to make any long range predictions? Do the perimeter and area "behave" in similar ways?

7. Someone makes the claim that, even though the area is getting larger, it can't go beyond a certain value. How would you respond to this claim? Could a similar claim be made about the perimeter?

Activity 8.12—Properties of Equations

<u>Addition Property of Equations</u>
Solve the following equations for the variable.

1. $x + 3 = 9$ 2. $a - 8 = 10$

3. $3w - 14 = 1$ 4. $-2b + .5 = 2.5$

To find the values of the variables, you used the Addition Property of Equations. Using what you know about addition and equations, make a conjecture about what is the Addition Property of Equations. Try to state it as precisely and concisely as possible.

<u>Multiplication Property of Equations</u>
To solve #3 and #4 above, you used the Multiplication Property of Equations. Using what you know about multiplication and equations, make a conjecture about what is the Multiplication Property of Equations. Try to state it as precisely and concisely as possible.

<u>Substitution Property of Equations</u>
The following two examples make use of the Substitution Property of Equations.

5. $2(x + 4) = 20$ and $2x + 8 = 20$ 6. $(b + 3)(b - 3) = 0$ and $b^2 - 9 = 0$

Using what you know about substitution and equations, make a conjecture about what is the Substitution Property of Equations. Try to state it as precisely and concisely as possible.

Activity 8.13—Using Properties to Solve Equations

Solve each equation for the variable by showing all the steps involved. State the property you are using at each step.

1. $3x + 5 = 2x = -8$

2. $-.5a + 36 + 4a = -9a - 12$

3. $5(c + 3) - 2c + 9 = 2(c - 1) + 13$

Activity 8.14—Investigating Distance vs. Time Motion
(Optional—Requires TI-82 (or TI-83 or TI-92) and CBL Unit)

Experiment Setup Procedure

1. Instructor downloads program HIKER into one TI-82 in each group. Collected data will be stored on this calculator. After data collection is complete, each group will download data and program so each calculator has the same data.

2. Connect the CBL unit to the TI-82 calculator with the unit-to-unit link cable using the I/O ports located on the bottom edge of each unit. Press the cable ends in firmly.

3. Connect the motion detector to the SONIC port on the left side of the CBL unit.

4. Turn on the CBL unit and the TI-82 calculator.

5. Place the motion detector on the table so it will detect the movement of a student walking away from or towards the detector.

The CBL system is now ready to receive commands from the calculator.

Experimental Procedure

1. Clear a walkway in the area designated by your instructor. Make sure that the walkway is wide enough so that no one else except the walking student will have their motion detected by the motion detector.

2. The motion detector should be perpendicular to the line of motion of the walker and sitting flat on the table top.

3. The walking student must stay in the motion detector's beam and walk perpendicular to the detector. **Note:** The student must walk beyond 1.5 feet from the motion detector because the detector cannot detect objects closer than that distance.

4. The detector takes measurements in feet every 0.1 seconds for 6 seconds and displays the graph of the collected data on the calculator.

5. Make sure the CBL is turned on. Start the program HIKER on the TI-82. The program will pause with a message "PRESS ENTER TO START GRAPH". When you and the walker are ready, tell the walker to start walking after you press ENTER and hear the clicking sound from the motion detector.

6. A graph of Distance (y-axis) vs. Time (x-axis), is plotted on the TI-82 as the data is collected. When the walker has a reasonably good graph, move to the analysis section of the lab (below). To get the data (ordered pairs) needed for the analysis, press TRACE and move along the plotted points.

Analysis

1. Take turns being the walker for each of the following graphs. Draw a rough sketch of your graph, and discuss with your group what the walker had to do to obtain the graph. Write a careful and complete explanation of what the walker did.

    Express the Distance as a function of Time either by using TRACE on the graph to find the coordinates of end points of the line or by analyzing the data table if you have stored it already.

a. Line with a positive slope

b. Line with a steeper positive slope

c. Line with a negative slope

d. Line with a less steep negative slope

e. Line with a slope of zero

f. Parabola opening down

2. Compare and analyze all the graphs you made and answer the following questions:

a. What does a graph look like when a person is not moving? Give some examples.

b. How can you tell from a graph whether a person is walking or running? Give some examples.

c. How can you tell which direction a person is moving from a graph ?

d. How can you tell where a person started from by looking at a graph?

3. The following graphs were obtained using the CBL-motion detector system (distance vs. time). Describe as fully as possible the walks represented by these graphs and explain the differences between them.

a.

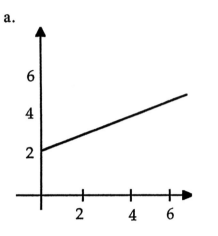

b.

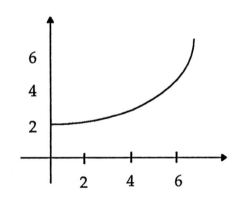

c.

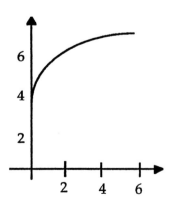

Things to Know from Chapter 8

Words to Know
- data
- dependent variable (output)
- domain of a function
- equation
- function
- graph
- independent variable (input)
- iterated function
- range of a function
- rate of change
- rule
- slope
- variable

Concepts to Know
- what a variable is
- what a function is and what it means for two quantities to have a functional relationship
- what is the relationship between the independent and dependent variable, and the domain and range of a function
- the relationship between the function and its domain and range
- what rate of change is and what it means in functional relationships
- what it means to say that a function iterates
- what it means to find an optimal solution
- the relationship between functions and equations

Procedures to Know
- identifying functional relationships from tables, graphs, symbols
- generating output values when given input values
- identifying a rule for a function from a table or graph
- determining the domain and range for a function
- using properties to solve equations for a variable
- finding rate of change of a function from a table, graph, or equation

Exercises & More Problems

Note: The exercises and problems at the end of the other chapters in this book are grouped into four categories: Exercises, Critical Thinking, Extending the Activity, and Writing/Discussing. The exercises and problems in this chapter have not been grouped in this way because so many of the exercises and problems belonging to different categories are associated with a table or graph (e.g., items 1 - 5 are associated with the chart shown below). There are, however, Writing/Discussing tasks at the end of these exercises and problems.

In the chart below are estimates for the world population during the 20th century:

Year	Population (in billions)
1900	1.7
1910	1.8
1920	1.9
1930	2.1
1940	2.3
1950	2.5
1960	3.0
1970	3.7
1980	4.5
1990	5.3

1. What was the rate of change of the world population, in people per year, between 1900 and 1910? Between 1900 and 1990?

2. What was the rate of change of the world population, in people per *minute*, between 1980 and 1990.

3. Based on the data, what do you predict will be the world population in 2000? Explain how you arrived at your estimate.

4. It has been predicted that the world population will "stabilize" around the year 2200, with a population of more than 11 billion. What factors do you think would contribute to this stabilization?

5. *(Optional)* For an interesting look at world population statistics, visit the World Wide Web at http://www.census.gov/cgi-bin/ipc/popclockw

The graph below shows the United States population from 1900 to 1990, as determined by the U.S. Census:

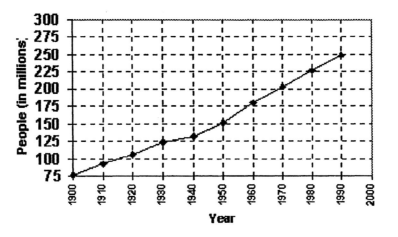

United States Population (by Census)

6. What was the rate of change of population, in people per year, from 1900 to 1990? Is this faster or slower than the rate of change of population from 1980 to 1990?

7. How can you tell, without doing any calculations, which of two time periods has the higher rate of change in population?

8. On average, according to the U.S. Census Bureau, there is a baby born every 8 seconds. At this rate, how many babies per year are born?

9. What do you predict will be the United States population in 2000?

10. Beside the birth and death rate, what other factors might contribute to the population of the United States?

11. Where on the graph do you see the lowest rate of change in population? What factors might have contributed to this decrease?

12. Plot a line graph that shows the relationship between the length of one side of a square, and the area of that square. Plot a line graph that shows the relationship between the radius of a circle, and the area of that circle. How are the square graph and the circle graph similar? How are they different?

13. Plot a line graph that shows the relationship between the diameter of a circle (plotted on the horizontal axis), and the circumference of that circle (along the vertical axis). What is the slope of the resulting line?

14. The mass of an average American young person, in kilograms, is a function of the person's age in years. Below are some sample data. Choose reasonable scales for axes on a graph and plot the given data. Then write a sentence describing the pattern in the graph and what it says about the relation between the two variables.

Age (years)	0	2	4	6	8	10	12	14
Mass (kg)	3	11	15	20	26	31	38	49

Source: *The World Almanac*. 1992.

15. You wish to construct a rectangular lot for your dog, and enclose it with a fence. Suppose you want the lot to have an area of 400 square feet, and you have 240 feet of fence available, but would like to have some fence left over.
   a. Suppose one side of the lot measured 10 feet. In all, how many feet of fence would you need to make the lot cover 400 square feet?
   b. Make a table and a graph that show the relationship between the length of one side of the lot and the amount of fence you need for that lot.
   c. What is the least amount of fencing needed to create the desired lot? Explain how you arrived at your solution.
   d. Is it possible to create a lot with an area of 400 square feet, and which uses all of the available fence?

16. Suppose you have two natural numbers {1, 2, 3, ...} whose sum is 50. What is the largest possible *product* of these numbers? What is the smallest possible product?

17. Suppose you have *three* natural numbers whose sum is 20. What is the largest possible *product* of these numbers? What is the smallest possible product?

18. Suppose you have *some* natural numbers whose sum is 100. What is the largest possible product of these numbers?

19. At a grocery store, peanuts cost $2.29 per pound. Plot a graph of the relationship between weight (in pounds, along the horizontal axis), and cost (in dollars, along the vertical axis). The resulting graph will be a line. What will be the slope of that line? Explain how to find that slope without using a graph.

20. The Department of Mathematics is trying to decide between two new copying machines. One sells for $20,000 and costs $0.02 per copy to operate. The other sells for $17,500, but its operating costs are $0.025 per copy. The department decides to buy the more expensive machine. How many copies must the department faculty and staff make before the higher price is justified? Explain how you arrived at your solution.

21. A swimming pool with dimensions of 20 feet by 30 feet is surrounded by a sidewalk of uniform width x. Find the possible widths of the sidewalk, if the total area of the sidewalk is to be greater than 200 square feet but less than 360 square feet.

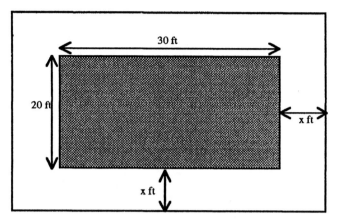

22. For problem 21, write an equation that gives the area of the sidewalk in terms of x.

23. For problem 21, write an inequality that is an algebraic representation of the problem situation.

24. A group is taking an outing and they can rent a bus for $180 per day. The organizer of the trip decides to charge every member of the party an equal amount for the ride. How will the size of each person's contribution depend upon the size of the group? Create a function to express the relationship.

25. A photographic service develops film for $2 (a fixed price for processing) plus 25¢ for each print. How does the cost of developing a film vary with the number of prints you want developed? Write down a function to express the relationship.

For each of the rules given below, complete the table of values.

26. Rule: Add five to the input and multiply the result by 3 to get the output.

Input	Output
1	
2	
3	
	42
x	
	a

27. Rule: Take 6% of the input and add the result to the input to get the output.

Input	Output
50	
60	
70	
	424
x	
	a

28. Rule: Find the average of the input and 20 to get the output.

Input	Output
14	
-20	
20	
	125
x	
	a

29. Rule: Subtract three from the input and divide the result into twenty to get the output.

Input	Output
2	
4	
6	
	1
x	
	a

In each of the following situations you are given data relating two variables. In each case, choose reasonable scales for axes on a graph and plot the given data. Then write a sentence describing the pattern in the graph and what it says about the relation between the two variables.

30. The average weight of an American baby, in pounds, is a function of the baby's age in months. Here are some sample data.

Age (months)	Mass (lb.)
0	7
3	13
6	17
9	20
12	22
15	24
18	25
21	26
24	27

31. The price of a bag of mangoes is a function of the number mangoes bought. Here are some sample data.

Number of Mangoes	Price (dollars)
2	5
4	10
6	15
8	20
10	25
12	30
14	35
16	40

32. The displacement of a mass hung from an oscillating spring is a function of time. Here are some sample data.

time (sec)	displacement (in)
0	1.0
1	0.4
2	-0.3
3	-0.5
4	-0.25
5	0.1
6	0.2
7	0.15
8	0
9	-0.1
10	-0.05
11	0
12	0.05

33. Think about functional relationships that you experience in everyday life. Many times we think of functional relationships where time is the independent variable. List two functional relationships involving time, where time is the *dependent* variable. Then sketch a graph of the function. For example, the amount of time it will take me to shovel my driveway can be thought of as a function of the depth of the snow.

Sketch a graph illustrating the relation between the variables in each of the following situations. Be sure to label your axes.

34. During the spring and summer, the height of a corn stalk is a function of growing time.

35. At a fruit stand, the price of a bag of apples is a function of the weight of the package.

36. When boiling water is poured over a tea bag, its temperature is a function of time.

37. Animal populations tend to rise and fall in cycles. Suppose the following data shows how squirrel populations in a central Pennsylvania city varied from 1975 to 1984. Plot a graph of this data. Then, write a headline and opening paragraph for an article designed to inform readers about squirrel population patterns.

Year	'75	'76	'77	'78	'79	'80	'81	'82	'83	'84
Population	750	500	520	680	730	650	550	625	780	700

38. Find at least 3 different ways to fill in the next number in this series: 1, 2, 4, 7, ___. Explain how you arrived at each.

The Celsius scale for temperature was designed to make it easy to look at some common temperatures—those between the freezing point of water (known as 0° Celsius), and the boiling point of water (known as 100° Celsius). The Fahrenheit scale for temperature is set up differently, with the freezing point of water being 32° Fahrenheit, and the boiling point of water known as 212° Fahrenheit. Knowing this, and knowing that that the relationship between degrees Celsius and degrees Fahrenheit is *linear*, answer

39. If an object has a temperature of 50° Celsius, what is its temperature in degrees Fahrenheit? Explain how you found your answer.

40. In degrees Celsius, what range of temperatures might be appropriate for wearing shorts and a T-shirt while outside?

41. In degrees Celsius, what would a normal body temperature be?

42. At what temperature would the number of degrees Celsius be equivalent to the number of degrees Fahrenheit?

43. Find and describe a relationship between degrees Celsius and degrees Fahrenheit that could be used to help someone convert from one scale to the other.

44. Suppose someone suggests that an easy way to convert *approximately* from degrees Celsius to degrees Fahrenheit is to "double it and add 30." That is, multiply the number of degrees Celsius by 2 and add 30 to the product. How appropriate is this rule?

45. *Doubling a temperature in Celsius is the same as doubling a temperature in Fahrenheit.* Is this statement always true, sometimes true, or never true? Explain your reasoning.

A newspaper delivery person's weekly pay is a function of the number of papers delivered each day. Here are some sample data:

Papers delivered	50	100	150	200	300	500
Pay (dollars)	70	120	170	220	320	520

46. Plot a graph of this data. Suppose you were writing an advertisement to convince people to become newspaper carriers. How could you accurately describe the relationship between the number of papers delivered and the pay the carrier receives, in a way that would be "attractive" to newspaper carriers?

47. According to wildlife experts, the rate at which crickets chirp is a function of the temperature; that is, $C = T - 40$, where C is the number of chirps every 15 sec and T is the temperature in degrees Fahrenheit.
    a. Sketch the graph of this function
    b. Describe this function using as many descriptors as possible.
    c. Describe and explain what you think are the minimum and maximum values for this function.

48. Rebekah borrowed $250 from her mother to purchase a deluxe grass-catching lawn mower for her new lawn-mowing business. She created the table below to chart her summer business prospects. She wants her summer earnings to be no less than $1,000.

# of lawns mowed	Profit in $
0	-250
5	-200
10	-150
15	-100
20	-50
25	0
30	50

    a. How much is Rebekah charging per lawn?
    b. Develop a rule relating the number of lawns mowed and Rebekah's profit.
    c. How many lawns must Rebekah mow to reach her goal of $1,000?
    d. Suppose Rebekah decides to buy a less expensive lawn mower for $195 instead of the $250 one. Develop a rule relating the number of lawns mowed and Rebekah's profit.
    e. How many lawns must Rebekah mow to reach her goal of $1,000, given that she starts with a $195 debt?

Writing/Discussing
49. Make a concept map for functions and explain the links and connections you made.

50. Describe the difference between a dependent (output) and independent (input) variable.

51. Write a paragraph explaining, in your own words, what you think a function is.

52. Is it possible for a set of data to not have a rule that describes the relation between the input and output values? Make up a data set for which there is no rule. Is it always possible to find a rule to describe the relation between the input and output values if you are only given two input-output values? Explain.

53. Describe an everyday relationship that would not be a function and explain why not.

54. Write a paragraph explaining, in your own words, what you think a linear function is.

55. Make a second concept map about functions. Write a reflection comparing your first and second maps and explaining your present understanding of functions.

Chapter 9: Geometry

Chapter Overview:

Geometry is among the richest and oldest branches of mathematics. We think of geometry as the study of space experiences. This study focuses mainly on shapes as abstractions from the environment, which can be informally investigated and analyzed. In this chapter, you will explore 2-dimensional shapes (although most of the ideas are equally valid for 3-dimensional shapes as well). Particular attention is given to making conjectures and attempting to verify them—that is, to develop proofs for your conjectures.

Big Mathematical Ideas:

problem-solving strategies, shape & space, congruence, similarity, verifying, conjecturing, generalizing, decomposing

NCTM Standards Links:

K - 4:   Mathematics as problem solving; Mathematics as communication; Mathematics as reasoning; Mathematical connections; Geometry & spatial sense

5 - 8:   Mathematics as problem solving; Mathematics as communication; Mathematics as reasoning; Mathematical connections; Geometry

Chapter Outline:

Activity 9.1—Communicating with Precise Language

For this activity, you will need to work with a partner. You and your partner will sit across from each other and erect a barrier (e.g., an open book or binder placed in a vertical position) so that neither of you can see what the other person is doing.

Your instructor will give each person a set of tangrams, and will give one person in each pair a figure that should be kept hidden from the partner. The object for this activity is for the person with the figure to make this figure using a set of tangrams. Then this person will describe to the partner how to make the figure using the other set of tangrams. The person who gives directions cannot describe the final figure (e.g., "It's a house."). The person following the directions may ask to have directions repeated or clarified, but neither person can look across or around the barrier unless the directions have been completed. No hand waving or signaling are allowed either! Once the person giving directions has completed them, and the person following the directions is satisfied that he or she has followed them correctly, you may remove the barrier and check your work.

Once you have checked your work, switch roles and ask your instructor to give the person giving directions this time the second tangram figure to complete. Repeat the steps outlined above.

Activity 9.2—Definitions: What is Necessary and What is Sufficient?

What makes for a good definition? Writing a good definition involves carefully considering *necessary* and *sufficient* conditions, and verifying that the definition says what you think it says. In this activity, your instructor will lead you in discussing definitions for some geometric terms. Use this page to record the class's progress towards good definitions of the geometric concepts you discuss.

Activity 9.3—Tangram Puzzles: Exploring Geometric Shapes

The seven polygons below comprise the ancient Chinese Tangram puzzle.

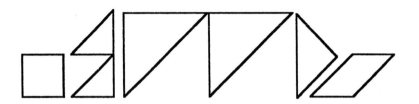

The puzzle involves manipulating the square, parallelogram, and five triangles into various silhouette patterns of people, animals, and other figures. For example, the silhouette of the person to the right can be formed with the seven tangram pieces.

1. Use your tangram pieces to form this figure.

Is it possible to form a square using all seven tangram pieces? Is it possible to form a trapezoid using only five of the pieces? The answers to such questions may not be immediately obvious. By exploring the sizes and shapes of the pieces, you may make some discoveries that can help you to complete the chart below. As you explore, if you discover any relationships among the pieces, write them down so that you may share them with others.

2. In the chart below, use your tangram pieces to determine whether the given shapes can be formed. Record your solutions so that you may later share them.

Using only...							
Can you form a...	1 piece	2 pieces	3 pieces	4 pieces	5 pieces	6 pieces	7 pieces
Square							
Non-square rectangle							
Trapezoid							

3. A student made the claim that if two figures are made of the exact same tangram pieces, then they must have the same area. Is this claim true or false? How can you convince others?

4. Another student claimed that if two figures are made of the exact same tangram pieces, then the must have the same perimeter. Is this claim true or false? How can you convince others?

Activity 9.4—Constructing Geometric Relationships

For generations, geometers were interested in knowing which geometric figures could be constructed given some geometric elements such as points, segments, lines, angles or circles and using <u>only</u> a straightedge (no markings on it) and a collapsible compass.

The following diagrams show how to perform some basic compass and straightedge constructions. Use them to do the constructions on the following pages.

A.   Construct a segment on a line l congruent to a given segment AB.

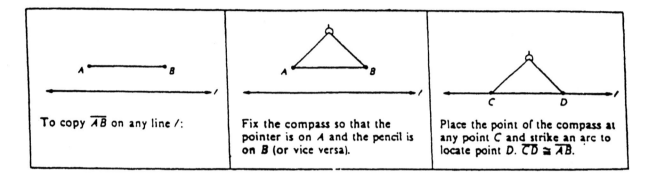

B.   Copy an angle (i.e., construct a congruent angle).

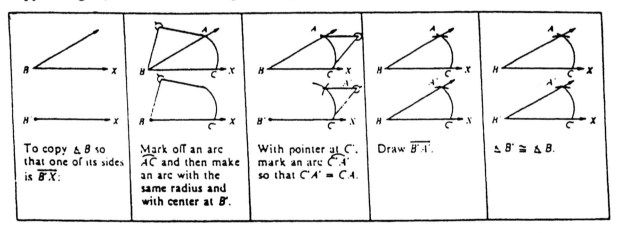

C.   Through a given point P, construct a line parallel to a given line l, using the rhombus method.

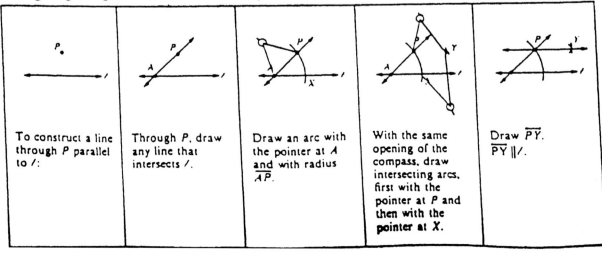

D.   Construct a perpendicular to a line from a point not on the line.

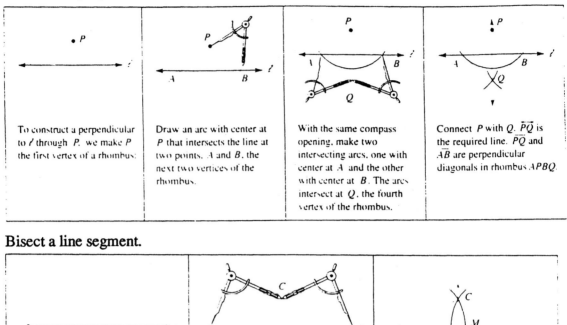

| To construct a perpendicular to *l* through *P*, we make *P* the first vertex of a rhombus: | Draw an arc with center at *P* that intersects the line at two points, *A* and *B*, the next two vertices of the rhombus. | With the same compass opening, make two intersecting arcs, one with center at *A* and the other with center at *B*. The arcs intersect at *Q*, the fourth vertex of the rhombus. | Connect *P* with *Q*. $\overrightarrow{PQ}$ is the required line. $\overrightarrow{PQ}$ and $\overline{AB}$ are perpendicular diagonals in rhombus *APBQ*. |

E.   Bisect a line segment.

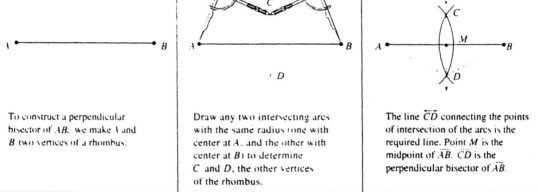

| To construct a perpendicular bisector of *AB*, we make *A* and *B* two vertices of a rhombus: | Draw any two intersecting arcs with the same radius (one with center at *A*, and the other with center at *B*) to determine *C* and *D*, the other vertices of the rhombus. | The line $\overleftrightarrow{CD}$ connecting the points of intersection of the arcs is the required line. Point *M* is the midpoint of $\overline{AB}$. $\overleftrightarrow{CD}$ is the perpendicular bisector of $\overline{AB}$. |

F.   Construct a perpendicular to a line from a point on the line.

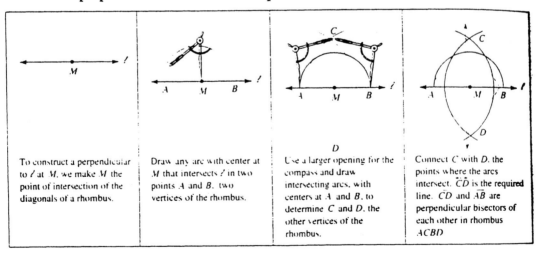

| To construct a perpendicular to *l* at *M*, we make *M* the point of intersection of the diagonals of a rhombus. | Draw any arc with center at *M* that intersects *l* in two points *A* and *B*, two vertices of the rhombus. | Use a larger opening for the compass and draw intersecting arcs, with centers at *A* and *B*, to determine *C* and *D*, the other vertices of the rhombus. | Connect *C* with *D*, the points where the arcs intersect. $\overleftrightarrow{CD}$ is the required line. *CD* and *AB* are perpendicular bisectors of each other in rhombus *ACBD* |

1.   Construct a segment congruent to $\overline{PQ}$ on the given line m.

2.   Construct a segment congruent to 2PQ on the given line n, where $\overline{PQ}$ is as in question 1.

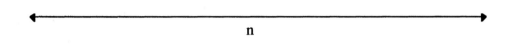

3.   Construct an angle congruent to 2 • m∠ A below which has $\overrightarrow{PX}$ as one of its sides.

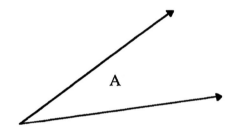

P   X

4.   Construct a line through point P that is parallel to the given line k.

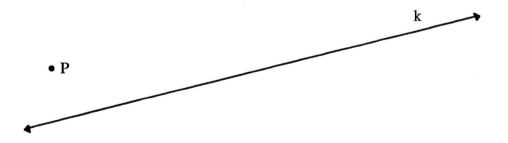

5. Using only a compass and a straightedge, construct a right triangle with one of its legs twice the length of the other.

6. Using only a compass and straightedge, construct an equilateral triangle ABC (make each side approximately 4 inches—estimate this length) with base of segment BC. Now bisect the two base angles of the triangle (<B and <C) and extend these angle bisectors until they meet at point D. Connect points B and D, and points C and D. Make a conjecture about the shape of triangle BCD. Check your conjecture by measuring.

Activity 9.5—Exploring Lines and Angles

For this activity, your instructor will give you a paper triangle. Color each angle of the triangle a different color (e.g., red, yellow and green). Draw a straight base line near the middle of a blank sheet of paper. Line one side of the triangle along one end of the base line. Trace the other two sides of the triangle.

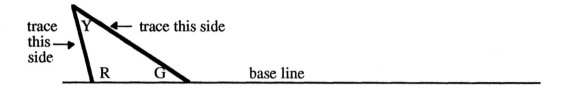

Now rotate the triangle so that the angle marked Y fits snugly against the base line and the side common to angles Y and G fits against its tracing. Then trace the side common to angles Y and R.

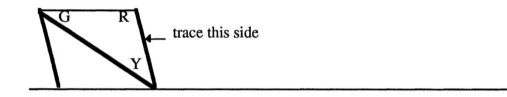

Continue to rotate the triangle and trace the sides of the angle Y to create a "SAW". Color each angle Y as you make it.

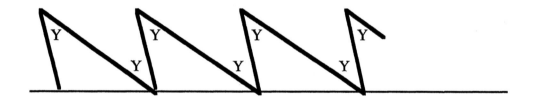

1. Alternate sides of the saw "teeth" form _____ lines and the angles

    within the saws are _____ .

To create a "LADDER", draw another base line, this time towards the lower end of your blank paper. Place one side of the triangle along the base line at one end of it. Of the two sides not on the base line, trace the side closest to the end of it. Mark the point where the third vertex meets the base line.

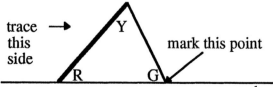

Now slide the triangle along the base line until the vertex of angle R lies on the marked point and repeat—trace the same side and mark a point using the same vertex as before.

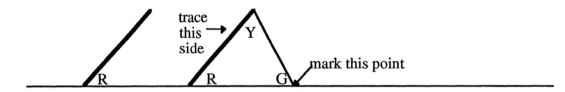

Keep sliding the triangle and tracing the side of angle R which is not on the base line. These sides appear as the "rungs" of a ladder. Color each angle R as it is made.

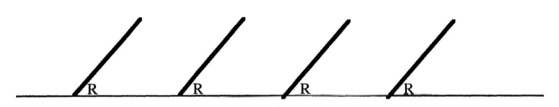

2.   The rungs of the ladder form _____ lines and the angles on the same

   side of each rung are _____ .

Interior Angles

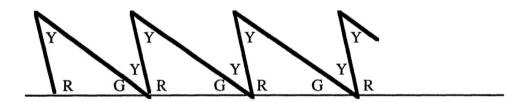

3.   Using both the saws and ladder patterns one gets the above figure. Make a conjecture about the interior angles of a triangle.

Angles Formed by the Intersection of Two Lines

Using a straightedge, draw two intersecting lines. Label each of the four angles and use those labels to answer the following questions.

4. Using a protractor, measure each of the angles and record your measurements below.

5. What do you notice about the measures of the angles opposite each other?

6. What do you notice about the measures of the angles adjacent to each other?

7. Do you think these relationships will always be true whenever two straight lines intersect each other? Why or why not?

Angles Formed by the Intersection of a Transversal Line and Two Other Lines

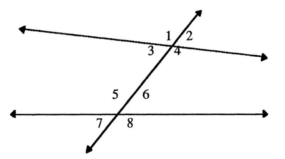

8. <1 and <5 are a pair of corresponding angles. Find three more pairs of corresponding angles.

9. <3 and <6 are a pair of alternate interior angles. Find another pair of alternate interior angles.

10. <2 and <7 are a pair of alternate exterior angles. Find another pair of alternate exterior angles.

11. Based on the Saws and Ladders activity, make conjectures about corresponding angles and alternate interior angles when a transversal line intersects two parallel lines.

12. Do you think these relationships will always be true whenever two parallel lines are cut by a transversal? Why or why not?

Activity 9.6—Defining Angles and Lines

Use the examples and non-examples below to define the following types of angles and lines.

1. Define *right angle*

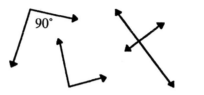

Right Angles   Not Right Angles

(Note: a small square in the corner of an angle indicates that its measure is 90°)

2. Define *acute angle*

 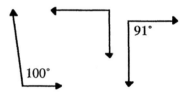

Acute Angles   Not Acute Angles

3. Define *obtuse angle*

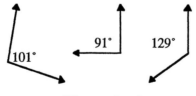 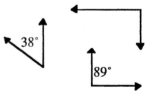

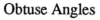

Obtuse Angles   Not Obtuse Angles

4. Define *pair of adjacent angles*

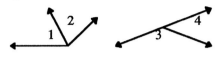

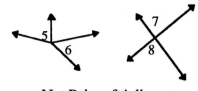

Pairs of Adjacent Angles

Not Pairs of Adjacent
Angles

5. Define *pair of complementary angles*

$m\angle 1 + m\angle 2 = 90°$

Pairs of Complementary Angles

Not Pairs of
Complementary Angles

6. Define *pair of supplementary angles*

$m\angle 3 + m\angle 4 = 180°$

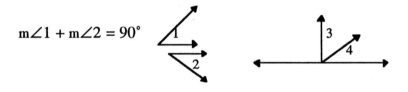

Pairs of Supplementary Angles

Not Pairs of
Supplementary Angles

7. Define *pair of vertical angles*

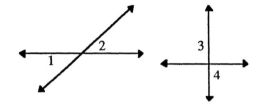
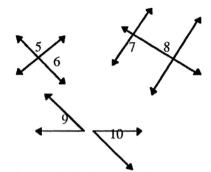

Pairs of Vertical Angles   Not Pairs of Vertical Angles

8. Define *linear pair of angles*

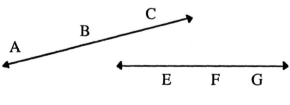

Linear Pairs of Angles   Not Linear Pairs of Angles

9. Define *collinear points*

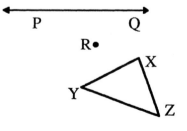

Collinear Points   Non-Collinear Points

10. Define *coplanar points*

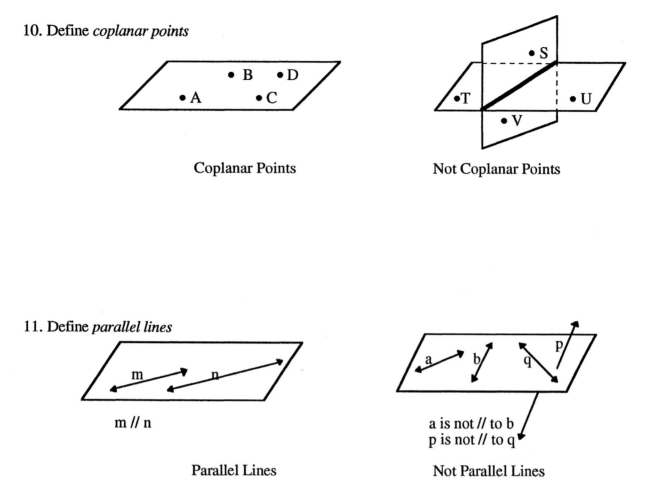

Coplanar Points   Not Coplanar Points

11. Define *parallel lines*

m // n

Parallel Lines   Not Parallel Lines

a is not // to b
p is not // to q

(Note: // means is parallel to)

12. Define *perpendicular lines*

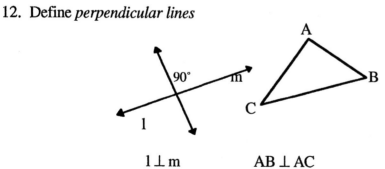

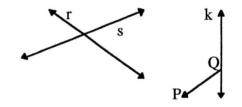

1 ⊥ m   AB ⊥ AC   r is not ⊥ to s ,   k is not ⊥ to $\overrightarrow{QP}$

Perpendicular Lines   Not Perpendicular Lines

(Note: ⊥ means is perpendicular to)

Activity 9.7—Exploring Polygons

1. Given below are some examples and non-examples of polygons.

Polygons   Not Polygons

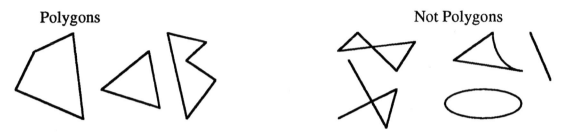

    a. Give a definition of a polygon based on these examples and non-examples.

    b. Quadrilaterals and triangles are examples of polygons. What are some other polygons?

    c. A <u>regular</u> polygon is one with equal sides and equal angles. What do we call a regular quadrilateral?

    d. The first two polygon examples are of <u>convex</u> polygons. The third is a <u>concave</u> polygon.

       i.   Draw a concave quadrilateral.

       ii. Which polygon is always convex?

Activity 9.8—Exploring Quadrilaterals

A quadrilateral is a polygon with four sides. Look carefully at the convex quadrilaterals below and answer the following questions.

1. Which quadrilaterals have at least one pair of parallel sides?

2. Which quadrilaterals have two pairs of parallel sides?

3. Which quadrilaterals have two distinct pairs of consecutive angles congruent?

4. Which quadrilaterals have two distinct pairs of consecutive sides congruent?

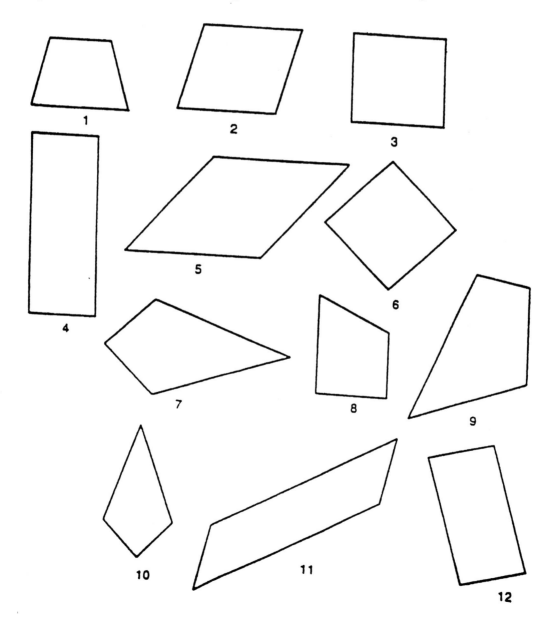

5. Match the twelve quadrilaterals with the names below. For each name, list all the quadrilateral numbers that fit this name. Note that we will define a trapezoid as a quadrilateral with at least one pair of parallel sides (instead of other definitions that require exactly one pair of parallel sides).

    a. parallelogram

    b. square

    c. polygon

    d. trapezoid

    e. rectangle

    f. kite

    g. rhombus

    h. isosceles trapezoid

6. Fill in the blanks using "All" or "Some".

    a. _____ parallelograms are rhombi.

    b. _____ kites are squares.

    c. _____ rectangles are trapezoids.

    d. _____ squares are quadrilaterals.

    e. _____ isosceles trapezoids are parallelograms.

Activity 9.9—Properties of Quadrilaterals

1. Complete the table on the next page which lists different properties that quadrilaterals could possess. Some of these you may already know. Others you may check using a tool like the *Geometer's Sketchpad™*, paper and pencil constructions, or manipulatives that the instructor has available. Make sure you understand what the various terms mean. Discuss these in your group and ask the instructor if you are still unsure.

2. After you have completed the table, use it to complete the tree diagram below relating the following quadrilaterals: isosceles trapezoid, kite, parallelogram, rectangle, rhombus, square, trapezoid.

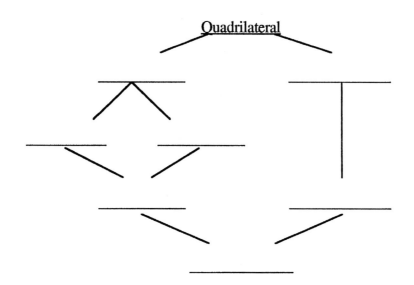

3. Use the table and your tree diagram to consider the number of side properties of each quadrilateral. What happens to the number of side properties as you move down the tree diagram?

4. Consider the number of diagonal properties of each quadrilateral. What happens to the number of diagonal properties as you move down the tree diagram?

5. Describe any connections you see between the relationships among the quadrilaterals and the properties they possess.

PROPERTIES	QUADRILATERALS						
	Parallelogram	Rectangle	Rhombus	Square	Trapezoid	Isosc. Trap	Kite
Side Properties							
4 sides	X	X	X	X	X	X	X
At least 1 pair of parallel sides							
2 pairs of parallel sides							
All sides congruent							
At least one pair of opposite sides congruent							
Opposite sides congruent							
2 pairs of congruent adjacent sides							
Angle Properties							
Interior angle sum = 360°							
All angles are right angles							
Opposite angles are congruent							
Adjacent angles are supplementary							
Diagonal Properties							
Diagonals bisect each other							
Diagonals are congruent							
Diagonals are perpendicular							
Diagonals bisect vertex angles							
1 diagonal forms 2 congruent triangles							
Diagonals form 4 congruent triangles							
Symmetric Properties							
Number of lines of symmetry							
Rotational Symmetry							

Activity 9.10—Defining Triangles

A triangle is a polygon with three sides. Based on the examples and non-examples given below, define the following geometric terms.

1. Define *right triangle*.

Right Triangles

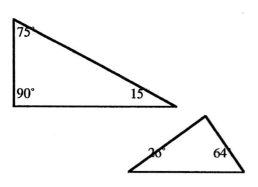

Not Right Triangles

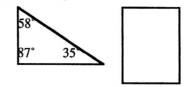

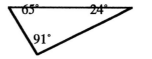

2. Define *acute triangle*.

Acute Triangles

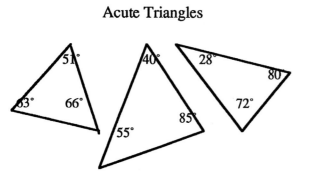

Not Acute Triangles

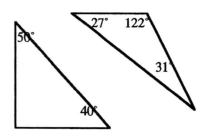

3. Define *obtuse triangle*.

Obtuse Triangles

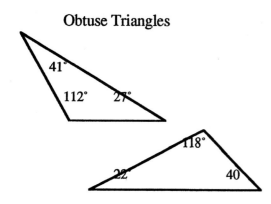

Not Obtuse Triangles

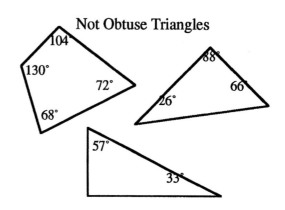

4. Define *scalene triangle*.

Scalene Triangles

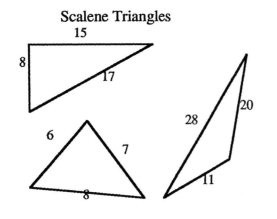

Not Scalene Triangles

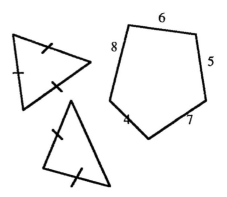

5. Define *isosceles triangle*.

Isosceles Triangles

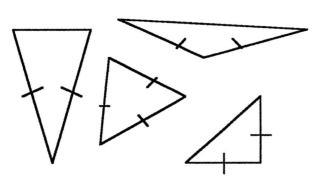

Not Isosceles Triangles

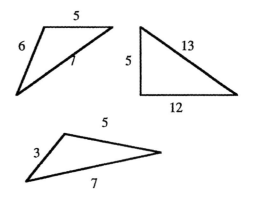

In an isosceles triangle, the angle between the two sides of equal length is called the <u>vertex angle</u> and this vertex is called the <u>apex</u>. The side opposite the vertex angle is called the <u>base</u> of the isosceles triangle. The two angles opposite the two sides of equal length are called the <u>base angles</u> of the isosceles triangle.

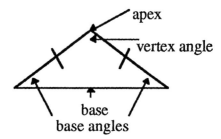

6. Define *equilateral triangle*.

Equilateral Triangles

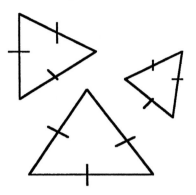

Not Equilateral Triangles

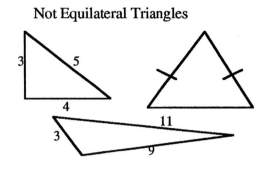

7. Define *median of a triangle*.

Medians of Triangles

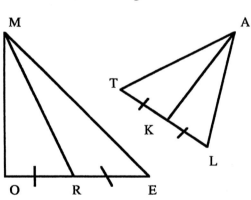

Not Medians of Triangles

Segments MR and AK are medians.

Segments PE and TO are not medians.

8. Define *altitude of a triangle*.

Altitudes of Triangles   Not Altitudes of Triangles

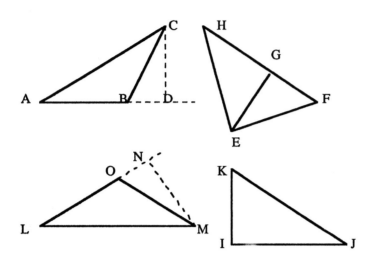

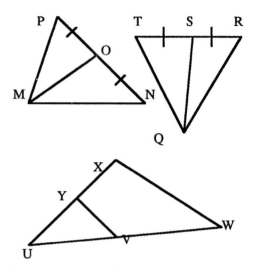

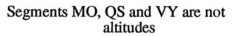

Segments CD, EG, MN and KI are altitudes   Segments MO, QS and VY are not
                                                                    altitudes

Activity 9.11—Exploring Side Lengths in Triangles

Try the following constructions on blank paper using only a compass and ruler.

1. Construct a triangle with side lengths 3 in, 5 in and 2 in. What happened?

2. Construct a triangle with side lengths 6 in, 2 in and 3 in. What happened?

3. Construct a triangle with side lengths 3 cm, 10 cm and 4 cm. What happened?

4. Construct a triangle with side lengths 7 cm, 4 cm and 6 cm. What happened?

5. Use the above to fill in the values in the chart below.

Side lengths a, b, c	a + b	b + c	c + a	What happened?

6. What do you notice when you compare the length of the third side to the sum of the lengths of the other two sides? State your observation in the form of a theorem in two different ways: In a general form as a statement about triangles and in an "If ...., then ...." form.

Activity 9.12—Exploring Triangle Congruence

1. Two things are said to be congruent if they are identical in all their parts. How would you define congruent triangles?

2. Using a ruler and compass, on a blank sheet of paper construct a triangle whose sides measure 2 in, 3 in and 4 in. On a second sheet of paper, construct in a different way another triangle with the same side lengths as the first. When you have finished, try fitting one triangle over the other (holding the two sheets of paper up to the light might help.) What do you find?

3. Use your triangle with sides of length 2 in, 3 in and 4 in. Can you construct a triangle with sides of length 2 in, 3 in and x in that is not congruent to the first? What did you take as x? What could you take as x?

4. In #2, what were the conditions on the two triangles you started with? Generalize these conditions so that they can be used as the hypothesis of a theorem. (Hint: the hypothesis is the "if" part of the theorem.)

5. In #2, what happened when you compared the two triangles? Will the same thing happen under the generalized conditions you stated in #4? Call this the conclusion of your theorem. (Hint: the conclusion is the "then" part of the theorem.)

6. Using your answers to #4 and #5, state your theorem below and give it a descriptive name.

7. Suppose we try a slightly different approach to making triangles. You are given the lengths of two sides of a triangle—2 in and 4 in—and the measure of the angle formed by the two sides (called the included angle)—30°. Using only your ruler and protractor, construct in different ways on two sheets of blank paper, two triangles with these measurements. What do you notice when you compare the two triangles?

8. Make two more triangles where the sides are 3 in and 7 in and the included angle is 45°. What do you notice when you compare them?

9. This time try something just a little different. Construct one triangle using lengths 3 in and 5 in and included angle 45° and the other triangle using lengths 3 in and 5 in and included angle 48°. Now compare the two triangle. What happened? Why?

10. State another theorem that gives necessary and sufficient conditions for the congruence of two triangles. Name your theorem.

Activity 9.13—Exploring Triangle Similarity

1. In this activity, you will use Δ ABC and point P on the next page. Follow the directions below to construct a new triangle from Δ ABC.

   - Construct the ray with endpoint P through point A.
   - Construct the ray with endpoint P through point B.
   - Construct the ray with endpoint P through point C.
   - Set your compass opening to the length PA.
   - Starting at P, mark off two lengths of PA along the ray PA.
   - Label this endpoint D.
   - Set your compass opening to the length PB.
   - Starting at P, mark off two lengths of PB along the ray PB.
   - Label this endpoint E.
   - Set your compass opening to the length PC.
   - Starting at P, mark off two lengths of PC along the ray PC.
   - Label this endpoint F.
   - Connect the points D, E, and F.

2. Make conjectures as to what the relationships are between Δ ABC and Δ DEF?

3. Explain why you think the conjectures you made in #2 are true.

4. Use the second Δ ABC on the page after the first ΔABC. This time notice that point P is inside Δ ABC. Repeat the steps in #1 above. What happens?

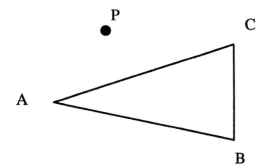

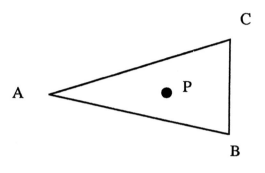

Activity 9.14—More On Similarity

1. In Activity 9.13, you explored similar triangles. What does it mean for one triangle to be similar to another triangle? What does it mean for one object to be similar to another? What are some objects in your everyday life that are similar to each other?

2. Some photocopy machines can be programmed to enlarge or reduce the original and both copies are similar to the original. An enlargement or reduction is called a <u>dilation</u>. Thus a similar figure can be obtained by dilating the original. A machine that is common in classrooms dilates an original. What is it? Does it dilate by enlarging or reducing, or both?

3. Your instructor will now lead the class in an activity that will enable you to discover the existence of the center of dilation and scale of dilation and how they are related. Use the rest of this page to record the class activity which will include a discussion of some properties of similar figures.

Activity 9.15—Constructing Proofs

Prove the following statements.

1.   In a triangle, angles opposite congruent sides are congruent.

2.   If both pairs of opposite sides of a quadrilateral are congruent, then the quadrilateral is a parallelogram.

3. In any triangle, the line segment formed by connecting the midpoints of two sides is parallel to the third side.

4. Draw a square ABCD. Draw the line segments connecting the midpoints of each side. Label the new quadrilateral EFGH. Prove that quadrilateral EFGH is also a square.

Activity 9.16—Sums of Measures of Angles of Polygons

1.   How could you show that the sum of the measures of the angles of any triangle is always 180°? How could you prove it? Write the proof.

2.   In any convex polygon with 3 or more sides, there is a relationship between the number of sides and the sum of the measures of the interior angles. Find the relationship. Justify your answer. Completing the table on the next page will help you in finding this relationship.

3.   Is there any difference in the sum of the angle measurements in regular polygons and in non-regular polygons? Why do you think this is the case? Justify your answer.

4.   Do these relationships hold for concave polygons? Why or why not?

Polygon	# of Sides	Sum of Angle Measurements	Measurement of Each Angle if Polygon is Regular
Triangle		180°	
Square		360°	
Pentagon	5		
Hexagon	6		
Heptagon	7		
Octagon	8		
Nonagon	9		
Decagon	10		
11-gon			
Dodecagon	12		
13-gon			
57-gon			
89-gon			
n-gon			

Activity 9.17—Spherical Geometry

True or False:
Through a point not on a line there is exactly one line perpendicular to the line. _____
If two lines intersect, their intersection contains only one point. _____

The sum of the angle measures of a triangle is 180°. _____

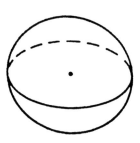

These statements are all true in the geometry developed by Euclid.
They are all false in *spherical geometry*. In spherical geometry a flat
surface is not used, but rather the surface of a sphere. A line in
spherical geometry is a great circle of the sphere. What is a great
circle? _____

_____

Do spherical lines have length? _____ What is the length of a line
in spherical geometry? _____

A point in spherical geometry is any point on the surface of a sphere.
How many points of intersection are there for two spherical lines?
_____ Why? _____

_____

In the figure at the right, points A, B and C are on the same great
circle. Are A, B and C collinear? _____
Which of the three points is between the other two? _____

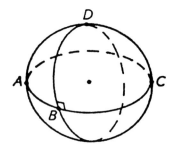

Suppose the spherical line through D is perpendicular to line AB. Are
there other lines parallel to line AB? _____ If so, how many? _____
Illustrate this in the diagram.

Are there any lines parallel to line AB? _____

Now consider special triangles. In spherical triangle ABC at the right,

is the sum of the angle measures 180°? _____

Is it greater or less than 180°? _____ How many right angles
can a triangle have in Euclidean geometry? _____
How many right angles can a triangle have in spherical geometry?
_____ Why? _____

_____

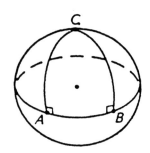

A triangle in Euclidean geometry can have only one obtuse angle.
How many obtuse angles can a spherical triangle have?
_____ Why? _____

An obtuse angle has a measure greater than 90° and less than 180°.
Thus, the sum of the angle measures of a spherical triangle is less than

_____

Things to Know from Chapter 9

Words to Know

- adjacent angles
- alternate exterior angles
- angle
- collinear points
- concave polygon
- convex polygon
- corresponding parts

- exterior angles
- interior angles
- parallel lines
- pentagon
- polygon
- ray
- regular polygon
- similarity
- supplementary angles
- triangle
- vertical angles

- alternate interior angles
- altitude
- circle
- complementary angles
- congruence
- coplanar points
- definition (necessary and sufficient conditions)
- hexagon
- octagon
- parallelogram
- perpendicular lines
- quadrilateral
- rectangle
- rhombus
- square
- trapezoid
- vertex

Concepts to Know

- what it means to define a term with necessary and sufficient conditions
- what it means to construct a geometric figure
- the relationships among various polygons (e.g., quadrilaterals, triangles)
- what it means to prove something
- the relationship among the side lengths of a triangle
- what congruence is, what similarity is, and the relationships between congruent and similar figures
- the relationship among the sum of the measures of the angles in a polygon and its number of sides
- what is spherical geometry and what is its relationship to Euclidean geometry

Procedures to Know

- writing definitions of terms with necessary and sufficient conditions
- recognizing and using various geometric figures and shapes
- constructing basic geometric figures
- classifying polygons according to their properties
- determining whether three given segment lengths could be used to form a triangle
- determining when two figures are congruent
- determining when two figures are similar
- using properties of figures to find angle measures and/or side lengths
- determining the sum of the measures of the angles in a polygon
- determining the measure of an angle in a regular polygon

Exercises & More Problems

Exercises

1. Determine how many lines are determined by the following:
   a. 4 non-collinear points   b. 5 points, where 3 are non-collinear

2. A classmate claims that if any two planes that do not intersect are parallel, then any two lines that do not intersect should also be parallel. What do you think?

3. Give a mathematical explanation of why a three-legged stool is always stable and a four-legged stool sometimes rocks.

4. Is it possible that a line is perpendicular to one line in a plane but is not perpendicular to the plane? Explain.

5. Determine whether the following triangles can exist (draw a picture if one does exist):
   a. an right scalene triangle   b. an obtuse isosceles triangle
   c. an acute scalene triangle   d. a scalene isosceles triangle

6. Determine which of the following are either congruent or supplementary, when a transversal intersects two parallel lines:
   a. alternate exterior angles   b. same side interior angles
   c. corresponding angles   d. vertical angles
   e. adjacent angles   f. alternate interior angles

7. If two angles are complementary and the ratio of their measures is 5:4, then what are their angle measures?

8. Using any of the three constructions shown in Activity 9.4, construct an isosceles triangle that has the following properties:

   a. the length of its base is congruent to $\overline{AB}$ and its base angles are congruent to $\angle Q$

   b. the length of its base is congruent to AB above and its equal sides are of length 2•AB

9. Using only a compass and straightedge, construct the following quadrilaterals:
   a. a square   b. a rectangle that is not square
   c. a parallelogram that is not a rectangle   d. an isosceles trapezoid that is not a rectangle
   e. a rhombus   f. a kite that is not a rhombus

10. a. Complete the following to obtain true statements. Remember, a theorem has no exceptions.
       i. A quadrilateral with four congruent sides is a _____.
       ii. A quadrilateral with three congruent sides is a _____.
    b. Consider statements i and ii below. If true, explain. If false, find a counterexample.
       i. A quadrilateral with all angles congruent is a square.
       ii. A quadrilateral with all angles congruent is a rectangle.

11. Sketch and carefully label each figure:
    a. an acute isosceles triangle
    b. an obtuse isosceles triangle
    c. a right isosceles triangle
    d. a scalene triangle with median
    e. an equilateral triangle with altitude

12. What is the minimum information needed to determine congruency for each of the following? Explain.
    a. two squares   b. two rectangles   c. two parallelograms

13. Which of the following are always similar? Explain.
    a. any two rectangles   b. any two circles   c. any two regular polygons

14. True or False?
    a. Any two isosceles triangles are similar.
    b. Any two equilateral triangles are similar.
    c. Any two isosceles right triangles are similar.
    d. A triangle has exactly one median.
    e. A triangle has at least three altitudes.

15. True or False? If false, give a counterexample.
    a. All circles are similar.
    b. All circles are congruent.
    c. All rectangles are similar.
    d. All squares are similar.
    e. All similar polygons are congruent.
    f. All congruent polygons are similar.

16. Determine whether a 5 x 8 rectangle is similar to either of the following:
    a. 10 x 16   b. 15 x 32   c. 30 x 54   d. 20 x 32

17. A series of six rectangles is shown below that have been nested according to size with the longer edge at the bottom and the lower left corners aligned.

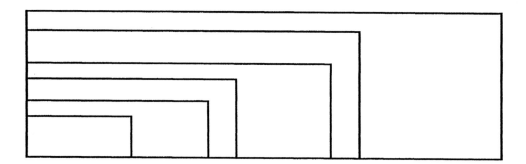

    a. Which rectangles do you think are similar? Carefully measure ratios of corresponding sides and check your guess.
    b. How do those you identified as similar nest together? What might be a test for determining similarity of rectangles?

18. Write a definition for the terms below. Remember to use necessary and sufficient conditions.
    a. A rectangle is a quadrilateral with . . .
    b. A rhombus is a quadrilateral with . . .
    c. A square is a quadrilateral with . . .

19. If quadrilateral ABCD is a parallelogram, and BF = 6, FC = 3 and BD = 7.5, find BE and ED. Explain your answer.

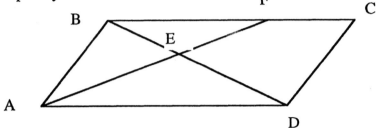

20. Using the chart below, write a formula for a in terms of s.

s	a
3	150
4	300
5	450
6	600
.	
.	
.	
n	

21. Find the sum of the interior angles of the polygon illustrated below. Justify your answer.

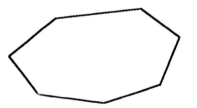

22. Consider the sets of quadrilaterals (Q): parallelograms (P), trapezoids (T), rectangles (R), rhombi (D), and squares (S). Draw a Venn diagram to illustrate the relationships among these sets of quadrilaterals and explain your diagram.

23. Consider the following diagram:

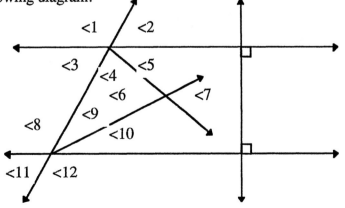

a. What is the relationship between <1 and <3?
b. What is the relationship between <6 and <7?
c. What is the relationship between <2 and <11?
d. What is the relationship between <8 and the sum of <4 and <5?

24. Given the figure below, with segment AX parallel to segment DY, find the following:
a. m<1
b. m<3
c. m<4
d. m<2
e. m<5

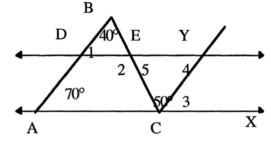

25. Find the measure of each interior angle of a regular hexagon. Explain your procedure.

26. Find the measure of each interior angle of a regular octagon. Explain your procedure.

Critical Thinking
27. How many regions would a plane be separated by two parallel lines? By two intersecting lines?

28. Is it possible for a line to be parallel to another line in a plane but not be parallel to the plane itself? Explain

29. Explain the similarities between rays, segments, and lines.

30. Explain the similarities between the terms collinear and coplanar.

31. Is it possible that a line can be perpendicular to two distinct lines in a plane and not be perpendicular to the plane? Explain.

32. If a line not in a given plane is perpendicular to two distinct lines in the plane, is the line necessarily perpendicular to the plane? Explain.

33. Justify why this is a good or bad definition of adjacent angles: two angles with a common side.

34. Justify why this is a good or bad definition of a square: a parallelogram with one right angle.

35. In the following diagram, a student claims that polygon ABCD is a parallelogram if m<1 = m<2. Is she correct? Justify your answer.

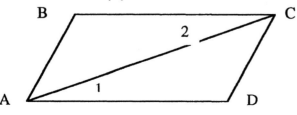

36. Is it possible for two triangles to be congruent but not similar? Explain.

37. What polygons are always similar regardless of the dimensions chosen.

38. If two sides of one triangle were congruent to two sides of another triangle, then what other part(s) must also be given in order for the two triangles to be congruent?

39. Suppose that in the figure below, segment AB is parallel to segment DE, BF is parallel to segment CD, and m<ABF = 90°, AB = 6, BF = 8, and DE = 3.

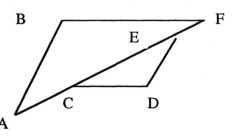

   a. What is m<CDE? Explain.
   b. What is the length of segment CD? Explain.
   c. What are the lengths of segments EC and AF? Explain.

40. A triangle ABC has the following side lengths: side opposite <A is length a, side opposite <B is length b and side opposite <C is length c.
   a. If a > b > c , what is the relationship between m<A, m<B and m<C?
   b. If a = b and each is less than c, what is the relationship between m<A, m<B and m<C?
   c. If m<B = m<C and each is greater than m<A, what is the relationship between a, b and c?

41. Determine whether each of the following statements are SOMETIMES, ALWAYS, or NEVER TRUE:
   a. If two triangles are congruent, they are similar.
   b. If two triangles are similar, they are congruent.
   c. If two triangles are both equilateral, they are similar.
   d. If two triangles are both isosceles, they are similar.

42. Reflect on the following statement and then answer parts a and b: "If a trapezoid is cut into four triangles by its two diagonals, at least two of the four triangles are congruent."
   a. Is the statement ALWAYS, SOMETIMES or NEVER TRUE
   b. If your answer to a. is ALWAYS or NEVER TRUE, give a reason why. If your answer is SOMETIMES, give an example of when it is true and an example of when it is false.

43. Is it sufficient to say that two triangles are similar if they have two pairs of congruent angles? Explain.

44. Is it sufficient to say that two triangles are similar if they have all pairs of corresponding sides in the same ratio? Explain.

45. Is it sufficient to say that two rectangles are similar if they have two pairs of congruent angles? Explain.

46. Is it sufficient to say that two rectangles are similar if they have four pairs of congruent angles? Explain.

47. Is it sufficient to say that two rectangles are similar if they have all pairs of corresponding sides in the same ratio? Explain.

48. a. Show by computing ratios that two triangles with sides length 4 in, 3 in, 2 in and 6 in, 4.5 in, 3 in respectively, have proportionate sides.
    b. Using only a compass and ruler, construct the above triangles. Using a protractor measure the interior angles.
    c. Does your conjecture in #44 hold true?

49. a. Using only a straight edge and a protractor construct two triangles that have the same interior angles—45°, 35° and 100° as follows: Start with base sides of unequal lengths and using your protractor and straight edge construct different pairs of the above three angles at the two vertices formed by the ends of the base. Extend the arms of the angles until they meet at the third vertex. (Measure this angle—it should be equal to the missing third angle. Why?)
    b. Using your ruler carefully measure the sides of each triangle and calculate the ratios of sides opposite congruent angles in the two triangles.
    c. Does your conjecture in #43 hold true?

50. In each of the following, find x and y if possible.

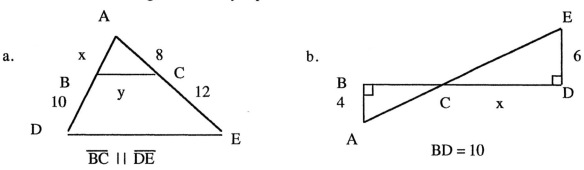

a. $\overline{BC} \parallel \overline{DE}$

b.   BD = 10

51. The symbol for "is congruent to" is ≅. When stating that two geometrical objects are congruent, the order of the letters used must correspond to congruent parts. For example Δ ABC ≅ Δ RST means that segment AB ≅ segment RS and <C ≅ <T. From the information given, determine the correct congruence statement for the following.

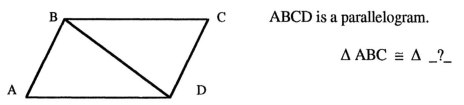

ABCD is a parallelogram.

Δ ABC ≅ Δ _?_

52. Prove that the side opposite the 30° angle in a 30° - 60° - 90° triangle is half as long as the hypotenuse. (Hint: Try making an equilateral triangle out of two congruent triangles.)

53. Find missing side and angle measures in the following pair of congruent triangles. Explain your reasoning.

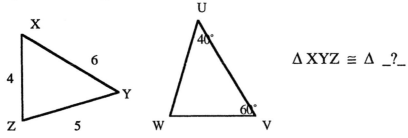

Δ XYZ $\cong$ Δ _?_

54. a. Make a conjecture about the base angles of an isosceles triangle.
    b. Prove your conjecture. (Hint: Remember that often it helps to introduce "something new". Draw the isosceles triangle and mark the congruent sides. Which of the following should you introduce into your picture to help you prove your conjecture: altitude, median or angle bisector from the apex to the base?)

55. Given Δ ABC with <BCA and <CDA right angles. Prove that <A is congruent to <DCB. Be sure to justify your statements.

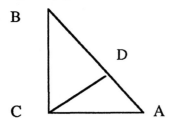

56. Moses said that he was sure that if two angles and the included angle of one triangle are congruent to two angles and the included side of another, respectively, then the two triangles will be congruent (ASA). Rebekah said (AAS) could also be used to prove two triangles are congruent. What do you think?

57. Prove the following theorems. (In each case, the results of one can be used to prove the next.)
    a. In any triangle, the line segment formed by connecting the midpoints of any two sides is parallel to the third side and equal to 1/2 the length of the third side.
    b. The quadrilateral formed by joining the midpoints of consecutive sides of any quadrilateral is a parallelogram.
    c. The quadrilateral formed by connecting the midpoints of consecutive sides of a rectangle is a rhombus.

58. In any triangle, the line segment connecting the midpoints of any two sides is parallel to the third side. Prove that the smaller triangle formed with this segment is similar to the original triangle.

59. Sketch the following triangles: Δ ABC is an isosceles right triangle with legs of length 4 cm. Δ DEF is an isosceles right triangle with legs of length 8 cm.

    a. Find measures of all angles and sides. Support your answers with logical reasoning and/or use of theorems.
    b. Prove or disprove the statement: "These triangles are similar."
    c. Prove or disprove the statement: "These triangles are congruent."
    d. Find the area of each triangle.

60. A student claimed that the sum of the measures in a 10-sided figure is 1800. Her proof was to connect a point in the interior with the 10 vertices to form 10 triangles. Thus, 10 • 180 = 1800. What do you think about her proof?

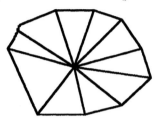

61. Find m<1 + m<2 + m<3 + m<4 + m<5 in any five-pointed star. Justify your answer.

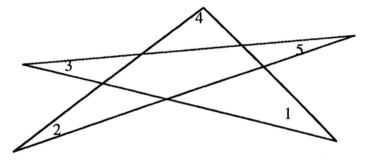

62. Find the sum a + b + c + d + e + f in the figure.

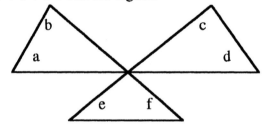

Extending the Activity

63. Define all seven types of quadrilaterals that you considered in Activity 9.9. Remember that a definition must include necessary and sufficient conditions.

64. Using the table you completed in Activity 9.9, consider the angle properties of each quadrilateral and note relationships between the number of angle properties a quadrilateral has and its position in the tree diagram.

65. Using the table you completed in Activity 9.9, consider the symmetric properties of each quadrilateral and note relationships between the number of symmetric properties a quadrilateral has and its position in the tree diagram. Count each line of symmetry once and count rotational symmetry once.

66. a. How many different triangles with a perimeter of 12 units can be made if the length of each side is a whole number? Find as many possibilities as you can, and after each, use toothpicks (1 toothpick = 1 unit of length) to verify that you have found numbers that work.
    b. Roll three dice. How likely is it that the three numbers you get can be the lengths of sides of a triangle?
    c. Without actually making any triangles, how can you determine if three numbers can be the lengths of sides of a triangle?

67. a. Suppose your home is 23 miles from Nearsville and 49 miles from Farsville. How far from Nearsville is Farsville?
    b. Find a way to determine how far apart two towns are if you know the distance from each of these two towns to a third town.

68. Suppose you have a stick with a length of 12 feet. If you drop the stick and it breaks into three pieces, how likely is it that the three pieces could be the sides of a triangle? How many different right triangles are possible?

69. a. On a blank sheet of paper, redraw the first $\triangle$ ABC in Activity 9.13 with point P outside the triangle. Instead of marking off twice the length, mark off three times the length. What happens? Do relationships change? If so, how?
    b. Instead of marking off integer multiples of the length, bisect the length. What happens to the new triangle? How do the relationships change?
    c. Redraw the triangle and place point P on the triangle. Follow the steps for constructing a new triangle. What happens?

70. In the discussion in class for Activity 9.14 you may have discussed that when the scale factor is n/1, the dilation has area n^2 times the area of the original. For example, when the scale is 2/1, the dilated area is 4 ($= 2^2$) times the original area. When the scale is 1/2, the dilated area is .25 ($= .5^2$) that of the original. Extend your conjecture to similarity in 3-dimensions. How many unit cubes (side length 1) would you need to make a (similar) cube whose side length is 2? length 3? length n?

71. Redraw the figure from #4 on Activity 9.15 starting with a rectangle instead of a square. Will the figure drawn by connecting the midpoints be a square? If yes, prove your answer. If not, state what shape it is and then prove your answer.

72. Draw a convex quadrilateral ABCD where all four sides and angles have different measures. Draw the line segments connecting the midpoints of each side. Label the new quadrilateral EFGH. Prove that quadrilateral EFGH is a parallelogram.

Writing/Discussing
73. Make a concept map about geometry. Discuss the links and connections you made in your map.

74. Discuss important factors to consider when writing definitions. Explain why you think these are important, any changes in your understanding of what makes a good definition, and what caused you to change your thinking about definitions.

75. Many times patterns for projects are shown in magazines. Since it is nearly impossible to show them to the correct measurements, scale drawings appear. How might you turn the scale drawing into an exact-size drawing?

76. Discuss the applications of various theorems to particular problems. How does one decide whether or not the theorem applies? What is the significance of meeting the conditions in the hypothesis before applying the theorem?

77. Discuss the importance of definitions in mathematical structures. How do you come to understand a definition? What role do examples and non-examples play in your understanding?

78. In the table in Activity 9.16 that lists angle measurements for polygons, there is a column for the sum of the measures of all angles in each of the polygons. Will that total be the same if the polygon is a regular polygon? Why or why not?

79. How does spherical geometry enable you to think differently about geometry in general?

80. Make a second concept map about geometry and explain the links and connections in the map. Then write a reflection comparing and contrasting your first and second concept maps.

Chapter 10: Measurement

Chapter Overview:

Perhaps no part of mathematics is more clearly applicable to everyday life than measurement, the focus of the activities in this chapter. As a consequence of the practicality of measurement in the real world, it is a very important strand in the elementary school mathematics curriculum. In particular, students learn extremely useful measurement skills (e.g., how to use a ruler), concepts (e.g., the concepts of area and perimeter), and key formulas (e.g., $A = l \cdot w$). Just as important is the fact that making measurements can be a source of many, very interesting problems. For example, did you know that two shapes can have the same perimeter, but different areas? One natural question that follows from this is can two shapes have the same area, but different perimeters? In this chapter you will investigate these and many other challenging problems.

Big Mathematical Ideas:

problem-solving strategies, conjecturing; verifying; generalizing

NCTM Standards Links:

K - 4: Mathematics as problem solving; Mathematics as communication; Mathematics as reasoning; Mathematical connections; Measurement

5 - 8: Mathematics as problem solving; Mathematics as communication; Mathematics as reasoning; Mathematical connections; Measurement

Chapter Outline:

Activity 10.1—Exploring Area and Perimeter

1. The area of a square of side 1 unit length is 1 <u>square unit</u>. What is the area of a square of side length 1 inch? 1 mile?

2. Use the square tiles given to you <u>to demonstrate a proof</u> that the area, A, of a rectangle of length x units and width y units is equal to xy square units (take x and y as whole numbers). Describe your proof below using a picture, if necessary.

3. Using the result A = xy for A, x and y as in #2 above, and knowledge that a square is a special kind of rectangle, give an explanation for the formula for the area of a square.

4. a. Determine a formula to find the perimeter P of a rectangle of length x units and width y units. Explain why the formula is valid.

   b. Determine a specialized formula to find the perimeter of a square of side s units. Explain they the formula is valid.

5. Devise a strategy for finding the area of the following polygon, and then find the area.

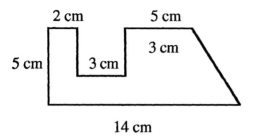

Activity 10.2—Area and Perimeter: Is There a Relationship?

For each of the following, try to find at least two rectangles that fit the conditions listed. You are limited to rectangles whose lengths and widths are whole numbers and which can be built using at most 25 square tiles, each tile having area 1 square unit. For a given condition, if no such rectangle exists or only one such example exists, explain why. Is it because you are limited to 25 tiles or does such a rectangle not exist at all?

1.   area between 10 and 16 square units

2.   perimeter between 8 and 15 units

3.   area less than perimeter

4.   area equal to perimeter

5.   area greater than perimeter

6.   area an even number

7.   perimeter an even number

8.   area an odd number

9.   perimeter an odd number

10. area a square number (but not a square)

11. perimeter a multiple of 4 without length or width being equal to 4 units

12. maximum perimeter

13. maximum area with less than 20 tiles

14. minimum perimeter with an area of 16 square units

15. maximum perimeter with an area of 16 square units

16. perimeter that is neither minimum or maximum for an area of 12 square units

17. area equal to a prime number

18. perimeter equal to a prime number

19. area is one more than perimeter

20. area that is more than perimeter by the same number that designates its width

Looking for a Relationship between Area and Perimeter

1. If two polygons have the same perimeter, can you make a generalization about their areas? Use a geoboard for exploration.

2. If two polygons have the same area, can you make a generalization about their perimeters? Use a geoboard for exploration.

Activity 10.3—Pick's Formula

In Activity 10.2, we found that there is not a direct relationship between area and perimeter in general. However, there is a relationship between area and perimeter for polygons on a lattice (like a geoboard) if we consider the interior and boundary points of the lattice.

In 1899, Georg Pick generated a formula for calculating the area, A, of a polygon that can be formed on a geoboard. The formula gives A in terms of just two easily determined numbers, I and B, where

$\quad$ I = the number of geoboard points in the interior of the polygon, and

$\quad$ B = the number of geoboard points on the boundary of the polygon.

Your task is to rediscover the relationship between A, I and B by exploring with geoboard polygons.

In order to do this effectively, you should consider some systematic way of obtaining your data and make a table to keep track of your results. Although the formula works for any geoboard polygon, you should work with those where you can easily determine their area. For example, it is easy to see that polygon #1 below has an area of 8 square units (why?), but that of polygon #2 is not found as easily. However, once you have discovered the formula, you can find the area of polygon #2 in terms of its values for I (6) and B (9).

#1 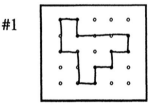   #2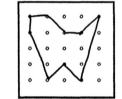

Activity 10.4—Investigating Length

In each of the figures below, the distance between a dot and any horizontally or vertically adjacent dot is 1 unit. For each square below, find the square's area and side length. Be prepared to describe how you calculated the area.

1.

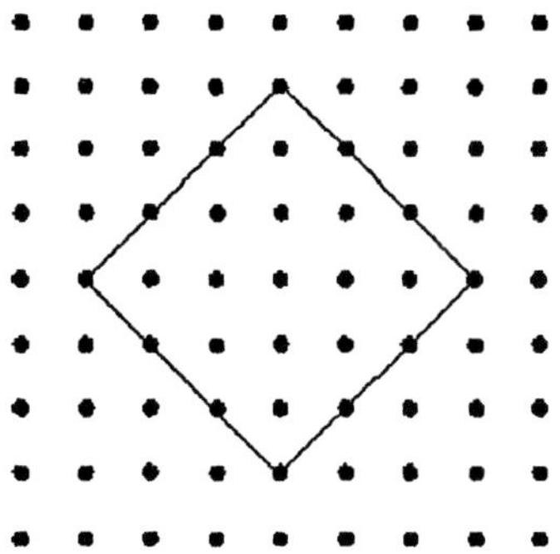

Area of square = _____

Length of side = _____

2.

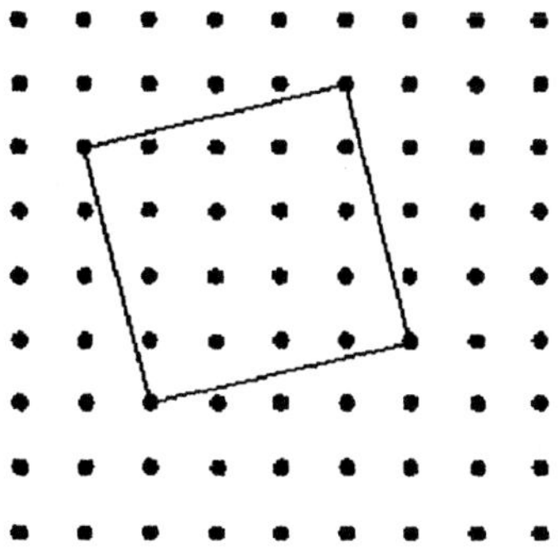

Area of square = _____

Length of side = _____

3.

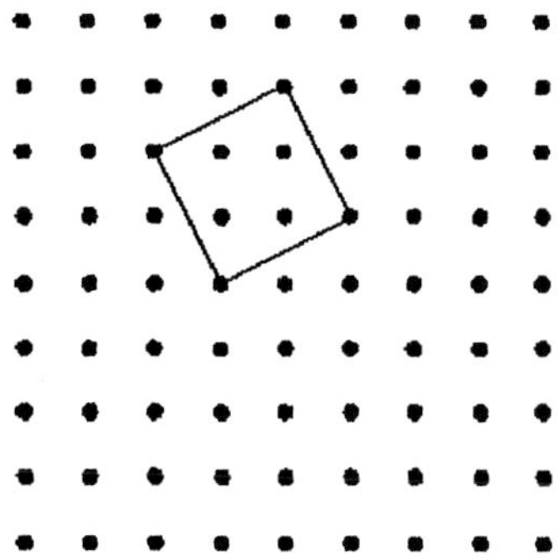

Area of square = _____

Length of side = _____

4. Describe a procedure for finding the area and side length of any square tilted on a geoboard.

5. Can you use the same or a similar method to find the area and side length of this square?

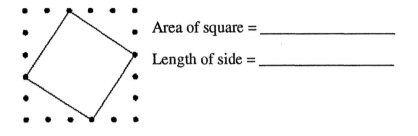

Area of square = _____

Length of side = _____

6. Using the ideas explored above, find the length of the hypotenuse (longest side) of this right triangle.

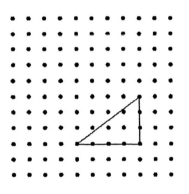

Activity 10.5—Pythagoras and Proof

The Pythagorean theorem is probably the most famous theorem in all of mathematics. The simple equation, $a^2 + b^2 = c^2$, would probably be recognized by anyone who ever took a high school mathematics class, whether they remembered what it meant or not.

Pythagoras was a Greek philosopher who lived around 500 B.C. Although he is credited with the theorem, a number of different cultures around the world—Arabic, Chinese, Indian, European and probably others—both before and after Pythagoras' time, discovered the right triangle relationship, or at least specific cases to which it applies, independently of one another. Pythagoras' claim to fame is that he *proved* the theorem, although ironically, nobody is sure what Pythagoras' proof of the theorem was.

Pythagoras lived and traveled throughout the Mediterranean and Asia Minor, studying and teaching in Egypt, Babylonia and what are now Italy and Greece. Babylonia was an important center of world commerce, and during his time there Pythagoras had the opportunity to study with Babylonian, Egyptian, Chinese and Indian scholars who may have known the theorem. No one knows whether Pythagoras came upon the theorem in his studies or discovered it himself independently. On his return to Greece, Pythagoras established a school that had a lasting influence on the study of mathematics. In violation of the laws of the time, he allowed and encouraged women scholars. His wife and daughters kept the school active long after his death. Pythagoras' proof may be the proof found in Euclid's *Elements*, or one of the simpler proofs you will try in class.

Introduction of Pythagorean Theorem

Your instructor will first lead the class in a discussion of the meaning of the Pythagorean theorem's familiar result: $a^2 + b^2 = c^2$. A proof of the theorem will then be obtained based on the diagram below. The proof uses ideas of congruence of triangles and decomposition of areas. You should participate in the discussion and write your own proof below the diagram.

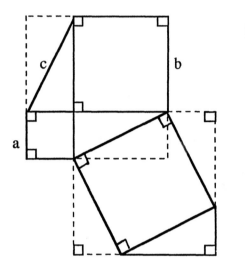

Pythagorean Proof #1

Group Work on Proofs

Although the Pythagorean theorem is so famous, what is not so well known is that there are numerous ways to prove it. You have already discussed one proof of it. On each of the following pages is a diagram that suggests a particular version of proof. You will now get to prove the theorem based on the diagram assigned to your group. Be ready to present your proof to the class at the end of 20 minutes.

Pythagorean Theorem Extensions

The Pythagorean Theorem is usually thought of in terms of the additivity of the areas of squares on the two sides of a right triangle (e.g., some of the proofs that were done today used this idea). Instead of drawing only squares, is it possible to draw other figures, such as the ones below? Does the idea of additivity of areas from the Pythagorean Theorem hold for these figures? Why or why not?

1.

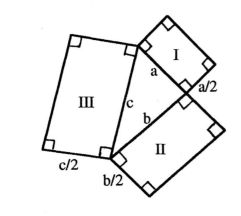

2.

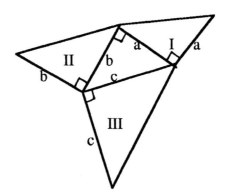

3.

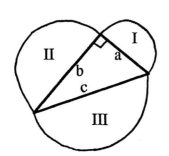

Pythagorean Proof #2 (The Simplest Dissection)

The following figure appears in very old texts and you may have even seen it in decorative tile designs. Nobody knows, but it may have been the proof known to Pythagoras, as it seems to have been known in China and India, and Pythagoras studied with Chinese and Indian scholars while he was in Babylonia.

The Pythagorean Theorem: If a right triangle has legs of length a and b and hypotenuse of length c, then $a^2 + b^2 = c^2$

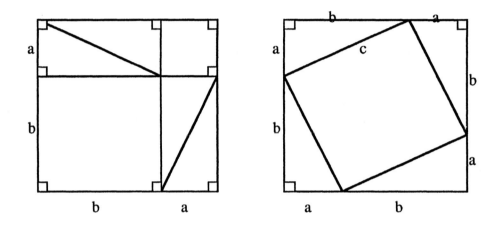

Pythagorean Proof #3 (Perigal's Proof)

Many proofs of the Pythagorean theorem have ancient origins, but were rediscovered later by people unfamiliar with the older sources. This proof was "discovered" by mathematician Henry Perigal in 1873, but was probably known to the Arabian mathematician Iabit ibn Qorra a thousand years before.

The Pythagorean Theorem: If a right triangle has legs of length a and b and hypotenuse of length c, then $a^2 + b^2 = c^2$

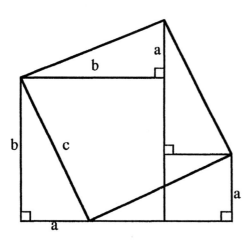

Pythagorean Proof #4 (Presidential Proof)

James Abram Garfield (1831 - 1881), the country's twentieth president, discovered a proof of the Pythagorean theorem in 1876, while he was a member of the House of Representatives, five years before he became President of the United States. An interest in mathematics may not be a prerequisite for the Presidency, but it had been common at the time. One of Garfield's predecessors, Abraham Lincoln, credited Euclid's *Elements* as being one of the books most influential to his career as a lawyer and a politician, saying he learned from it how to think logically. Garfield's proof of the theorem is illustrated with a relatively simple figure: a trapezoid.

The Pythagorean Theorem: If a right triangle has legs of length a and b and hypotenuse of length c, then $a^2 + b^2 = c^2$

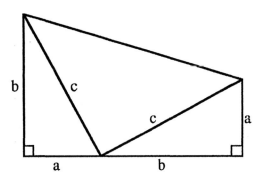

Pythagorean Proof #5 (Behold!)

The twelfth century Hindu scholar, Bhaskara, wrote the single word "Behold!" to accompany his figure demonstrating the Pythagorean theorem. Bhaskara must have felt the figure spoke for itself! Perhaps it does speak for itself, but you can gain a deeper understanding by constructing a proof based on the figure. Incidentally, this figure is also found in an ancient Chinese text, making it another candidate for being a proof known to Pythagoras.

The Pythagorean Theorem: If a right triangle has legs of length a and b and hypotenuse of length c, then $a^2 + b^2 = c^2$

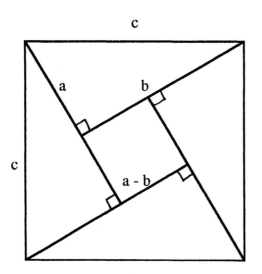

Pythagorean Proof #6

This figure is attributed to Saunderson (1682-1739) but probably came from the twelfth century Hindu mathematician Bhaskara (see Proof #5).

The Pythagorean Theorem: If a right triangle has legs of length a and b and hypotenuse of length c, then $a^2 + b^2 = c^2$

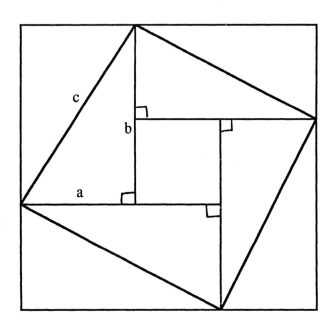

Pythagorean Proof #7 (Similar Triangle Proof)

The similar triangle proof has the dual distinction of being the shortest when written out as well as being the proof most commonly found in geometry books. It is also the basis of a generalization of the Pythagorean theorem that will be discussed at the end of the class period.

The Pythagorean Theorem: If a right triangle has legs of length a and b and hypotenuse of length c, then $a^2 + b^2 = c^2$

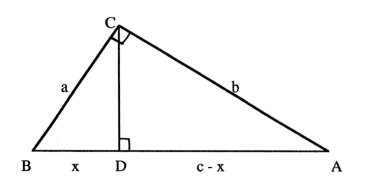

Activity 10.6—Investigating Circles

The circle is a geometric shape that is all around you. Some societal uses are wheels, circular gears and machinery parts, potter's wheels, clocks, windmills and compact discs. Great advances to civilization have been based on the applications of circles and spheres. In this activity your group will examine and define parts of a circle: the center, radius, diameter, chord, secant, tangent, central angle and inscribed angle. The following figure is referred to as *circle O* , since the center is at O:

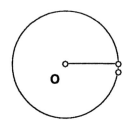

A line segment from the center to a point on the circle is called a *radius*.

Write a definition of each geometric term after discussing the following examples with your group members.

1. Define *chord.* _____

_____

chord

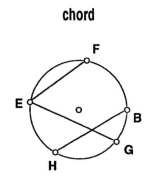

not a chord

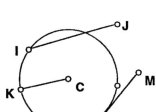

2. Define *diameter* _____

_____

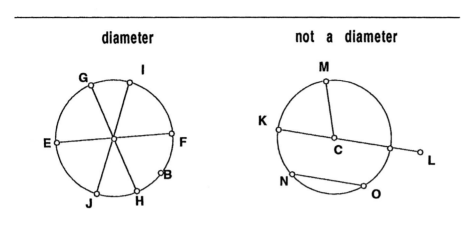

3. Define *secant* _____

_____

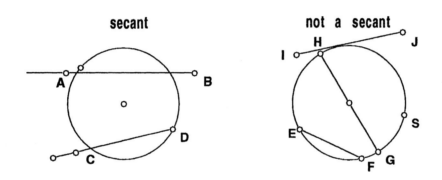

4. Define *tangent* _____

_____

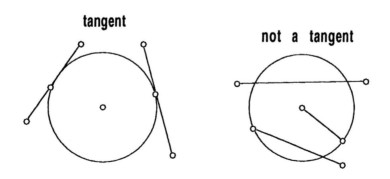

5. Define *inscribed angle* _____

_____

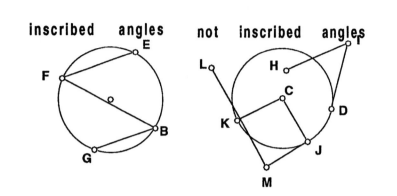

6. Define *central angle* _____

_____

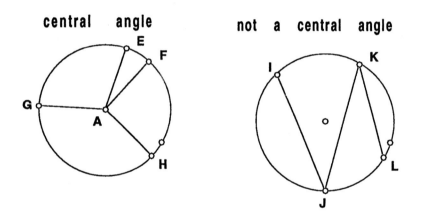

Activity 10.7—Investigating the Circumference to Diameter Ratio

In a polygon, the distance around the figure is called the perimeter. In circles, the distance around the figure is called the *circumference*. In this activity, your group will discover (or perhaps rediscover) the relationship between the diameter and the circumference of every circle. Once you know the relationship, you can measure a circle's diameter and calculate it's circumference.

Part 1: Investigation
Materials: Your instructor will give you two circular objects to class, and string, and a yardstick.

Step 1:   With the string and yardstick, measure the circumference and diameter of each round object to the nearest tenth inch.

Step 2:   Make a table and record the circumference (C) and diameter (D) measurements for each round object.

Step 3:   Calculate C/D and enter each answer in the corresponding column in your table.

Step 4:   Calculate the average of your C/D results.

Record your table below and be sure to include the name of the object.

Part 2: Discussion
Each group will list their average ratio on the chalkboard and be prepared to discuss the similarities and differences between these averages. Give a formula definition of the ratio C/D:_____.

If you solve this formula for C, you get a formula for finding the circumference of a circle in terms of the diameter.

The formula is: _____.

The formula can be rewritten in terms of the radius: _____.

Activity 10.8—Investigating the Area of a Circle

In this activity, your group will discover a formula for calculating the area of any circle. Each group member will perform a separate part of the investigation.

Part 1: Investigation

Materials: Each group member will need a compass, a pair of scissors, a sheet of construction paper, and a glue stick.

Step 1:   With your compass, make a circle with a radius of approximately three inches. Cut out the circular region.

Step 2:   Fold the region in half. Fold it in half a second time. Fold it in half a third time. Fold it in half one last time.

Step 3:   Unfold the circular region and cut it along the folds into 16 wedges.

Step 4:   Glue onto the construction paper, a row arrangement of the 16 wedges, alternating tips up and down to form a shape that resembles a parallelogram.

1.   What would the shape resemble had you cut more wedges?

2.   Since no area has been lost or gained in this change from a circle to the new shape, could you say the area of this new shape is the same as the area of the original circle?

3.   Sketch your wedge shape below and label the dimensions. Give a reasonable algebraic and written argument for your group's conjecture of the area of circle.

Part 2: Application
Discuss the following problems within your group. Decide how to solve them and provide a
detailed solution based on that agreement. Include diagrams and reasons for steps you take and
why certain formula(s) are necessary.

1. A small college TV station can broadcast its programming a radius of 60 km. How many
square kilometers of viewing audience does the radio station have? Use 3.14 for π. Explain
why your answer is in terms of square kilometers.

2. The strength of a bone or a muscle is proportional to its cross sectional area. If a cross section
of one muscle is a circular region with a radius of 3 cm and a second identical type of muscle
has a cross section that is a circular region with a radius of 6 cm, how many times stronger is
the second muscle?

Activity 10.9—Surface Area and Volume of Rectangular Prisms

1. A cube is a familiar polyhedron.

    a. Describe some common objects that have the shape of a cube.

    b. Describe as many properties of a cube as possible.

    c. Define a cube.

    d. What is the volume of a cube with edge 1 cm?

2. *A rectangular prism is a polyhedron with all its faces rectangular.* Discuss why this definition forces a rectangular prism to have exactly 6 faces. [Hint: Think about what is an interior angle of a face and how many such faces can meet at a vertex so as to form a solid.]

3. Using cubic blocks, demonstrate a proof that the volume V of a rectangular prism of length x, width y and height z units is given by V = xyz cubic units. Assume a cubic block has volume 1 cubic unit and that x, y and z are whole numbers. Describe your proof.

4. The surface area of a solid is the sum of the area of all its faces. What is the surface area S, of a rectangular prism with length x, width y and height z units? Explain your answer.

5. Use your result in question #4 and knowledge that a cube is a special kind of rectangular prism to determine the surface area, S, of a cube of edge s units.

Activity 10.10—Drawing Rectangular Prisms

1. A rectangular prism is a 3-dimensional object. To draw a representation of a 3-dimensional object on a 2-dimensional paper is usually not easy, but doing so for rectangular prisms (especially cubes) is not too difficult.

    To draw a cube, first draw a square to represent its front face and a slightly smaller square behind it to represent the back face.

    Now join the corresponding vertices of the two squares using straight line segments.

    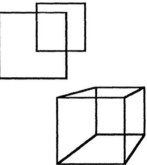

    a. We indicate which edges of the cube cannot be seen by the viewer by using dotted lines. In each of the following pictures of cubes, describe using one from each of the following two groups of qualifiers where the viewer is in relation to the cube: above/below and left of/right of/in front of.

    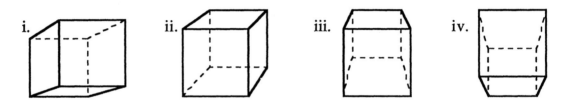

    b. Draw a picture of a cube of edge length 5 cm viewed from slightly above and to the left.

2. The drawings of cubes in #1 captures the impression that objects further away from the viewer (like the back face of the cube) appear smaller. This is a characteristic of <u>perspective drawing</u>, which tries to convey a feeling of depth on a 2-dimensional plane.

The drawings in #1 were all examples of perspective drawing with one-point perspective, where a face of the cube was taken parallel to the plane of the paper so that all lines, which cannot be contained on a plane parallel to that of the paper, meet in a single point when extended.

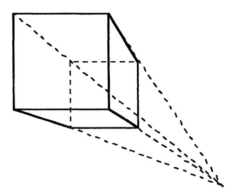

In this drawing, the single point is below and to the right of the cube. Where is the viewer in relation to the cube?

3.   An example of a two-point perspective drawing of a cube is shown below.

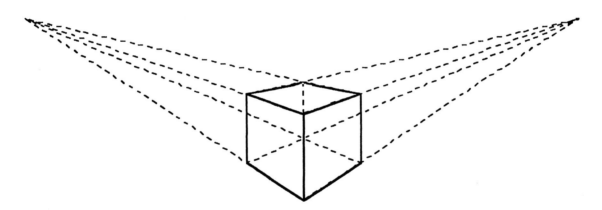

a.   Is a face of the cube parallel to the plane of the paper?

b.   Which part of the cube is closest to the viewer?

4.   A technique similar to that used for drawing cubes in question #1 can be used to draw any rectangular prism. Use it to draw a rectangular prism of dimension 5 cm x 4 cm x 4 cm so that:

a.   the square faces are parallel to the plane of the paper and the rectangular prism is viewed from slightly below and to the right.

b.   a pair of non-square faces is parallel to the plane of the paper and the rectangular prism is viewed from slightly above and directly in front.

Activity 10.11—Exploring the Surface Area of Cones

A cone has three important linear dimensions. They are the *radius, height,* and *slant height.*.

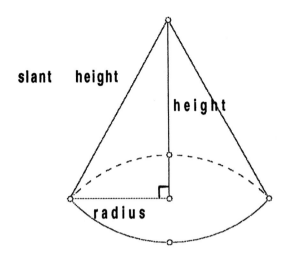

Cut out the circle on page 343. Cut through to the center of the 8 cm radius line. By placing the cut line on top of the lettered surface of the circle and moving the edge of the cut line to one of the lettered positions, the lateral surface of a cone is formed. Use a paper clip to hold it in place. Slowly move the cut edge from letter A to B to C, and so on. The height of the cone will increase.

1. Does the radius increase, decrease, or remain the same?

2. What does the slant height do?

3. What is the longest radius possible?

4. What is the greatest height possible?

This time open the model of the cone from a tightly overlapped position by moving the edge back toward the letters C, B, and A. The height of the cone will decrease.

5. At what height is the lateral area the greatest?

6. At what height is the area of the base the least?

7. a. As the height of the cone decreases, the lateral area increases. What happens to the area of the base?

    b. What happens to the total area?

8. a. As the cone is opened, the area of the base approaches the area of the original 8 cm circle. Does the lateral area approach the same value?

    b. Does the total area approach the same value?

9. Make the cone formed by placing the cut line on D. Find the altitude of the cone.

10. Using an 8 1/2 by 11 cm piece of paper, what is the maximum altitude you could have when making a cone?

11. If the circumference of the cone is 3 cm and the lateral surface area is 25 square cm, can you find the altitude of the cone? If yes, do it. If no, why not?

12. Given the circumference and the slant height of any cone, can you find the lateral surface area of the cone? Explain.

13. Is it possible for two cones to have the same lateral area and different altitudes? Explain.

14. Is it possible for two cones to have the same base area, different altitudes, and the same lateral area?

15. If you know the lateral area, can you predict the altitude? If yes, explain your answer. If no, give an example.

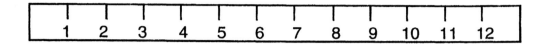

Use this centimeter strip for measuring.

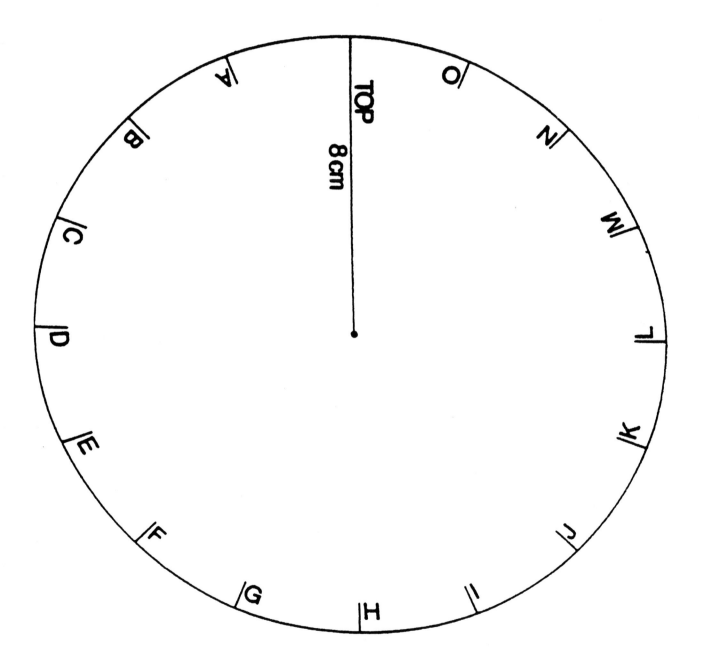

Activity 10.12—Investigating the Volumes of Cylinders and Cones

In this investigation, your group will build a cylinder-cone pair with congruent bases and the same height. The following definitions will help familiarize you with these objects:

*A **cylinder** is a solid composed of two congruent circles in parallel planes, their interiors, and all the line segments parallel to the axis with endpoints on the two circles.*

The circles and their interiors are the **bases**. The **radius (r)** of the cylinder is the radius of a base. The **altitude** of a cylinder is a perpendicular segment from the plane of one base to the plane of the other. The **height (h)** of a cylinder is the length of an altitude.

If the axis of a cylinder is perpendicular to the bases, then the cylinder is a **right cylinder**.

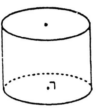

Use your knowledge of the area of a circle and that volume is a three dimensional measure to give a formula for the volume of the below "disk" whose height is 1 unit:

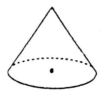

Now generalize this formula for the volume of any cone: _____

*A **cone** is a solid composed of a circle, its interior, a given point not on the plane of the circle, and all the segments from the point to the circle.*

The circle and its interior make up the **base** of the cone. The **radius** of the cone is the radius of the base. The point is the **vertex** of the cone. The **altitude** of a cone is the perpendicular segment from the vertex to the plane of the base. The **height** of a cone is the length of the altitude.

If the line segment connecting the vertex of a cone with the center of its base is perpendicular to the base, then it is a **right cone**. In this investigation, you will discover the formula for the volume of a cone.

Build a Cylinder-Cone Pair

Your instructor will provide your group with the following needed materials:

* a large, clean, empty can
* a manila folder
* scissors and tape
* a paper bag filled with a quantity of rice sufficient to fill the can

Step 1:   Force a manila folder rolled into a cone into the can until the tip firmly touches the bottom of the can. With the help of another group member, adjust the open end of the cone so that it is tight against the rim of the can. Tape the cone securely.

Step 2:   Mark a circle on the cone where the rim of the can touches the cone. Cut off the excess manila folder along the circle.

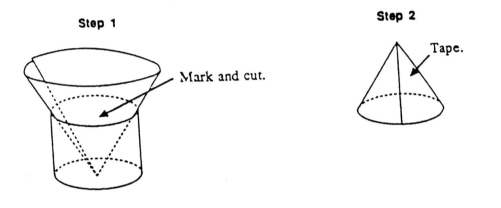

You now have a cylinder and cone with congruent bases and the same height.

Step 3:   Discuss within your group how you might discover the formula for the volume of the cone using the rice. Determine the best procedure to use and then carry it out. [Hint: use the rice!]

Explain and describe your procedure and conjecture. What did you discover to be the formula for the volume of your cone?

Maximizing the Volume of a Cone

This investigation will allow your group to explore what happens to the volume of a cone when various dimensions change. You will need to cut out the circle on page 347 and use the centimeter strip for measuring. Obtain a paper clip from your instructor.

Make the cone tighter by moving the edge from letter A to B to C, and so on. The height will increase and the area of the base will decrease.

1. Describe in your own words what happens to the volume.

2. Discuss within your group what position forms the cone with the greatest volume. Take your model and set it at that position. Paper clip it in place.
    Letter _____

3. Measure, to the nearest 0.5 cm the height of the cone in that position. Find the radius.
    Radius _____

4. Carefully measure to the nearest 0.5 cm the height of the cone in that same position.
    Height _____

5. Find the volume for the cone at this position. Use 3.14 for π and show work.
    Volume _____

6. Plot your radius and volume on the same axes below. Then plot the volume for at least four different radius values.

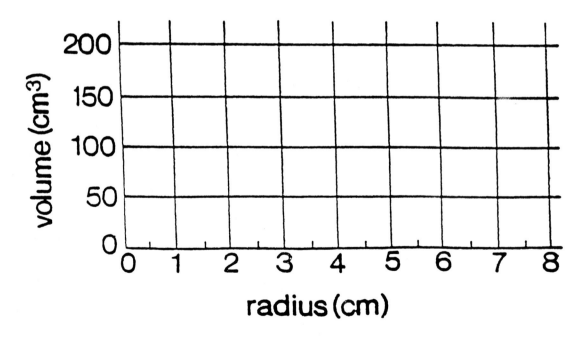

Explain how dimension changes affect the volume. What does the data tell you about maximum volume?

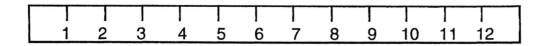

Use this centimeter strip for measuring.

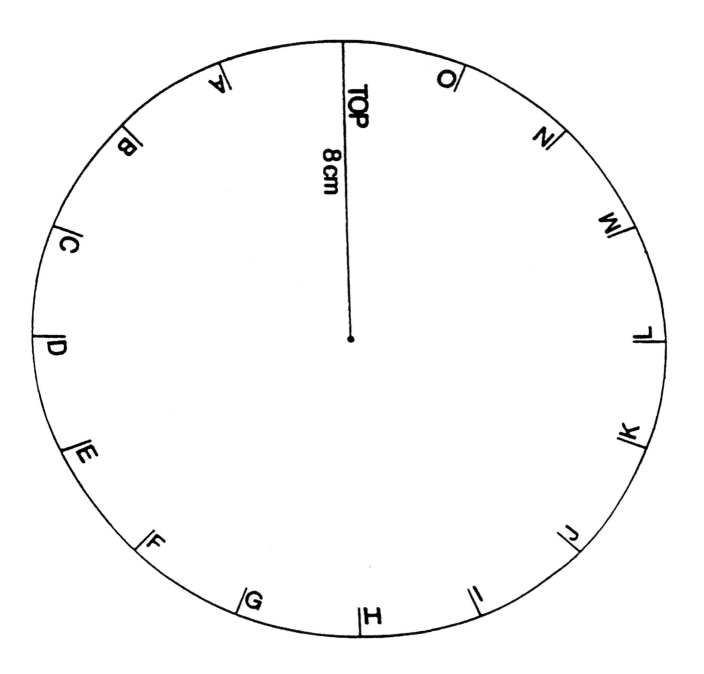

Activity 10.13—Geoboard Battleship: Exploring Coordinate Geometry

Form two teams within your group. Each team gets a 5 x 5 geoboard and three rubber bands. Team A places rubber bands on their geoboard, which is hidden from Team B, to represent their "fleet" which consists of:

- A gunboat, represented by a square of side 1
- A destroyer, represented by a square of side 2
- A submarine, represented by a 1 x 2 rectangle

The sides of all three rectangles must be parallel to an edge of the geoboard, and none of the ships may touch the others.

Team B tries to sink the fleet by trying to guess the exact location of each ship. A geoboard peg is specified by two coordinates (column #, row #). The far left column is column 1, and the bottom row is row 1.

Team B should call out "shots" by specifying their coordinates (always using whole numbers). Team A must specify whether the shot is a "miss" (in the water), or a "hit." If the shot is a hit, team A should specify whether the shot is *within* the ship, on a *vertex*, or on the *perimeter* (excluding the vertices). At no time should team A reveal *which* ship is hit. Team B should keep an organized record of each shot: whether a "hit" or a "miss" and, if a hit, what kind.

The game ends (and teams switch roles) when team B correctly identifies the precise location of each ship in the fleet. The goal is to discover the location of each ship in the fewest number of shots possible. When team B is sure that they have correctly identified all the locations, they should mark those locations on their own geoboard, and compare with team A.

Once both teams have played both roles, answer the following questions:

1. If a shot fell *within* a ship, which ship got hit?

2. When team A places its ships, how many choices do they have for the placement of the gunboat? of the destroyer? of the submarine?

3. If the destroyer has been placed, how many choices are there for placing the gunboat?

4. When team B makes its first shot, what is the probability that it lands in the water?

5.   In a certain game, team B made their first shot and immediately knew the precise location of the destroyer. Which guesses could have led so quickly to this discovery?

6.   Describe a situation, including the coordinates of the fleet and of the guesses, in which team B could discover the location of all three ships with only two shots.

7.   Suppose this game were played with the same ships, and the same rules, but on a 6 x 6 geoboard. In a "best-case" scenario, what is the fewest number of shots needed to find the fleet?

Activity 10.14—Investigating Translations using the *Geometer's Sketchpad*™ (Optional—Requires use of *Geometer's Sketchpad*™)

There are many ways to explore translations with the *Geometer's Sketchpad*™. In this activity, however, you will work with only one of these, *Translation by a Marked Vector*. A vector represents part of a line which has length and direction. You will investigate and then define a translation. [Reminder: Before choosing a menu item for an object, you must "select" the object with the arrow tool. For more than one object, hold the shift key while "selecting" the objects.]

Sketch
Step 1:   Open a New Sketch and use the point tool to create the vertices of a polygon (e.g., a letter or other shape). **Construct the polygon interior.**

Step 2:   Create a segment less than two inches long and not far from your polygon. Label the endpoints A and B using the label tool. Select the two endpoints of your segment, noting the order of selection.

Step 3:   Under the **Transform** menu select **Mark Vector,** noting the name of the vector.

Step 4:   Select your polygon then under the **Transform** menu select **Mark Vector.**

Step 5:   When the Translate window appears, choose **By Marked Vector.**
          What happens?

EXAMPLE:

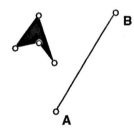

Investigation
1.   Using the arrow tool, investigate what happens when you move any point of the pre-image. What effect does this have on the image?

2.   Move one end of your segment which defines the translation vector. What happens to the translated image of your polygon?

3.   Measure the length of the sides of your polygon and the area (labels may be useful here). What are similarities or differences you observe between moving point(s) of the pre-image and endpoints of the vector?

4. Discuss with your classmates and determine the effect of a translation on an object. State as many conjectures as you can. Give an informal definition:

Extension: Construct a parallelogram using Transformations by Marked Vector.

Sketch
Step 1: On a New Sketch, create two translation vectors which share a common point.

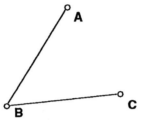

Step 2: Select points B and A (in that order) and choose **Mark Vector** under the **Transform** menu. Select segment BC and translate it by marked vector BA.

Step 3: Select points B and C (in that order) and choose **Mark Vector** under the **Transform** menu. Select segment BA and translate it by marked vector BC.

5. What happens when you change the position of the points A, B and C?

6. Does your definition hold for the parallelogram? Why or why not?

Activity 10.15—Investigating Rotations using the *Geometer's Sketchpad*™ (Optional—Requires use of *Geometer's Sketchpad*™)

There are several ways to directly rotate objects using this software. In this activity, you will be rotating your selection by a fixed angle around a point marked as center. You will be able to examine effects of this transformation and define it informally.

Sketch

Step 1:   Open a New Sketch and under **Graph** menu choose **Show Grid**. This background graph will help you to analyze the rotations.

Step 2:   In the first quadrant, construct a triangle or other polygon of your choice.

Step 3:   Select the origin and choose **Mark Center** in the **Transform** menu. The object will now rotate around this center point.

Step 4:   Select the polygon interior and choose **Rotate** under the **Transform** menu. Choose 90 degrees for your first investigation.

Step 5:   Give your new image a different color or shade.

Step 6:   Keep Rotating: select the new image each time and choose **Rotate** under the **Transform** menu.

Investigation

1.   Investigate and state what happens when you move any point of the original polygon.

2.   Compare measurements of the original polygon with those of the rotated images (labels may be useful here). What are some similarities or differences between the pre-image and images? Note your measurements. Obtain a printout of your sketch.

3.   Open a New Sketch and repeat the Steps twice. Each time choose angles different from 90 degrees. (Note: *Sketchpad*™ cannot evaluate angles greater than 180 degrees.) Compare your findings with your investigation of the 90 degree rotation. Obtain a printout of each of the above sketches.

4. Discuss with your classmates and determine the effect of a rotation on an object. State as many conjectures as you can. Give an informal definition:

5. State any similarities between your investigation of translations and rotations.

Activity 10.16—Investigating Reflections using the *Geometer's Sketchpad*™ (Optional—Requires use of *Geometer's Sketchpad*™)

Sketchpad™ will reflect a selected object across a line, ray or axis marked as a mirror. In this activity, you will investigate the images of objects reflected across segments using *Mark Mirror* . You will be able to informally define the effects of this transformation.

Sketch

Step 1:   Open a New Sketch and create a triangle on the left side of the screen. Use the point tool then select all three points at once using the shift key. Choose **Segment** under the **Construct** menu so that the three sides of the triangle appear. Label the vertices.

Step 2:   Using the segment tool draw a vertical segment in the middle of the screen (holding the shift key while drawing the segment will insure a straight segment). While the segment is still selected, choose **Mark Mirror** from the **Transform** menu.

(If you don't see this as an available option then you either have something else selected as well as your segment or your segment is not selected. Select the vertical segment and try again.)

Step 3:   Select your whole triangle by dragging the mouse with the button pressed from top left to bottom middle of your screen (a dotted rectangle should appear—make sure your triangle is completely contained in the rectangle). On releasing the mouse button all objects that were in the rectangle should be selected.

Step 4:   With your triangle selected, choose **Reflect** from the **Transform** menu. A mirror image of your triangle should appear on the other side of your "mirror" segment.

Investigation

1.   Investigate what happens when you move points of the original triangle. What happens to the mirror image? Move your triangle around, make it bigger, smaller, move it closer to the mirror, further away.

2.   Compare measurements of the original triangle with the image (labels may be useful here). What are the similarities or differences? Obtain a printout of your sketch.

3. Create a horizontal mirror perpendicular to the vertical mirror and reflect both triangles across it. Explore and predict the motions of the three image triangles when you change your original triangle. How are the images alike? Different? Obtain a printout of your sketch.

4. Explore what happens when you change the relative positions of the two mirror segments. How do the images change? Stay the same?

5. Discuss with your partner and determine the effect of a reflection on an object. State as many conjectures as you can. Give an informal definition:

Activity 10.17—Tessellations: One Definition

1. A **polygonal region** is a polygon together with its interior. Some polygonal regions can be used to tile a plane. For example, many public places have floors tiled with squares, hexagons, or rectangles. Some people use combinations of shapes—like octagons and squares or hexagons and triangles—to tile various rooms in the house. Notice that the only region the polygons have in common is their sides and that there are no empty spaces between the polygonal regions. Also notice that some of these arrangements have the polygonal regions placed so that all the corners meet at a vertex, while other arrangements have corners that do not meet at the vertex. For example, the rows of bricks used on the outside of a house are alternated; the corners do not all meet at the same place. When the corners do not necessarily meet at a corner, they are called **tilings**. When the polygonal regions are arranged so that all corners meet at a vertex, they are called **tessellations**. Identify the tessellations and tilings below.

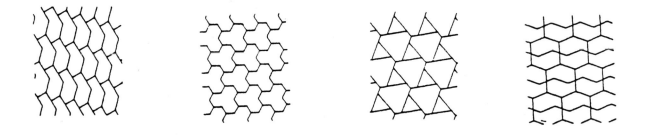

2. When the polygonal regions are arranged so that the corners always meet at a vertex, we can describe the tessellation by listing its **vertex arrangement**. We write vertex arrangements by listing the number of sides in each polygonal region that meets other regions at that vertex. While it is not important whether we move around the vertex in a clockwise or a counterclockwise direction, it is important to move in a circle rather than randomly listing the number of sides. Some tessellations and their vertex arrangements are shown below.

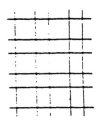

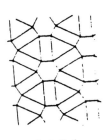

4.4.4.4   **3.4.6.4**

3. A tessellation is a **regular tessellation** if it is constructed of regular polygons. Some arrangements of polygonal regions that tessellate the plane use only one regular polygon. That is, if the arrangement uses pentagons, no other shapes are used with the pentagons. Your instructor will give you some regular shapes so that you have at least 10 equilateral triangles, squares, regular pentagons, regular hexagons, regular heptagons, and regular octagons in your group like the ones on the next page. Try tessellating the plane with each of these figures. Find the regular polygonal regions that will tessellate the plane. List them below. Be prepared to give an analytical (or algebraic) reason why these are the only shapes that will work.

4. A tessellation is a **semi-regular tessellation** if it is made with regular polygons such that each vertex is surrounded by the same arrangement of polygons. A few semi-regular tessellations are shown below.

    a. How many such arrangements are possible? Be able to justify your answer. [Hint: There are more than five and less than 10 arrangements.]

    b. List the vertex arrangement for each of the patterns. [Hint: You may want to recall the angle measurements of regular polygons from Activity 9.16. It will help you if you are systematic in keeping track of your work.]

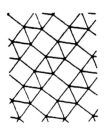

3.3.3.4.4

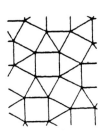

4.3.4.3.3

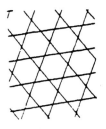

3.6.3.6

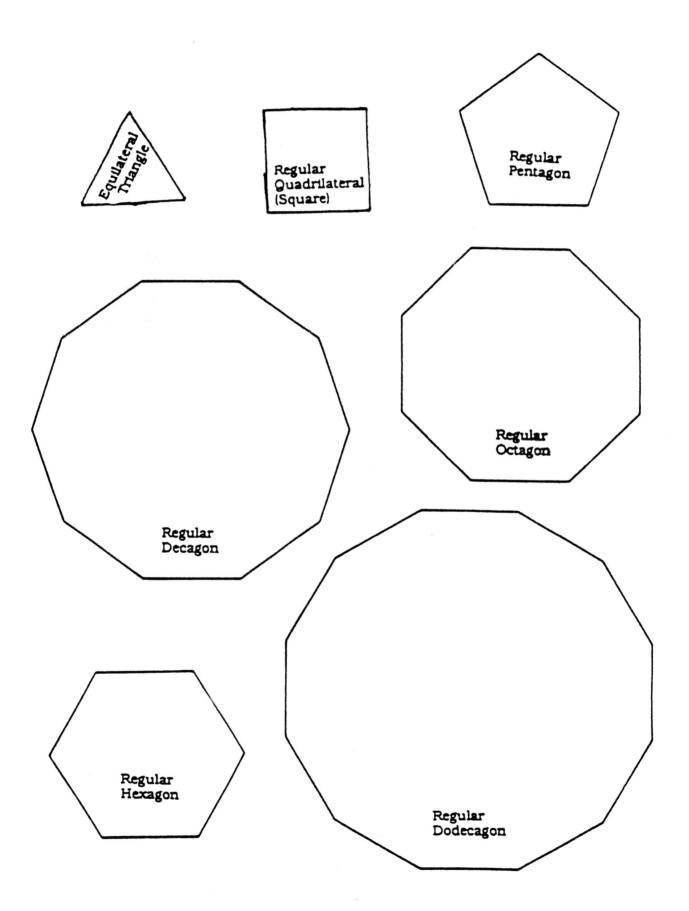

Equilateral Triangle

Regular Quadrilateral (Square)

Regular Pentagon

Regular Decagon

Regular Octagon

Regular Hexagon

Regular Dodecagon

Activity 10.18—Tessellations: Another Definition

1. In Activity 10.1, we began our discussion about tessellations by defining a regular tessellation to be constructed entirely of one regular polygon. If we change the definition of tessellation to include all tilings of the plane, must we change the definition of regular tessellation in order to have the identical pictures of regular tessellations that we had in Activity 10.1? If you think we need to change the definition, write your new definition below. Test all possible ways of interpreting your definition by drawing all the pictures that fit your new definition. If you think the definition is still okay, test all possible ways to interpret it by drawing pictures that fit the old definition.

2. Does this new definition of tessellation change the definition of semi-regular tessellations? Explain your answer.

3. The **dual of a tessellation** is the tessellation obtained by connecting the centers of the polygons in the original tessellation that share a common side. The dual of a tessellation of regular triangles is the tessellation of regular hexagons. Find the dual of the other regular tessellations, using either definition of regular tessellation.

4. Will the dual change depending on the definition you use? Explain.

5. Is there any predictable relationship between a tessellation and its dual?

Things to Know from Chapter 10

Words to Know

- altitude
- base
- chord
- circumference
- cube
- diameter
- height
- lateral area
- perimeter
- polygon
- polyhedron
- Pythagorean Theorem
- rectangular prism
- regular tessellation
- rotation
- secant
- slant height
- surface area
- tangent
- tiling
- translation
- vertex arrangement

- area
- central angle
- circle
- cone
- cylinder
- dual of a tessellation
- inscribed angle
- line symmetry
- pi (π)
- polygonal region
- prism
- radius
- reflection
- right [cone, cylinder, prism]
- rotational symmetry
- semi-regular tessellation
- solid
- symmetry
- tessellation
- transformation
- vertex
- volume

Concepts to Know

- what length is
- what area is
- what surface area is
- what volume is
- what is the relationship, if any, between perimeter and area of a polygon
- what the Pythagorean Theorem tells us
- how to prove something
- what a circle is and its relationship to a polygon
- what π represents
- the relationships among various polygons and polyhedra
- how translations, rotations, and reflections transform figures
- what tessellations and tilings are
- why some regular polygons tessellate the plane and some do not
- why some polygons always tessellate the plane
- how different definitions may change the structure of some ideas

Procedures to Know

- finding length, area, perimeter/circumference, surface area, volume of various figures
- generating rectangles to meet specific criteria
- finding the length of a side in a right triangle when given the other two sides
- proving the Pythagorean relationship
- identifying various parts of two- and three-dimensional figures
- drawing rectangular prisms from different views
- translating, rotating, reflecting figures
- making tessellations
- identifying vertex arrangements for tessellations

Exercises & More Problems

Exercises

1. The length of a rectangle is 20 in. The width is 10 in.
   a. What is the area?
   b. What is the perimeter?

2. The area of a rectangle is 24 cm². One dimension is 6 cm. What is the perimeter? Show how you found this answer.

3. The area of a rectangular parking lot is 24 yd². Find all the possible whole-number dimensions in yards of the parking lot.

Find the area of the polygons in #4 and #5 in square feet. The scale is 1 unit = 1 ft.

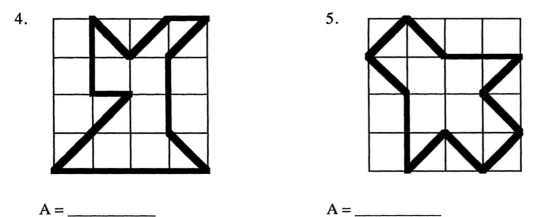

4.

A = _____

5.

A = _____

6. In a right triangle if the hypotenuse is 11 cm and the length of one side is 4 cm, then what is approximately the length of the third side?

7. What is the area of a triangle with an altitude measuring from side AC to vertex B equaling 13, and the length of that same side AC equaling 7?

8. If the area of a rhombus measured 20 cm² and the height measured 5 cm. Then what would the length of each side be?

9. If the area if a trapezoid is 75 cm² and the lengths of the two parallel sides are 7 cm and 3 cm. What is the height of the trapezoid?

10. If the ratio between the sides of two squares is 5:7, what is the ratio of the areas? Explain your result.

11. The ratio of the lengths of the corresponding sides of two similar rectangles is 2:1. What is the ratio of their areas?

12. Draw three rectangles that have the same perimeter but different areas.

13. Determine whether the following can be lengths of the sides of a right triangle:
   a. 4, 7, $\sqrt{69}$ b. 6, 8, 10   c. 4, 5, 6

14. If the radius of a ball is 6 cm, what is the surface area of the ball? What is the volume of the ball?

15. What is the surface area of a cylindrical metal food container with diameter 5 cm and height 10 cm where the top cover is removed?

16. If the dimensions of a rectangular prism are 2 cm x 4 cm x 8 cm. What would the dimensions be of a cube that had the same volume?

17. Which of the following is a better bargain? An orange with radius 4 cm that costs 18 cents or an orange with radius 5.5 cm that costs 37 cents. Explain.

18. A round waterbed mattress measures 7 feet in diameter by 8 inches thick. How many gallons of water are in this waterbed? Use 22/7 for π.

19. What solid would result if you spun each two-dimensional figure 1-7 about the axis indicated? Match each two-dimensional figure on the top row with a solid of revolution on the bottom row.

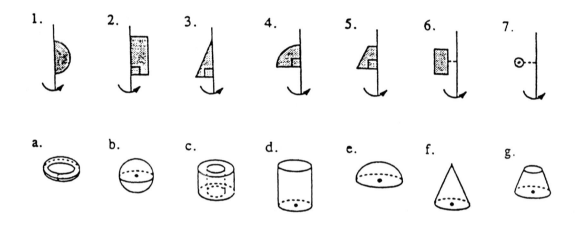

20.   Match each 3-D figure sliced by a plane with its cross section.

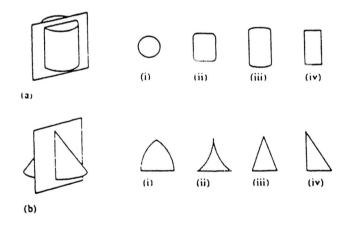

21. Construct a polygon of your choice and then perform the following rotations. Determine which rotations ended in the same result:
a. 90°   b. 180°   c. -270°   d. -90°

22. If a triangle with the coordinates A (3,6), B (9,2), and C (-1,-2) is translated three units to the right and 2 units up. What would the new coordinates be?

23. What words produce the same word when reflected through a horizontal line? What about a vertical line?

24. Which of the following properties are not effected by a size transformation. Explain:
    a. the angle measurements   b. lengths of sides   c. proportionality of sides

25. A geometric figure has a *line of symmetry*, l, if it is its own image under a reflection in l. Draw all the lines of symmetry for the figures below.

a.

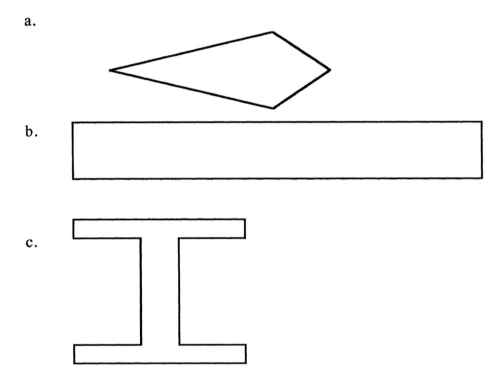

b.

c.

26. Half of a miniature golf hole is drawn below. Complete the figure so that the line shown is a line of symmetry.

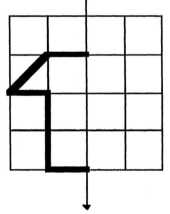

27. Draw the following polygons and determine how many lines of symmetry exist:
    a. square   b. rectangle   c. equilateral triangle   d. rhombus

28. A figure has *rotational symmetry* when the traced figure can be rotated less than 360° about some point so that it matches the original figure. Determine what rotational symmetries the figures in #27 have.

Critical Thinking

29. If a rectangular field is 80 m x 70 m. How can you determine the dimensions of square field that has the same area? If you were fencing in this area how would you determine the lengths of this new square field?

30. How could you represent on a graph the relationships between the length and width of all rectangles with perimeters of 16 cm?

31. Find the areas of the following polygons on the simulated geoboard.
    a. Area of A = _____   b. Area of B = _____

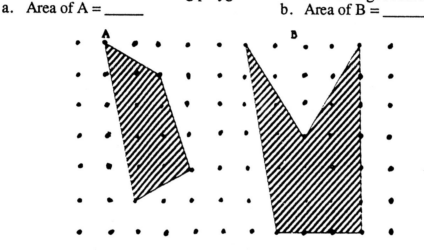

32. Find the perimeter and area of the geoboard figure below:

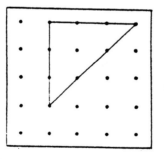

33. Around the world in eighty days? If the diameter of the earth is 8,000 miles, calculate your speed in miles per hour if you were to take 80 days to circumnavigate the earth about the equator. Use 3.14 for π.

34. The Pizza Palace is known throughout the city for its delicious pizza with extra thick crust around the edge. Their small pizza has a 6 inch radius and sells for $9.75. The medium size sells for $12.00 and is a savory 8 inches in radius. The large is a hefty, mouth-watering 20 inches in diameter and sells for $16.50. Since the edge is the thickest part of a Palace pizza, calculate which gives the most edge per dollar. Find the circumference of the pizza.

35. Give as much information as you can about each of the following figures:

12 inches

a.

12 inches

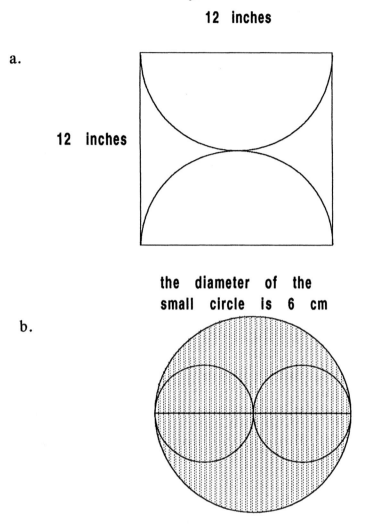

the diameter of the
small circle is 6 cm

b.

36. Explain why rotations sometimes, always, or never result in a similar transformation as a reflection.

37. Do all quadrilaterals tessellate the plane? Explain.

38. a. Which regular polygons tessellate the plane by themselves?
     b. What does the vertex arrangement 3.6.3.6 mean?
     c. Draw (a sufficient portion of) the semi-regular tessellation with the vertex arrangement 3.6.3.6.
     d. Why does the vertex arrangement 3.6.3.6 form a tessellation?

39. Adam wants to completely cover his bathroom walls with tiles in the shape of some regular polygon (all tiles used must be the same). List his choices and make a sketch showing what each would look like.

40. Could 4.4.6.8 describe a vertex point of a semi-regular tessellation? Explain.

41. It costs $50 for paint to cover a chalkboard at school. How much would it cost for paint to cover a board half as long and half as wide?

42. A stack of rectangular paper sheets weighs 3 lbs. What will be the weight of a stack of sheets of the same paper quality that is 3 times as high with sheets three times as long and three times as wide?

43. Suppose a wire is stretched tightly around the earth. The radius of the earth is approximately 6400 km. If the wire is cut, its circumference increased by 20 m, and the wire is then placed back around the earth so that the wire is the same distance from the earth at every point, could you walk under the wire? Justify your answer.

44. Explain two methods for approximating the area of a circle.

45. Draw and label the units of a polygon that has a larger numerical value for its perimeter than it does for its area. Do the same for a polygon that has a larger numerical value for its area than it does for its perimeter.

46. A circular flower bed is 6 m in diameter and has a circular sidewalk around it 1 m wide. Find the area of the sidewalk in square meters.

47. If the ratio of the lengths of the corresponding sides in two similar triangles is 3:1, what is the ratio of their areas?

48. If two trapezoids are similar and the ratio of their corresponding parts is 3:1, what is the ratio of their areas? Explain.

49. a. If the length and width of a parallelogram are each doubled, is the area of the parallelogram doubled? Explain.
    b. If the base and height of a triangle are each doubled, what happens to the area of the triangle?

50. Congruent circles are cut out of a rectangular piece of tin, as shown below, to make lids. Find what percent of the tin is wasted.

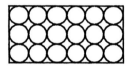

51. Suppose the ratio of the radii of two circles is 2:1.
    a. What is the ratio of the areas of the two circles? Explain.
    b. What is the ratio of the circumference of the two circles? Explain.
    c. If two cylinders of equal height have the circles above as bases, what is the ratio of the volumes of the two cylinders? Explain.
    d. If two cones of equal height have the circles above as bases, what is the ratio of the volumes of the two cones? Explain.

52. Does doubling the radius of a cylinder increase the volume more than doubling the height? Explain.

53. If you were asked to determine the volume of a shape that does not have a specific formula, how would you go about determining the volume? Draw an example of such an irregular figure and determine the volume of it.

Extending the Activity

54. Find the area of the octagonal shaped miniature golf hole whose dimensions are given below. Show and explain all your work.

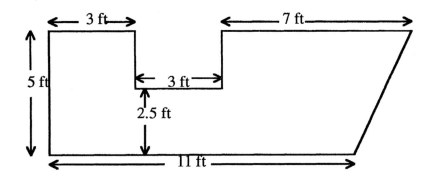

55. Find the area of the miniature golf hole shown below. Explain how you obtained your answer.

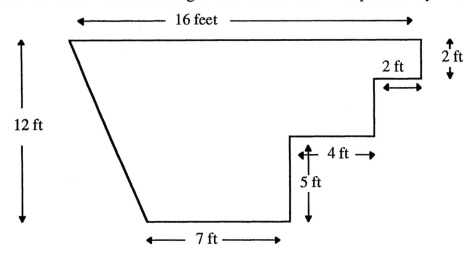

56. If two polygons on a geoboard have the same number of boundary pins, will they also have the same perimeter? Explain.

57. How many non-congruent polygons on a geoboard can be constructed that have 5 boundary pins and 2 interior pins? Explain.

58. If two polygons on a geoboard have 5 boundary pins and 2 interior pins, do they also have the same perimeter? Do they have the same area? Explain.

59. Draw a proof without words to show that $1 + 2 + 3 + 4 + ... + n = n(n + 1)/2$
    Proving this is the same as proving $2(1 + 2 + 3 + 4 + ... + n) = n(n + 1)$.
    Hint: The Cereal Box and Patio Tile problems in Activity 1.3 may help.

Write the explanation for each of these "proof without words" in 60 - 62.

60. Area of a parallelogram is b x h

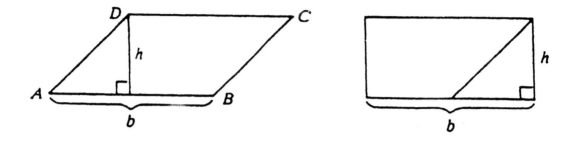

61. Area of a trapezoid is   1/2 (b₁ + b₂)h

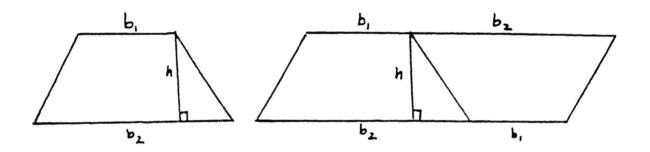

62. Area of a circle is πr^2

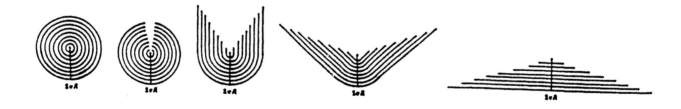

63. Create a semi-regular tessellation out of at least two regular polygons. Your design should cover a minimum of a 8 inch square section of paper.

64. a. Only three regular polygonal regions can be used to tessellate the plane by itself. Which shapes are these?
    b. Other tessellations are made of combinations of regular polygonal regions. Is it possible to tessellate the plane with non-regular figures? For example, can you tessellate the plane with any triangle? Any quadrilateral? Any pentagon? Any hexagon? Justify your answers.
    c. Make a general statement about non-regular figures that will tessellate the plane.
    d. So far we have only used convex polygonal regions. Is it possible to tessellate the plane using concave polygonal regions? What criteria must the shape meet in order to tessellate the plane?
    e. Draw at least one concave figure that will tessellate the plane and then draw the tessellation. Will every quadrilateral tessellate the plane? Explain.
    f. Find a semi-regular tessellation anywhere outside of the classroom. Sketch it and identify the location of the tessellation.

65. Suppose you need to find the height of a tall tree but have no way of measuring it directly. Use the diagram below to write a complete explanation of how you could determine the tree's height.

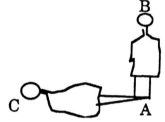

Writing/Discussing
66. Why do you think throughout history civilizations have developed measurement systems? Why do you think the measurement systems have changed over time?

67. Discuss any beliefs you have or may have had concerning the relationship(s) between perimeter and area. Has your thinking changed? If so, how?

68. When finding area of shapes on a geoboard how could you use ideas of decomposition?

69. In Activity 10.5, how did you see ideas of multiple representations being used?

70. Choose one of the proofs of the Pythagorean Theorem and write up the proof so that someone could read and understand it without you being there to explain what you wrote.

Solutions to Exercises & More Problems

Chapter 1

1. various solutions are possible; one possibility is: 8, 16, 32; another possibility is 7, 11, 16

3. 116, 159, 209

5. 16, 19, 22

7. answers will vary

9. a. The following table shows one way in which Rebekah could get 6 cups and 1 cup of water. It lists the amount of water at each step in each of the cups. Only one transfer has been made at each step. Remember, since it is water that is needed Rebekah could afford to throw away the unused quantities of water.

5 cup vessel	8 cup vessel
0	8
5 (throw away)	3
3	0
3	8
5 (throw away)	6 --> Amount needed for the recipe

   b. 5   1

   c. Once Rebekah gets 1 cup of water, she can get any other quantity (in whole cups), by storing the 1 cup in another vessel, and adding on any more cups of water.

11. a. You can get all those and only those values that are sums or multiples of 5 and 8; that is all those values that are of the form $8x + 5y$, where x and y are non-negative whole numbers. The numbers 7, 14 and 17 cannot be obtained. The following combinations show some possible amounts.
$18 = 8 \cdot 1 + 5 \cdot 2$
$31 = 8 \cdot 2 + 5 \cdot 3$
$41 = 8 \cdot 2 + 5 \cdot 5$
$43 = 8 \cdot 1 + 5 \cdot 7$
$52 = 8 \cdot 4 + 5 \cdot 4.$
In fact, every number greater than 27 can be obtained.

   b. The numbers 1, 2, 3, 4, 6, 7, 9, 11, 12, 14, 17, 19, and 27 cannot be obtained.

13. a. $23.01.
   b. At the end of December; at the end of March the following year.

15. 9 minutes.
Adam can put the first two waffles into the griddle, and let the first side of both cook—this takes three minutes. He then flips over one waffle, but removes the second one from the griddle, and puts in the third one. At the end of end of another 3 minutes, both the sides of the first waffle, and one side each of the second and the third waffles are done. So he removes the first waffle and lets the second side of both the second and third waffles cook for another 3 minutes. Thus, total time taken is $3 + 3 + 3 = 9$ minutes.

17. The first number is larger. It can be explained by using the distributive property, and the formula for the sum of the first n numbers.

19. Pull out a ball from the box marked "Red and White Balls." This should give us the solution. For example, if the ball you extract is white, then this box should be marked "White Balls," the one marked "White Balls" should be marked "Red Balls" and the one marked "Red Balls" should read "Red and White Balls."

21. The order is: Tom - 156 lbs., Harry - 152 lbs., Max - 138 lbs., John - 135 lbs., Eric - 130 lbs., and Kevin - 120 lbs.

23. The plants could be arranged as follows:

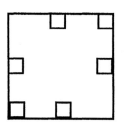

25. 28th day

27. Sara—$39, Cathy—$21, Tina—$12

29. 1

31. first move should be to the middle peg

33. if you have an even number of disks, the first move should be to the peg which is not the target peg; if you have an odd number of disks, the first move should be to the target peg

35. You always get a number of the form nnnnnn, where n is the original number. Thus, with 3 you get 333333, and with 5, 555555. This happens because $273 \cdot 407 = 111111$. You could factor 111111 differently to get other numbers in place of 273 and 407.

Chapter 2

1.	72	▼ ◀▼▼	∩∩∩∩∩∩∩ΙΙ	...	LXXII
	1,273	◀◀ ▼ ◀▼▼▼	𝕃↱ᴾϿϿ∩∩∩∩∩∩ΙΙΙ		MCCLXXIII
	1,813	◀◀◀ ◀▼▼▼	𝕃↱ᴾϿϿϿϿϿϿϿϿ∩ΙΙΙ		MDCCCXIII
	1,965	◀◀◀▼▼ ◀◀◀◀▼▼▼▼▼	𝕃↱ᴾϿϿϿϿϿϿϿϿϿ ∩∩∩∩∩∩ΙΙΙΙΙ		MCMLXV
	121	◤▼ ▼	Ͽ∩∩Ι		CXXI
	231	▼▼▼ ◀◀◀◀◀▼	ϿϿ∩∩∩Ι		CCXXXI

3. a. A numeration system is said to be a place value system if the value of each digit in a number in the system is determined by its position in the number. The place value of a digit is a description of its position in a given number that determines the value of the digit. In the given number, 2 represents 200, 5 represents 50, 4 represents 4, 7 represents 7/10 and 1 represents 1/100.

   b. A numeration system is said to be multiplicative if each symbol in a number in that system represents a different multiple of the face value of that symbol. In the given number, the 2 represents the multiple $2 \cdot 10^2$, the 5 represents $5 \cdot 10^1$, the 4 represents the $4 \cdot 1$, the 7 represents $7 \cdot 10^{-1}$, and the 1 represents $1 \cdot 10^{-2}$.

    c. A numeration system is said to be additive if the value of the set of symbols representing a number is the sum of the values of the individual symbols. In the given number, the value of th number is equal to $200 + 50 + 4 + .7 + .01$.

    d. A numeration system is a unique representation system if each numeral refers to one and only o1 number, since there is only one number that is represented by 254.71.

5. answers will be of the form 53x0, where x represents any digit but could also have digits in the places higher than thousands

7. a. 5,546   b. 206   c. 371   d. 244,107

9. a. x = five   b. x = seven

11. Starting with 20_{four} means you have 2 longs. Trade in one long for 4 units. Now you have 1 long and 4 units. Removing 1 long and 3 units leaves you with one unit.

13. base three: 1 cube, 2 longs, 2 units; base six: 5 longs, 5 units

15. $3 \cdot 5^2 + 2 \cdot 5^1 + 4 \cdot 5^0 + 1 \cdot 5^{-1} + 2 \cdot 5^{-2} + 2 \cdot 5^{-3}$

17. a. i. 326, 057   ii. 1,802,036

      b. i.   ii.

19.

	31	41	43
21	52	102	104
34	105	115	121
51	122	132	134

21. $7006000T_{eleven}$

23. 3 gal 2 qts 1 cup; base 4

25. 2 yd 2 ft 8 in; no base

27. trade and regroup as needed

29. 1 yd 3.5 in

31. 1 qt 15 Tbsp

33. even though these situations do not have one consistent base, these conversions are similar to converting a number from one base to another because of the method of looking for the largest pow of a unit (base), subtracting that amount, and repeating this process

35. Using an organized list and looking for a pattern is one way to find the solution to the Sultan problem. The place of the first wife to receive a ring in the nth round is 3^{n-2} more than the place of the first wife to receive a ring in the (n -1)st round, where $n \geq 2$. Thus, the generalized solution is

    $1 + \Sigma\, 3^k$, where k = 0 to n - 2.

The answer is 9842 wives. This number is 111111112base three. Writing the number in base three will help you better understand the problem and where the idea of multiples of three fits in.

37. Draw out one coin from the box labeled 35¢. If it is a dime, then the box should be labeled 20¢, and if it is a quarter, then it should be labeled 50¢. Given that all the three boxes are labeled incorrectly, it is now easy to work out the other labels. (This problem is similar to #19 in Chapter 1.)

39. 222222 is the largest six-digit base three numeral since if you add 1, you would have 1000000 (a seven-digit numeral)

41. They were using base 7, while the adventurer was using base 10.

43. four weights—1, 2, 4, and 8 grams; six weights—1, 2, 4, 8, 16, and 32 grams; 63 grams

45. 8 is the larger number; 5 is the larger numeral

47. a. 6 weights—1, 2, 4, 8, 16, and 32 ozs.
    b. 1 weight—1 oz.
    c. 4 weights—1, 3, 9, 27 ozs.
    d. base two, base three
    e. both use base two system

Chapter 3
1. a. $(3 + 4) + 8 = 3 + (4 + 8)$
   b. $7 \cdot 5 = 5 \cdot 7$
   c. $4 + 0 = 4$
   d. $3 \cdot 1/3 = 1$

3. a. Yes, a is the additive identity because a added to any element will equal that element.
   b. Yes, order in adding does not change the result; the table is symmetric.
   c. Yes, b has c for an inverse since $b + c = a$.

5. $4 \div (8 - 4) \neq (4 \div 8) - (4 \div 4)$ because $1 \neq -1/2$.

7. word problems will be similar to those in Activity 3.3

9. b, g, h, b, a

11. illustrations will be similar to those in Activity 3.4

13. a.

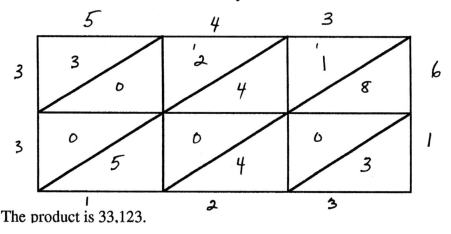

The product is 33,123.

b.

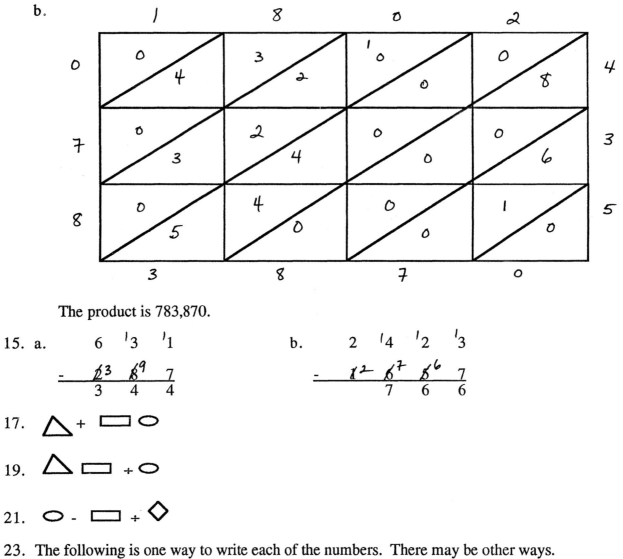

The product is 783,870.

15. a.   6 ^{1}3 ^{1}1
          $-$ $\cancel{6}^3$ $\cancel{8}^9$ 7
          ————————
             3   4   4

b.   2 ^{1}4 ^{1}2 ^{1}3
      $-$ $\cancel{1}^2$ $\cancel{6}^7$ $\cancel{8}^6$ 7
      ————————————
         7   6   6

17. △ + ▭ ○

19. △ ▭ ÷ ○

21. ○ - ▭ ÷ ◇

23. The following is one way to write each of the numbers. There may be other ways.
    $1 = (4 \div 4) + (4 - 4)$
    $2 = (4 \div 4) + (4 \div 4)$
    $3 = (4 + 4 + 4) \div 4$
    $4 = 4 + ((4 - 4) \cdot 4)$
    $5 = (4 + (4 \cdot 4)) \div 4$
    $6 = 4 + ((4 + 4) \div 4)$
    $7 = (4 + 4) - (4 \div 4)$
    $8 = 4 + 4 + 4 - 4$
    $9 = 4 + 4 + (4 \div 4)$
    $10 = (44 - 4) \div 4$

25. word problems will be similar to those in Activities 3.4 and 3.5

27. The set must be $\{1, 2, 3, 4, \dots\}$ = Natural numbers. Since the set is closed under addition and 1 is in the set, then $1 + 1 = 2$ is in the set. Then $2 + 1 = 3$ is in the set, and so on.

29. - x does not mean that - x is negative; it simply means the opposite of x. If $x < 0$, then $|x| = -x$.

31. a.
$$\begin{array}{cccc} & \overset{2}{2} & \overset{1}{3} & 4 \\ & 1 & \cancel{5}3 & \cancel{5}1 \\ & & \cancel{4}1 & 2 \\ & \cancel{5}2 & 0 & 2 \\ + & \cancel{5} & 1 & 0 \\ \hline 2 & 1 & 2 & 5_{\text{six}} \end{array}$$

b.
$$\begin{array}{ccccc} & & \overset{3}{1} & \overset{2}{\cancel{4}6} & 5 \\ & & & 3 & \cancel{4}3 \\ & & \cancel{5}1 & 2 & 1 \\ & & & \cancel{4}3 & 0 \\ + & 1 & \cancel{5} & \cancel{2} \\ \hline 1 & 2 & 2 & 0_{\text{six}} \end{array}$$

33.
$$\begin{array}{ccccccc} & & & & -3 \\ & & & -3 & & 0 \\ & & -2 & & -1 & & 1 \\ & 3 & & -5 & & 4 & & -3 \\ 5 & & -2 & & -3 & & 7 & & -10 \end{array}$$

35. 26 floors.
The answer can be found as follows: $4 + 10 - 6 + 15 - 3 + 2 + 4 = 26$.

37. a. No, if 7 is removed, the set will not be closed any more under addition (e.g., $4 + 3 = 7$ does not belong to the set).
   b. If 7 is removed, the set will still remain closed under multiplication since the only way to have a product of 7 is to multiply 7 and 1.
   c. If 6 is removed from the set, the set will lose the property of closure under both addition and multiplication, since $2 \bullet 3 = 6$.

39. a. The property of distribution of multiplication of multiplication over addition.
   b. Consider the multiplication of 54 by 13 in the standard algorithm.

$$\begin{array}{r} 54 \\ \times\ \underline{13} \\ 162 \\ \underline{540} \\ 702 \end{array}$$
$162 = 150 + 12 = 50 \bullet 3 + 4 \bullet 3$
$540 = 500 + 40 = 50 \bullet 10 + 4 \bullet 10$

   Thus, the process of the multiplication is the same as in standard multiplication, but the number of steps is increased, and the multiplication is with the multiple of the nearest power of 10 in this case.
   c. answers will vary
   d. Multiplication by powers of 10 makes the operation easier.

41. Her students would find $42 \div 6$ by repeatedly subtracting 6 and counting the number of times they were able to subtract 6 until they reached 0. Since division can be thought of as repeated subtraction, this algorithm works.

Chapter 4
1. a. $2 \bullet 3 \bullet 5 \bullet 7$ b. $2^3 \bullet 17$ c. $2 \bullet 3^3$
   d. $2^3 \bullet 5^3$ e. $2^4 \bullet 5^3$

3. $110 = 2 \bullet 5 \bullet 11$ $204 = 2 \bullet 2 \bullet 3 \bullet 17$
   start by dividing numbers by since they are both even, then continue dividing by factors until reach prime number

5. 7, 29, 43, 57, and 143 are prime. The others are composite.

7. a. 12/28 = 3/7; looked for greatest common factor for 12 and 28, which is 4, and then divided the numerator and denominator by 4
    b. 90/105 = 6/7; wrote prime factorization for each number, looked for greatest common factor, which is 15, and then divided the numerator and denominator by 15
    c. $\dfrac{2 \cdot 5^2 \cdot 11}{3 \cdot 7}$; looked for common factors to divide out of numerator and denominator

9. 310 has more than 6 factors because its prime factorization is 2 • 5 • 31. Thus, its factors are 1 & 310; 2 & 155; 5 & 62; 10 & 31

11. 3 and 7

13. a. yes, because it meets the requirements for divisibility by 3 <u>and</u> 8
     b. yes, because it meets the requirements for divisibility by 5 <u>and</u> 8
     c. no, because it does not meet the requirements for divisibility by 9
     d. yes, because it meets the requirements for divisibility by 4 and 9

15. a. 44   b. 3   c. 16   d. 8

17.
```
0  1  2  3
1  2  3  0
2  3  0  1
3  0  1  2
```

     a. 1   b. 2   c. 0

19. a. 1   b. 3   c. 3   d. 2   e. 5   f. 2   g. 4
     h. 7   i. 4   j. 0   k. 4   l. 0   m. 1   n. 3
     o. 6   p. 2

21. a. 3, since 5 • 3 = 15 = 1 (mod 7)
     b. there is no multiplicative inverse for 6 (mod 9)
     c. 3, since 3 • 3 = 9 = 1 (mod 4)

23. p^{13} has 14 factors: $p^0, p^1, p^2, p^3, \ldots, p^{13}$

25. No, one integer would have to be even and therefore not prime.

27. a. perfect   b. not perfect   c. not perfect   d. perfect

29. A number in the form p^4 has exactly 5 divisors. Some examples are 16, 81, 625.

31. a. 0, 2, 4, 6, and 8
     b. 3, and 9
     c. 5

33. GCD $(x^2, y^2) = 1$. Since x and y do not have any common factors other than 1, the products x • x and y • y will still not have any other common factors.

35. If a number is divisible by 3 and 4, it is divisible by 12.

37. a. false   b. true

39. 1, 2, 3, 4, 6, 8, 9, 12, 16, 18, 24, 36, 48, 72, and 144 rows

41. 600 days; least common multiple

43. N is greater than 1 because it is 1 more than the product of some whole numbers so it must be positive also. None of 2, 3, 5, . . ., p can divide N because it is one more than a multiple of each of these (since 1 was added to the product).

45. Since zero cannot be multiplied by any number to get a certain number n, zero is not a factor of any number. This is why division by zero is undefined.

47. answers will vary

49. 51 eggs

51. container 4

53. a. If every digit in the number appears exactly thrice, then the sum of the digits of the number will be a multiple of 3, and hence will be divisible by 3.
    b. We can make a similar conjecture for the number 9.

55. Writing a three digit number and then repeating it to get a six digit number is the same as multiplying the three digit number by 1001. Also, 7 • 11 • 13 = 1001. Hence when we divide successively by 7, 11, and 13, we actually divide the number by 1001, thus getting the original number.

57. 23; Look at the multiples of 7 increased by 2, until you find the required number.

59. a. The arrangement was (1 + 100) + (2 + 99) + (3 + 98) + ... + (50 + 51). The sum of every pair of numbers within the paranthesis is 101, and there are 50 such pairs (one-half of 100). Thus, the sum of the numbers is 50 • 101 = 5050.
    b. We may try the above process with different sets of numbers. This will help to generalize the method. Thus, the general formula will be (n/2)(n+1).

61. a. some numbers that have a large number of factors are 24 (8 factors), 30 (8 factors), 36 (9 factors), 40 (8 factors)
    b. some numbers that have only two factors are 29, 31, 37, 41, 43, 47

63. a. False; 16 is divisible by 4 but it is not divisible by 12.
    b. True; since 4 is a factor of 12, any number that is divisible by 12 is also divisible by 4.

65. Mod 7 and base 7 are alike in that both use 7 digits; in base 7 the digits are 0-6, and in mod 7 the digits are any seven consecutive digits but usually we use 0-6 or 1-7 (for clock arithmetic). They are also alike in that in both cases grouping is done by sevens (although the grouping is different) and when a group of seven is obtained the situation (counting, performing an operation) changes. In mod 7, this change takes the form of starting over at 0 (or the first digit). In base 7, this change takes the form of regrouping groups of seven. Mod 7 and base 7 are different in that mod 7 is a mathematical system with properties of a mathematical system. Base 7 is a numeration system with properties of a numeration system.

67. answers will vary; some possibilities are: 4 - 5 = 5, 2 - 5 = 3; 0 - 3 = 3; 3 + 5 = 3; 2 + 4 = 2; 1 + 5 = 5

69. the nth term of a triangular number is equal to the nth term of a square minus the (n-1)st term of a triangular number; in other words

$$n(n+1)/2 \quad = \quad n^2 - n(n-1)/2$$

71. The pattern of squares is 1^2, 2^2, 3^2, ... At the nth stage, the number of squares will be n^2. There may be other patterns.

73. 33,552

75. c. the sum of the numbers in the circle is twice the number two rows directly below the number surrounded by the circled numbers

77. Let x be the first number a Fibonacci sequence. Then the first 10 consecutive Fibonacci numbers are: x, x, 2x, 3x, 5x, 8x, 13x, 21x, 34x, 55x. The sum of these 10 numbers is 143x which is divisible by 11, so the sum of any ten consecutive Fibonacci numbers is a multiple of 11.

Chapter 5
1. a. $6 \cdot 6 \cdot 6 = 216$ elements
   b. The set of vowels considered is {a, e, i, o, u}. There are $26 \cdot 5 \cdot 26 = 3,380$ "words." If the letter "y" is considered as a vowel, which it sometimes is, there are $26 \cdot 6 \cdot 26 = 4056$ "words." Note that this solution allows for vowels in the first and third positions of each "word." If vowels are not allowed in these position, there are either $21 \cdot 5 \cdot 21 = 2,205$ or $21 \cdot 6 \cdot 21 = 2,646$ "words."
   c. $52 \cdot 51 = 2,652$ possible sets of 2 cards.
   d. $2 \cdot 2 \cdot 2 \cdot 2 \cdot 2 = 32$ possibilities

3. For five sandwiches and four drinks, there are $4 \cdot 5 = 20$ sandwich-drink combinations we can choose. If there are an additional three desserts. Then, there are $4 \cdot 5 \cdot 3 = 60$ combinations of sandwich-drink-desserts from which to choose.

5. The sample space for the experiment is as follows:

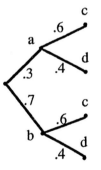

   a. P(a & d) = .3 $\cdot$ .4 = 0.12,
   b. P(a or d) = P(a & c) + P(a & d) + P(b & d) = .3 $\cdot$ .6 + ..3 $\cdot$ .4 + .7 $\cdot$ .4 = .58

7. There is a total of $(2)^4 = 16$ possible outcomes. The subset of the sample space that is favorable to an outcome of *at least* 3 heads is E, where E= {HHHT, HHTH, HTHH, THHH, HHHH}. Hence, P(at least 3 heads) = 5/16.

9.   a. $9,000 (about 75% of $12, 000)
     b. $15,000. The value is $5,000 (about 25% of $20,000), so the car has depreciated by $15,000.
     c. $7,000 (about 35% of $20,000)
     d. Dani should do it *within 2 years!* (By the time the car is 2 years old, it has depreciated by more than 50%.

11. According to the table, we must sum 5.5%, 10.0%, 12.8%, and 19.4%. So, the answer is 47.7%

13. In 1970, 21.3% of the population had taken one or more years of college. This percent is the sum of 10.6% and 10.7%. 10.7/21.3 = 50.2%, which is the percent of people who had begun college and who had finished a 4-year degree.

15. Post secondary education has steadily increased since 1970 and the percent of people who have not completed high school has steadily decreased.

17. In this problem, unlike the situation in #16, order does not matter. So, we get (31 • 30)/2 = 315 possible double scoops are possible.

19. In bowling, the bowler can knock down 0 - 10 pins on the first roll. The table below summarizes the possibilities:

No. of Pins Knocked Down	No. of Ways
0	1
1	10
2	45
3	120
4	210
5	252
6	210
7	120
8	45
9	10
10	1
Total	1024

21. answers will vary; Here is one example: Two cards are drawn from a standard deck and the first card is not replaced before drawing the second card. Find the probability of drawing two red cards.

P(red and red) = 26/52 • 25/51 = 650/2652 = (about) 24.5%

23.

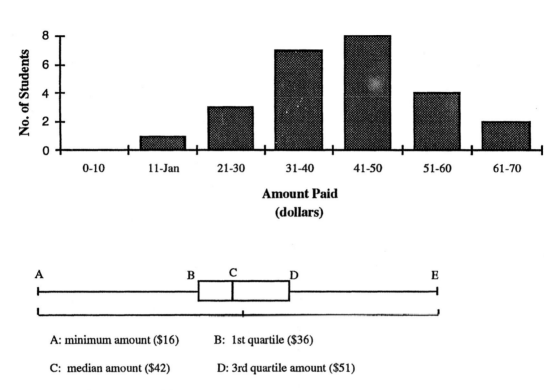

A: minimum amount ($16)   B: 1st quartile ($36)

C: median amount ($42)   D: 3rd quartile amount ($51)

E: maximum amount ($62)

d. The value of the 3rd quartile is not a whole number because it falls between 50 and 51. Notice that if 50 is chosen as the 3rd quartile amount, only 17 values are below it, which is 68% and if 51 is chosen as the 3rd quartile amount, 19 values fall below it, which is 76%. So the true 3rd quartile value must be between these two amounts.

25. a. The factors of 35 are, 1, 5, 7, and 35. But only 1, 5, and 7 are in the spinner. Hence, P(factor of 35) = 3/8.
   b. P(multiple of 3) = 2/8 = 1/4 since there are only two multiple of 3 on the spinner, namely 3 and 6.
   c. P(even number) = 4/8 = 1/2.
   d. P(6 or 2) = 2/8 = 1/4.
   e. P(11) = 0. *This event is not possible!*
   f. A composite number is a number, not equal to 0 or 1, that is *not prime*. A *prime* number is a number other than one whose only factor are 1 and itself. The desired event consists of the elements of the set {4, 6, 8}. Hence, P(composite number) = 3/8.
   g. P(neither a prime nor a composite) = P(1) = 1/8.

27. Observe that there are (16 • 15 • 14 • 13)/(4 • 3 • 2 • 1) = 1820 ways to choose 4 batteries from a set of 16.
   a. If there are 6 defective batteries, then there are (10 • 9 • 8)/(3 • 2 • 1) = 120 different ways to choose 3 nondefective batteries. The fourth batteries has to be defective and there are 6 ways to choose it. So there are 120 • 6 =720 ways to choose 4 batteries of which exactly one is defective. Hence, the desired probability p is given by p = (720)/(1820) = 36/91.
   b. There are 10 nondefective batteries; and (10 • 9 • 8 • 7)/(4 • 3 • 2 • 1) = 210 different ways of choosing 4 nondefective batteries. Hence, the probability p is p = (210)/(1820) = 3/26.

c. The probability that at least one of the batteries is defective is the complement of the probability of that none are defective. Hence, the desired probability p that at least one of the batteries is defective is p= 1 - (3/26) = 23/26.

29. a. Sample Space = {1, 2, 3, 4, 5, 6}; Probability distribution: P(1) = P(2) = P(3) = P(4) = P(5) = P(6) = 1/6.
   b. Sample Space = {1, 2, 3, 4, 5, 6, 8, 10, 12, 9, 15, 18, 16, 20, 24, 25, 30, 36};
      Probability distribution: P(1) = P(36) = P(9) = P(16) = P(25) = P(36) = 1/36; P(2) = P(3) = P(5) = P(8) = P(10) = P(15) = P(18) = P(20) = P(24) = P(30) = 2/36 = 1/18; P(4) = 3/36 = 1/12; P(6) = 4/36 = 1/9.

31. a.

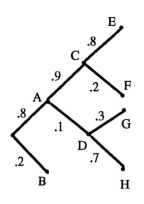

A: Sets alarm   E: Wakes in time

B: Does not set alarm   F: Does not wake in time

C: Alarm rings   G: Wakes in time

D: Alarm does not ring   H: Does not wake in time

   b. From the above tree, the probability that Jamal wakes in time for his 8:30 class is
      P(in time for class) = 0.8 • 0.9 • 0.8 + 0.8 • 0.1 • 0.3 = 0.6

33.

   a.

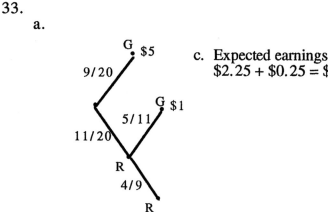

   c. Expected earnings = $5•9/20 + $1•(11/20)•(5/11) =
      $2.25 + $0.25 = $2.50

35. a. There are $(2)^8 = 256$ possible outcomes.
    b. There are 16 ways to have exactly 3 heads
    c. 247 outcomes have at least 2 heads.
    d. 203 outcomes have 4 or 5 heads.
    e. The entire sample space could be listed in a systematic manner and then inspected to see how many of them contain 2 or more heads. Another, more efficient way to determine how many outcomes have at least 2 heads is to determine how many outcomes have fewer than 2 heads and then subtract the result from 256.

37. a. 9/60 = 3/20
    b. 12/60 or 1/5

39. a. Both players have the same chance of winning because both can win in 2 ways of the 4 possible outcomes.
    b. Yes, the game is fair because the two players have the same likelihood of winning.

41. Let b= boy and g= girl.
    The sample space S is: S = {bbb, bgg, bgb, bbg, gbb, ggb, gbg, ggg}
    Favorable outcomes are bgg, bgb, bbg, gbb, ggb, gbg, ggg.
    Hence, the probability is 7/8.

    Alternatively, observe that P(at least one girl) = 1 - P(all 3 children are boys)
    But P(all 3 children are boys) = 1/8. Hence, P(at least one girl) = 1 - 1/8 = 7/8.

    You must assume that the probability of a boy being born is equal to the probability of a girl being born.

43. 45 matches

45. 45 handshakes

47. answers will vary

49. Various interpretations are possible. For example, one could compare Communist bloc (those that existed in 1988) countries with other countries and conclude that they won far more medals that non-Communist countries. The countries could be grouped by continent (viz., Africa, Asia, Australia, Europe, North America, South America) and draw conclusions about medal distribution (e.g., no South American countries were among the top 20 medal winners.)

51. The number of medals won by the USSR, East Germany, and the USA are outliers using the definition given.

53. The median probably best represents the average number of medals won by the top 20 countries—19 or 20. It would be a misrepresentation to eliminate the outliers by using the median of the other 17 countries. An even better indicator of the average number of medals won is probably the interquartile range because 55% of the values fall within this range.

Chapter 6
1. team

3. math is fun

5. answers will vary

7. a. 1/16; 1/4 • 1/4 = 1/16   1/12; 1/2 • 1/6 = 1/12
        1/4; 1/2 • 1/2 = 1/4   1/8; 1/2 • 1/4 = 1/8
    b. answers will vary

9. answers will vary; some possibilities are:
    a. 1/3, 2/6   b. -6/10, -9/15   c. 0/1, 0/5

11. a.78/77   b. 17/91   c. -17/45

13. a. 35/78   b. -32/63   c. 34/63

15. answers may vary
    a. 1518, 31/36   b. -17/28, -35/56   c. 144/209, 145/209

17. place appropriately in this order: .75 (b), 1.125 (c), 2 (d), 2.25 (a)

19. Divide the paper into tenths and shade two tenths. Show by folding, for example, that this is one-third of six tenths.

21. it would need to have a denominator with less than or equal value than the other

23. illustrations will vary; 9/10

25. 14

27. charge $3.33 for 576 square inches of material

29. 18 2/21 pizzas

31. when n is a multiple of two

33. 15 bookmarks; 3/4 inch left over

35. a. $a < c$ b. $b > d$ c. answers will vary; a/b = c/d

37. 5/6 = 1/2 + 1/3   13/12 = 1/3 + 3/4   13/36 = 1/4 + 1/9   26/21 = 2/3 + 4/7

39. There are infinitely many answers. Some possibilities are:
    a. 1/3, 4/5, 15/2   b. 2/3, 3/10, 1/10   c. 3/4, 1/2, 4/3

41. 2/3 ÷ 2/5 is asking "how many 2/5 are in 2/3?"; since there are 5/2 2/3s in 1 unit, then we must multiply 2/3 by 5/2 in order to find out how many 2/5 are in 2/3; illustration should demonstrate why there are 5/2 2/5s in one unit

Chapter 7

1. answers may vary; a block with 2 out of the 10 units shaded (or 20 out of 100 units, etc.)

3. a. 12.084   b. 1.625   c. 6

5. a. 3.2, 3.$\overline{22}$, 3.23, 3.$\overline{23}$, 3.2$\overline{3}$ b. -1.4$\overline{54}$, -1.$\overline{454}$, -1.45$\overline{4}$, -1.454, -1.45

7. write the decimals out to several more places and then compare

9. answers will vary; some possibilities are -2.295, -2.297

11. e

13. a. .625   b. $.\overline{3}$ c. $.91\overline{6}$

15. a. 13/30   b. 35/99

17. answers will vary; some possibilities are $\sqrt{(7/10)}$, $\sqrt{(.9)}$

19.

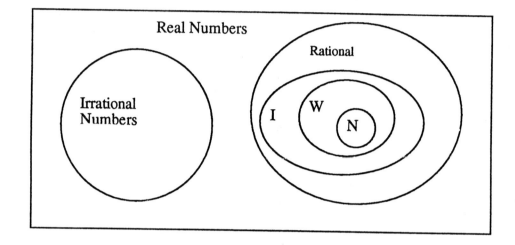

I = set of Integers, W = set of Whole numbers, N = set of Natural numbers

21. 3/5

23. the ratio of boys to girls will become smaller

25. you must consider that values exist continuously to the right of the repeated value

27. only after performing the multiplication or division is it essential to determine where the decimal place should be located

29. a. 88.6; 5 • 17 is 85   b. 15.6; 68 ÷ 4 is 17   c. 14.6; 6 • 17 is 102, 102 • .1 is 10.2
    d. .132; 16 • 8 is a three digit number, then divided by 1000 would be a three-digit decimal
    e. 4.71; .15 goes into .7 around 4 times   f. 4.68; 400 ÷ 80 is 5
    g. 2.2; .09 goes into .198 around 2 times   h. .7615; .9 goes into .7 around .7 times
    i. 2.096641; 5 • .3 is 1.5

31. A fraction can be written as a terminating decimal if it can be expressed with a denominator that is a power of 10. But 7, having prime factors other than 2 and/or 5, is not a factor of any power of 10.

33. 11 1/9%, 22 2/9%, 66 2/3%

35. Yes, each side of the square could be $\sqrt{11}$ cm, which is possible to construct. Construct right triangles with these sides: 1, 1, $\sqrt{2}$ and 1, 2, $\sqrt{5}$. Then using these hypotenuses ($\sqrt{2}$ and $\sqrt{5}$) as legs, construct a new triangle having a hypotenuse of length $\sqrt{7}$. Use this segment (of length $\sqrt{7}$ cm) and a segment of length 2 cm to construct another right triangle; this triangle

will have a hypotenuse of length √11 cm. Use this length to construct a square with sides of length √11 cm and the area will be 11 cm².

37. a. 4%   b. 32%   c. 64%

39. answers will vary; √2, .121221222..., √5

Chapter 8

1.   .01 billion per year between 1900 and 1910; .04 billion per year between 1900 and 1990

3.   answers may vary; One estimation is 6.1 billion people, as this is consistent with the prior two decades' increase of 0.8 billion people. (Another could be 6.2 billion.)

7.   1950 to 1960, and 1960 to 1970

9.   One reasonable answer is 273,000,000 people in 2000, as trends from the past few decades denote increases of just under 25,000,000 per decade.

11. Lowest rate of change during 1930-1940 decade. The Great Depression is a likely culprit.

13.

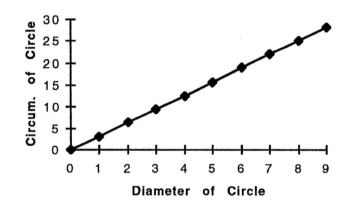

The slope of the line is π (3.14...).

15. a. 2(10) + 2(40) = 100 ft

b.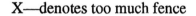

Side Length	Total Fence Needed
3.4	242 (X)
3.5	236
5	170
10	100
20	80
30	87
40	100
50	116
60	133
70	151
80	170
90	189
100	208
110	227
120	247(X)

X—denotes too much fence

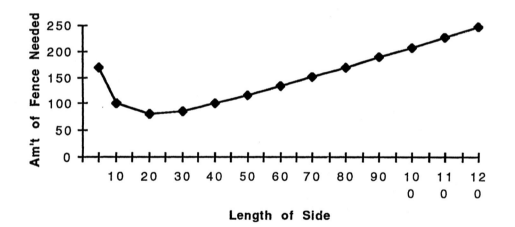

c. The least amount of fencing needed is 80 feet.
d. Yes, it is possible. The sides need to be 116.57 and 3.43 feet.

17. (6)(7)(7) = 294. (1)(1)(18) = 18.

19.

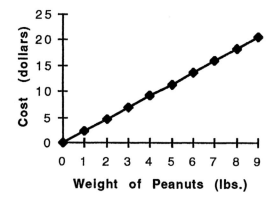

The slope of the line is 2.29. The slope is the rate of change of the cost and the cost increases at the rate of 2.29 per pound.

21. 1.8614 feet < x < 3.1923 feet

23. $200 < 4x^2 + 100x < 360$

25. The total cost, C(x), increases as the number of pictures developed increases. C(x) = 2 + .25x
The cost per picture, c(x), decreases as the number of pictures developed increases; c(x) = 2/x + .25

For each of the following (#s 26-29), the requested response is underlined.

26. Input	Output	27. Input	Output	28. Input	Output	29. Input	Output
1	18	50	53	14	17	2	-20
2	21	60	63.6	-20	0	4	20
3	24	70	74.2	20	20	6	20/3
9	42	400	424	230	125	23	1
x	3x+15	x	1.06x	x	x/2 + 10	x	20/(x-3)
a/3 - 5	a	a/1.06	a	2a - 20	a	(20/a) + 3	a

31.

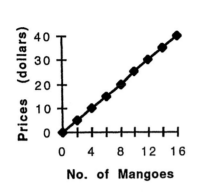

No. of Mangoes

The price of a bag of mangoes steadily increases as the number of mangoes increases. The rate of increase stays constant, as the price per mango is $2.50. The variables are positively and linearly related.

33. a. The amount of time it takes to mow the lawn with a push mower is a function of the height of the grass at the time of the mowing.

Height of Grass (in.)

b. The amount of time it takes to hand wash and wipe a certain number of dishes as a function of the number of people "doing the dishes."

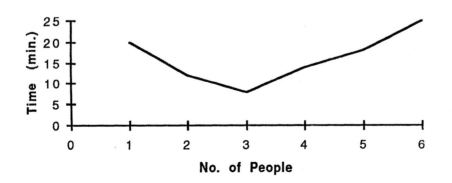

No. of People

35.

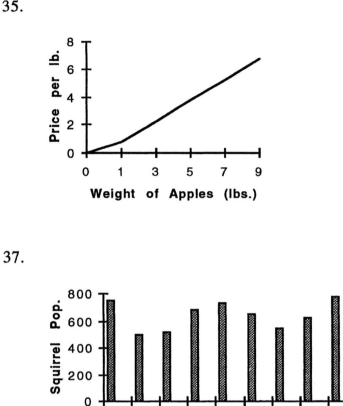

37.

Headline: "Squirrel Population Has Its Ups and Downs"
Opening Paragraph: (Paragraphs will vary, but all should indicate that the population of squirrels seems to have followed a pattern over the past 10 years (the period for which data was collected). The range in population has been from about 500 to nearly 800, but between these two extremes there is a definite rise and fall in approximately a sine curve.

39. $122°$ F; $50(9/5) + 32 = 122$

41. $98.6°$ F corresponds to $37°$ C

43. $F = (9/5)C + 32$; $C = (5/9)(F - 32)$

45. This is never true. First, $F = (9/5)C + 32$. Next, if the statement were true, then $2F = (9/5)2C + 32$. With substitution, $2[(9/5)C + 32] = (9/5)2C + 32$, which implies that $64 = 32$, which is not true.

47. a.

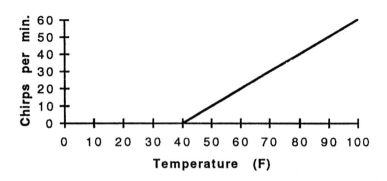

b. The function is linear, increasing from a temperature of 40 degrees on, is 0 below 40 degrees, and probably has no meaning after the temperature reaches some value above 100 degrees.

c. Minimum value for "chirps per minute" is 0. Maximum value is likely to be about 60 or 70 chirps per minute.

Chapter 9

1. a. 6   b. 10

3. three points always lie in the same plane (are coplanar) but four points may not be coplanar

5. a. yes   b. yes, as long as the obtuse angle is between the two congruent sides
   c. yes   d. no

7. 50° and 40°, respectively

9. constructions

11. a. 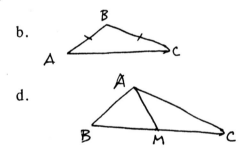 b.
    c. 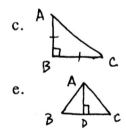 d.
    e.

13. a. any two rectangles are not always similar since their side lengths could be in different ratios
    b. any two circles are always similar since the ratio of the radii is constant
    c. any two regular polygons are always similar if they are the same polygon since their angles will always be congruent and the ratio of their side lengths will be the same for all corresponding sides

15. a. true   b. false, they may have different radii lengths
    c. false, their side lengths may be in different ratios   d. true
    e. false, their side lengths may not be congruent   f. true

17. a. the alternate rectangles are similar (i.e., every other rectangle)
    b. the diagonals of similar rectangles will line up when nested in this way

19. since △ BEF is similar to △ DEA by AAA, then BE = 3 and ED = 4.5.

21. use the formula (n - 2)180 or divide the polygon into triangles to find that the sum of the measures of the angles is 900°

23. a. <1 and <3 are supplementary
    b. <6 and <7 are vertical and therefore congruent
    c. <2 and <11 are congruent (alternate exterior angles)
    d. m<8 = m<4 + m<5 since they are alternate interior angles

25. 120°; there are 4 triangles that can be formed in a hexagon so the sum of the measures of the angles is 720°; since the hexagon is regular, all six angles are congruent, thus they must each be 120°

27. two parallel lines would form three regions and two intersecting lines would form four regions

29. they are all a set of points; a ray has one endpoint, a segment has two endpoints, and line does not have endpoints

31. yes, if all the lines are in the plane

33. this is not a good definition since the definition must include that the angles have a common vertex and no common interior points

35. no; m<1 = m<2 tells us that segment AD ∥ segment BC, but we do not have enough information to tell if segment AB ∥ segment CD

37. regular polygons

39. a. 90°   b. CD = 4   c. EC = 4, AF = 10

41. a. always   b. sometimes   c. always   d. sometimes

43. yes, since with two angles given, the third angles are determined and they must be congruent to each other; thus by AAA the triangles are similar

45. no, rectangles always have their angles congruent, but the sides could be in different ratios

47. yes, since all angles in rectangles are congruent

49. a. the sum of the measures of the angles in a triangle is 180°
    c. yes

51. CDA

53. m<w = 80°, UV = 6, UW = 5, WV = 4, m<Z = 80°, m<X = 60°, m<Y = 40°, VUW

55. use similar triangles ABC and CBD or that <DCB and <A are both complementary to <ACD

57. a. connect two midpoints and show that the newly formed triangle is similar to the original triangle by SAS for similarity; then since the ratio of two of the sides is 1 : 2, the thirds must also have this ratio so the third side is equal to 1/2 of the length of the original third side; also all angles must be congruent and so the line segment joining the midpoints must be parallel to the third side because corresponding angles formed by the transversal are congruent
   b. draw the diagonals in the quadrilateral and then connect the midpoints as specified; using the proof in a., pairs of opposite segments are parallel because they are both parallel to the diagonal drawn (the diagonals form triangles that allow us to use the results from a); since both pairs of opposite sides are parallel, the quadrilateral is a parallelogram
   c. draw the diagonals in the rectangle and then connect the midpoints as specified; from b. we have that the quadrilateral formed is a parallelogram; furthermore, since from a. the segments connecting midpoints are half the length of the diagonals, and the diagonals are congruent in a rectangle, all four segments are congruent; thus, the quadrilateral is a rhombus

59. a. the two base angles in each triangle are 45°; the hypotenuse in $\triangle$ ABC is $4\sqrt{2}$ cm and the hypotenuse in $\triangle$ DEF is $8\sqrt{2}$ cm
   b. the triangles are similar by AA similarity
   c. the triangles are not congruent because their corresponding sides are not congruent
   d. area $\triangle$ ABC = 8 square cm, area $\triangle$ DEF = 32 square cm

61. 180°

63. *trapezoid*—quadrilateral with at least one pair of opposite sides parallel; *parallelogram*—quadrilateral with both pairs of opposite sides parallel; *rhombus*—parallelogram with one pair of congruent adjacent sides; *rectangle*—parallelogram with one right angle; *square*—parallelogram with one pair of congruent adjacent sides and one right angle; *kite*—quadrilateral with two pairs of congruent adjacent sides; *isosceles trapezoid*—trapezoid with at least one pair of congruent opposite sides

65. the further down you go on the tree diagram, the more symmetry there is

67. a. between 26 and 72 miles apart
   b. You can determine the range by finding the difference (for the minimum distance) and the sum (for the maximum distance)

69. a. the new triangle is bigger; the ratio of the sides is 3 : 1
   b. the new triangle is smaller; the ratio of the sides is 1/2 : 1
   c. the new triangle is the same as the original

71. it will be a rhombus; draw the diagonals in the rectangle and then connect the midpoints as specified; we have that the quadrilateral formed is a parallelogram; furthermore, since the segments connecting midpoints are half the length of the diagonals, and the diagonals are congruent in a rectangle, all four segments are congruent; thus, the quadrilateral is a rhombus; we cannot prove that the angles of EFGH are right angles, so the most we can say is that the figure is a rhombus

Chapter 10
1. a. 200 square inches   b. 60 inches

3. 1 yd x 24 yd; 2 yd x 12 yd; 3 yd x 8 yd; 4 yd x 6 yd

5. 8 square feet

7. 45.5 square units

9. 15 cm

11. 4 : 1

13. a. no   b. yes   c. no

15. 56.25π cm^2

17. the better bargain is the 5.5 cm radius orange because its cost per square cm is less than the other orange

19. 1. b   2. d   3. f   4. e
    5. g   6. c   7. a

21. a and c produce the same result

23. answers will vary; some possibilities are: BOOK for horizontal line, MOM for vertical line

25. a. horizontal line through two opposite vertices
    b. horizontal and vertical lines, splitting rectangle in half
    c. horizontal and vertical lines, splitting figure in half

27. a. 4   b. 2   c. 3   d. 2

29. find the area of the field (5600 m^2) and take the square root; a square field with the same area should have a side length of approximately 74.83 m

31. Area of A = 9 square units; Area of B = 15 square units

33. if you traveled 24 hours per day, the average speed in miles per hour would be about 13.1 mph

35. a. area of square is 144 in^2, perimeter of square is 48 in, area of each semi-circle is 18π in^2, circumference of each semi-circle is 6π in

    b. area of the large circle is 36π cm^2, circumference of the large circle is 12π cm, the area of each small circle is 9π cm^2, the circumference of each small circle is 6π cm

37. yes, all quadrilaterals tessellate the plane. Each vertex point of the tessellation must be composed of each of the angles of the quadrilateral so that the sum of the angles at each vertex point is 360°.

39. equilateral triangle, square, regular hexagon

41. $12.50

43. yes, the wire would be approximately 3.2 meters above the earth

45. a 2 x 5 rectangle has perimeter of 14 units and area of 10 square units, while a 6 x 6 rectangle has perimeter of 24 units and area of 36 square units

47. $9 : 1$

49. a. no, it is quadrupled   b. it is quadrupled

51. a. $4 : 1$ b. $2 : 1$ c. $4 : 1$ d. $4 : 1$

53. divide the shape into figures that you know the areas of and then sum the individual areas

55. 126 square feet

61. Rotate a copy of the trapezoid into place as shown. A parallelogram is formed since both pairs of opposite sides are parallel (bases were already parallel and angles on non-base sides are supplementary). Thus the area of a trapezoid is $1/2(b_1 + b_2)h$ (1/2 the area of a parallelogram formed by two congruent trapezoids).

63. answers will vary

65. form similar triangles and set up a proportion using corresponding sides